Falling River

Falling River

Collected Poems ▪ 1976-2016

Al Rocheleau

Shantih Press

Published in the United States
by Shantih Press, Orlando, FL

Library of Congress Control Number.

ISBN-10: 1-946088-98-6
ISBN-13: 978-1-946088-98-7
Library of Congress Control Number: 2017946429

Front Cover Photo, Falls at Metacomet Mill, 2016:
Georgette Rocheleau

Interior Photo, Al Rocheleau, 1973:
B.M.C. Durfee High School

Back Cover Photo, Al Rocheleau, 2013:
Georgette Rocheleau

Back Cover Watermark, Greater Falls, c. 1940s
Fall River Herald News

Front Cover Design: Gary Broughman

Contents

Previous Publications

Confrontation

Saint Albert of the Asses

ArtWord Quarterly

The Iron Range
Reconsideration

Adirondack Review

Ant Farms
Seven Wonders
Under Construction

Nedge

Cantos from Fernald School
The Apparition of Vica
John of Revelation at the Rose Parade
Scott County
Cheyenne Requiem
Chain Letter

Dream International Quarterly

Träumerei
Lorca's Dream
Étude in E Major, Final Bar
Light Breakfast at the Alamo

Poetry Salzburg Review (pub. Austria)

The Salt Harvest
Trilobites

Poetry Depth Quarterly

Kites
A Birth Somewhere, Afar

Outerbridge

Anne Sexton

Homestead Review

Salinas

Evansville Review

Shostakovich Composes in Leningrad, 1944

Mockingbird

Cantilena: Bracelet of Similes

Mandrake Poetry Magazine (pub. Poland)

Trelawny (in the Second Person)
Postscript
Ernest and Gloria

Haight Ashbury Literary Journal

Smithsonian, 1975

Pennsylvania English

At This Moment

The Cortland Review

There Are Sprites of the Pities

Artisan: A Journal of Craft

Bobby Fischer Teaches Chess
The Clothed Woman
Ariadne of Naxos: A Reproduction

Pig Iron

Wyeth Paints Pictures of My Father

Sahara

Adagietto

Tule Review

Of the Relativity of Big and Small

Luna Negra

Niagara
For Your Penance
To the Potter's Field

San Fernando Poetry Journal

Instructions in the Faith
Continuum
Dalí: Smart Bomb in Anthropomorphic Echo
Something about Aryans and Jews
At This Moment (second publication)
Pilsner's Wake

Arts Connection, WMFE Radio

Poem Having to Do with Water
Christmas Song

Mobius

>Public Speaker
>Gaucho

Nebo, A Literary Journal

>Nashville, Answering Machine

FSPA Anthology # 33

>Monticello, May
>Barto in Mount Dora (II)
>Anniversary, Probably 1994

Ship of Fools

>Diva
>Lute (The Spinster)

PoetryMagazine

>Mayflies
>Myth of Bouncing Light
>The Innocents
>Yellow Flowers

Slant: A Journal of Poetry

>Orange Blossom Trail

Surratt House Museum

>The Innocents (second publication)

Iodine Poetry Journal

>Sun, the Moon, and Herbs

CHB Anthology # 3

A Marriage
Bombing the Muses

Contemporary American Voices

The Death in the Room
Tear (Rimbaud translation)
My Poems Are Little Cripples
You Need Not Fear the Catholics, Marianne
The Language of the Roll

Bread of Life Magazine (pub. Canada)

Lines from *Communion Sonata*
Mary's Nocturne
That January

Alpha Beat Soup

Equinox
Kerouac, Disembodied, Hears Side One of "The Fur
   Album" through a Car Window, above the Pacific
   Coast Highway at Big Sur

Illuminations

Rimbaud
Sleeper in the Valley (Rimbaud translation)

Broken Streets

Epistle of Saint Paul, on Rice Paper

Van Gogh's Ear (pub. France)

The House of Me

Poetic Realm

The Circle
Beneath My Religion
Aurore and Albert
Reunion (Durfee Prelude)
Thank You, Duncan Hines

The Journal (pub. England)

Vowels (Rimbaud translation)
The Star Wept Rose (Rimbaud translation)

Potomac Review

Young Coupling (Rimbaud translation)
Shame (Rimbaud translation)

Time of Singing

Poem, after the Greek
Twenty Views of the Baby Jesus (excerpt)

The Poetic Soul

Sea Grapes

My Legacy

Barto in Mount Dora (I)
For Rita, on Her Brother's Passing, from Evan,
    on the Eve of His Premature Birth
The Brief Outstanding
Aurore and Albert (second publication)

Plainsongs

Flood Plain

The Penwood Review

Rick's Envelope
Eighteen (Again)

Pulsar Poetry Magazine (pub. England)

For Ori

Providence Russian Festival

Mayakovsky
Morning
    (Mayakovsky translation with Victoria Richter)
Monstrous Funeral
    (Mayakovsky translation with Victoria Richter)

Poetry Forum

Progress in Eden

Lourdes Magazine (pub. France)

Passion of Saint Bernadette

Newsletter of the 26th Marines

An Inventory, 1968

Silver Wings

Savanna's Song

Current Accounts (pub. England)

Sapphire Bullets of Pure Love
Dalí's Old Man to the Left of the Sea

The American Chiropractor

The Lillard Bells

K9s for Veterans, Veteran's Day Event

Our Baghdad

St. Bernadette Institute of Sacred Art

Passion of Saint Bernadette (second publication)

The Plowman

Jesus of the Veldt

Revelry

Einstein's Corollary
Some People *(Thomas Burnett Swann Award)*
Blues
The Fishers
Body Poem of Pithecanthropus
Reaction
A Graft of Apples
Newton's Lament
At a Café, Longing
Crawfish among the Landed of Jackson
Eight Points

Postcards from My Head

George, a Ballad

Studio One

Deconstruction
Definition of Blank at the Teller's Window

26

Rose and Thorn

Kites (second publication)
The Innocents (third publication)
Myth of Bouncing Light (second publication)
Skydiver
Twenty-Seven Weeks

On Writing Poetry

Anne Sexton (second publication)
Ernest and Gloria (second publication)
Atlas, Revised
Jesus of the Veldt (second publication)
Epigram of the Fourth Grade (excerpt)
There Is Not
Milk of Magnesia of Human Kindness
     (Doggerel of Clichés)
Pre-Raphaelites
Communion Sonata (excerpt)
Doria
Copse of Birches
Something about Aryans and Jews (second publication)
Epistle of Saint Paul, on Rice Paper (second publication)
Among the Gas Giants (excerpt)
Sea Grapes (excerpt, second publication)
Taos (for Marjie) (excerpt, second publication)
Sestina for the Sixtieth Psalm
Confraternity of the Ghost of John Donne (I)
Junkies (Open Poetry Reading, 7 PM)

Poésie Française (pub. France)

Balles en Saphir de l'Amour Pur

Shemom

For Ori: The Christmas Letter

Fire (pub. England)

   The Water Goblin
   Taos (for Marjie)
   Voyeur
   Myth of Bouncing Light (third publication)

Red River Review

   An Ass and a Cow
   On Minds and the Noonward Race

Saison Poetry Library (pub. England)

   Taos (for Marjie) (third publication)
   Voyeur (second publication)

UCF School of Visual Art and Design

   Eight Points (second publication)

The Poet's Art

   Idyll
   Amaranths (Still Life for a Second Wedding)
   Greeting Card
   The Baker's Gift
   But Gone, Remain
   Mrs. Burt Plays Russian Dances

Peedeel's Blog (pub. England)

   Voyeur (third publication)

Earthshine

   Town of Luggalo
   Follower

Red Fez

Paradox

Neon (pub. England)

Metaphor
The Raga of Choices
God's Version of a Cézanne Charcoal

Great American Catholic Eulogies

The Innocents (fourth publication)

Tipton Poetry Journal

Double in a Diner, Afternoon

Ygdrasil, A Journal of the Poetic Arts (pub. Canada)

Gooseberry Island
Galatians Two
Les Québécois à la Cabane à Sucre
Watuppa Pond; The Ice House
This Thirst

FSPA Anthology # 34

Alms

Wild Goose Poetry Review

Gale Farm

Wild Violet

Streets of Fall River

Falling River ...

The Quequechan River, for more than five decades almost completely hidden from view, powered the many mills of Fall River, Massachusetts, a city of 100,000 known across parts of two centuries as the leading textile producer of the nation. The river at first lolls along from Lake Watuppa, then falls over shelves of Ice-Age rock that form eight cataracts, settling at the sea-level confluence of the brackish Taunton River, which flows south into Mount Hope Bay and the Atlantic. The name "Quequechan" in the Wampanoag language means "Falling River," lending title to the city and to this book.

The falls of the Quequechan were caught by large wheels that powered broad saws and spun the cotton thread of the early mills. Later, channeled into a narrow course of concrete and stone and slowed by dams, faux-ponds of its water filled along its route to supply and cool the steam turbines of the newer, larger mills. As the city expanded, guided by families enriched off the labor of a dozen different strains of immigrants, the river was further used and abused, and more and more of its course was compromised and covered over. Today, only glimpses of the river and its still-hurtling water remain above ground. Efforts are ongoing to fully clean the course and reveal the river to daylight. Regardless, it flows.

The recent cover photo of the river falling behind the old Metacomet Mill betrays a natural power impossible to stall completely. It's like life— mine and I hope, yours too.

A. R.

Notes from the Author

This collection, containing almost all the work that I have produced to date, spans forty years. During that time, like most people, I have worked regular day jobs (night ones too), provided for a family, lived a life. Those things have been more important than the writing, and I hope all of this living continues a while. But the writing was important, too; in fact, it had to be. I've wondered if it was a bit much to collect the poems now; even as I write this introduction, I think it. But here it is.

Many of these poems have been published in journals in the United States, Canada, and many countries abroad. Some are master translations out of French or Russian. Some of my own pieces in English are also translated into French. There are all kinds of poems of various forms, intents, and levels of ambition, poems heavy and light, sacred and profane. Those last two adjectives trouble me to the extent that a reader may gravitate to one kind of work and take me to task for the other. But it is all me. Style also changes over decades, as predilections, learning, and experience accrue. The poems are not in any chronology. Not only might you not be able to guess in what year they were written— beyond what decade, I might be similarly puzzled today.

Much of the work has not appeared elsewhere; some likely would never have appeared but for this book. The three smaller collections, *A Granite Symphony, Love and Blues,* and *Flying Machine* may reflect a general period of living and of observation, poems that were ordered for inclusion at the time. The final section, marked *Other Poems,* contains everything else: new poems, unpublished older poems, translations, songs, occasional poems, light work, and sketches of lyrics from the libretto of the opera, *Helen Keller.*

Now, I said that the work is "all me." It could be just as accurate to say it is "all you" or "all us." If we would admit it, our lives are remarkably similar, give or take one or another triumph or tragedy. I think there are prisms to reflect one another without, even as our lights refract within. We inhabit a beautiful world if we consider it so, person to person, and on that we may agree, but not always. The magic of the aesthetic wave is that it resonates in the beautiful as well as the ugly, and in the happy as well as the sad, granting us individual perspective within powerful poles. You might say we live to gain the aesthetic wave, a wave of such short length it aspires to the point of no wave at all, to the state of pure spirituality. And as we sense it, we return upon it a companion wave just as near-spiritual and powerful, one of admiration, of love in all its forms.

Beyond natural aesthetic waves that we perceive (the sunset, the surf, the baby's smile), comes a different kind of aesthetic, that created or re-imagined by the artist. What the artist lifts and the receiver re-creates we can call the *poetic* wave, because we *make* it. For writers, it is done using the graphic symbols of our expression; for poets, the expression condenses to the level of an essence, rising word by word, phrase by phrase. It is something precious. As the poet makes these waves lift and perceives the result, it becomes something of an addiction.

Poets don't get rich. Rather, the work itself enriches the poet and others. Each poem as it is polished, as it is finished and said orally or read silently, comes to the world from a universe of poets— new ones, working ones, masters and grandmasters, part of a legacy of poetry drawn from every age. From privileged and common persons alike, from people engaged in the necessary affairs of their place and their time, and who may have mostly written on the side, each were and are yet driven to create a real thing, a needed thing, a perfectly sounded, ordered, meaningful and affecting object that elevates us now, and that may be counted on to elevate, in decades or centuries ahead of us, those who find such objects waiting in books like these.

Al Rocheleau

by Lucie Winborne

That Al Rocheleau is a master poet doesn't necessarily mean he was born a poet. As he has said, "When I was young it was all about the short story and preparing to be a novelist. I submitted my first story to a magazine when I was fourteen. By high school, I wanted to be the next Thomas Wolfe." Then fate intervened through the medium of a "brilliant, just brilliant" English teacher in his home town of Fall River, Massachusetts.

"I was introduced to the gamut of English poetry, from Chaucer to Shakespeare, Keats to Eliot," with a new light dawning as he absorbed "The Love Song of J. Alfred Prufrock." He went on:

"I couldn't believe that such an amount of craft and fathomless profundity could be pressed into such a form. I was hooked."

And hooked ever since. Fortunately, Al hasn't kept such treasures, or his pursuit of poetic expression, to himself. Almost all writers seek the validation of sharing their work with the public both on and off the page—isn't that the purpose of the gift of language?— and Al's verse has appeared in more than eighty magazines in six countries. It can be found at websites as diverse as the Surratt House Museum in Washington, DC and the Saint Bernadette Institute of Sacred Art in New Mexico. It has been read on the radio ("Poem Having to Do With Water"), sung at the funeral of a beloved father-in-law ("George, a Ballad"), and earned honors such as the Thomas Burnett Swann Award from the Gwendolyn Brooks Writers Association ("Some People"). But it is not enough for Al to write and share what he writes. He is an innovative teacher who for many years hosted online workshops and served as Poetry Editor and Senior Columnist at the writers' website, Amazing Instant Novelist. His articles on poetic craft reside in the resource databases of numerous schools ranging from the middle grades to college; his lectures have been enjoyed at venues including the Florida Writers Association, the Florida State Poets Association, Emerson College, and the University of Massachusetts; and in 2012, he developed and launched an ambitious, one-of-a-kind seminar program called "The Twelve Chairs," a 180-hour course for poets of all skill levels, that offers full scholarships to high school students.

Al is also a musician who occasionally brings out his guitar at poetry salons he hosts, performing songs from Bob Dylan to John Keats, and tells his students to listen to the nocturnes of Chopin at least 100 times to absorb the poetic shifts of tone and flow. He teaches that poetry itself is music, and that words are actual physical objects transmuted and restored by the poet's symbols. He is an encourager who has helped friends bring their own collections to fruition by the power of his belief in them.

He is a synesthete, like Nabokov with his alphabet of vibrant, unchanging colors, with the ability to "see" sound or "taste" a painting, who, "even in free verse … will 'paint' the sounds of assonance, consonance, and internal rhyme." He is an author whose practical, down-to-earth manual, *On Writing Poetry: For Poets Made as Well as Born,* was published by Shantih Press in 2010 and has been distributed to schools and public libraries.

Al is a husband, a father, a "working man" of remarkable casting and roles. He cites among his artistic influences such icons as Miles Davis and Robert Altman, Salvador Dalí and Brian Wilson, John Donne and Jack Kerouac. Like Jack a generation earlier, Al "hit the road" as the untimely death of Anne Sexton ended his plan to study with her at Boston

University. He roamed the U.S. on a Greyhound Ameripass, landing in Berkeley, California, later returning to Fall River to marry and raise a family. And, in his "*real* work time," to write poetry.

But what qualifies as good poetry? I asked Al that in a blog interview, because most writers have as keen a desire to know whether they possess that elusive thing called talent as they do to get published. I offered him something I'd read from one editor: "If it looks good at 6:00 in the morning, it probably is good." To my amusement, Al responded, "I guess that depends on how awake you are at 6:00 a.m." Then he added, "A poem can be done in fifteen minutes, or not done in fifteen years." Most good poetry, like any other form of writing, takes work."Sometimes you find that shining nugget lying on the ground. Other times you have to mine the ore, and burn off the baser elements. When it's done, it's perfect. At 6:00 in the morning, or any other time."

The deep, definitive work herein has been rigorously mined and softly polished over four decades: the observant, tender, searing, questioning nuggets, and vignettes from the "real" world:

Gette, I come back to you,
to New England with a diamond
in a quirky setting, courtesy
of Standard Oil of California.

from "Memoirs of the Chevron Refinery…"

Laments for what might have been:

I'd like to think I would have been the one ingénue
of your unschooled, oh-so-wicked way to penetrate
and hold you fast, to steer you to the fast winds

eliminating the rowing toward God, and on green air
or water lilt and undulate, letting you seduce me
in a way that would offend no one, responding with psalms.

from "Anne Sexton"

Awash in the language of the senses:

I have not eaten sea grapes.

If you tell me, they are sweet
as pomegranates, as the voice
of Albanese in *Tosca*.

If you tell me, they are sour
as young lemons, or
the frisson of jealousy.

If you tell me, they are bitter
as lies, or salty
as tragedy.

from "Sea Grapes"

Read the poems aloud to enjoy the variances of sound. Read
them silently to be transported to another place. Read them to
view a reflection of the world at large. Read and give thanks for
the glorious gift of words.

Lucie M. Winborne
December 2016

Falling River

Collected Poems
1976-2016

A Granite Symphony

(2002)

"If Galileo had said in verse
that the world moved, the inquisition
might have let him alone."

— Thomas Hardy

for John Pietruszka

MYTH OF BOUNCING LIGHT

A child, I pressed my face to the hard pane
and, seeing me, wondered what I'd be
in that other world, that gay parallel,
the great and different sameness where

time emits a more evolved love
and spots are on the move, not safe or still
in the night's array, not static, ignored
as the reflection of Arcturus in a glass ashtray.

Older now, I wipe my breath from the cold
window wintering my content in opaque
function, unworried of light bending, or astronomy,
laurels, lingerings, latitudes of things

but plenty of dinner, God, the regular universe
where I seem to cross and commend myself,
a small soul in a dull house of nearly
grown children, losing their images, quickly.

JOHN OF REVELATION AT THE ROSE PARADE

Joined in progress.

And that was the float from Laodicea. I know your deeds!
Buy from me gold refined by fire, presenting in blooms
of forsythia.

This next one is really something.

A throne standing there in heaven, all of Hever Castle,
a variety of Japanese quince, and there The One
all in jasper of black narcissus, and carnelian
of bingo chrysanthemums.

There, the twenty-four, count them, surrounding thrones
of the elders in the slight contrast of Burpee's primrose, known
to experts as the Cosmos.

Those white garments, all carnations
with gold day-lily crowns. The flashes
of lightning are quince again,
the thunder, implied.

Around the major throne, the four creatures
covered with eyes of gold-rimmed, black pansies
front and back, the lion of orange zinnias,
ox of a million violets, the third has the face
of a man, in oxeye leucanthemum, and the fourth
a praying eagle, of juniper fronds.

But don't forget the scroll, or the Lamb!
The One holds a scroll of white roses, and
on the scroll are the seven seals to follow.
And there is the white geranium Lamb, bleeding gladiolus,
with seven horns of kale and seven petunia eyes,
grasping the news of the ages.

There it goes, my best of show.

In rapid succession, the seals are opened.
A white horse, fetlocks of St. Bernard's lily
on motors, wheeling. The rider's bow of twined
irises stands for menace, and he is crowned
in cornflowers.

Come forward!

Another horse, of pyracantha, fire-thorns.
The huge sword of hybrid tea roses
glistens with dew.

Come forward!

The black horse rider, all black narcissus
carries scales on which real wheat shafts
and barley are falling to a carpet of chamomile.

Come forward!

With the broken fourth seal the horse
of sickly green approaches in the horror
of cress and conifers. Its rider
is named Death.
And the netherworld, a selection
of scilla, dog roses, and moss follows in train,
a chaos of killing, famine and decay.

The fifth seal is opening to an altar of
peonies, with trailing arbutus for the
spirits beneath.

How long will it be! How long!

The sixth seal opens and its float
shimmers and quakes as if to render a cleave
down the middle of Colorado Street.
Figs shake loose.
The sun is all black olives.
The moon is bloodlike poppies, somnolent.

As the Lamb breaks open the seventh seal
there is silence.
One hundred and forty-four thousand stand waiting.
Countless others watch from behind.

And here comes the marching band, trumpets wailing.

Petals are circling in wind.
At the end of the street, the lead float
has reached the Rose Bowl.

Those with tickets follow.
We believe! We believe!

Good day for a game.

ANNE SEXTON

I'm like Dorothy, lining up for the balloon ride.
Dearest Anne, my vehicle of some emulation,
I believe I'll miss you most of all, but wait—

must I leave you behind, can't I sit with you
in the carriage, listening to soft radio, until
the shovel hung and plant-stakes turn to clouds,

turn to puffiest clouds of ether, or forgetfulness
and you could give me all those special lessons,
introduce me to your fey fire, your insouciance,

your friends passing by the window, Lowell harnessed
to his baggage, Sylvia on her Schwinn, Betsy Bishop
vodka-toasting a circle of the circle's shrinks

who wash their blood-hands of invisible ink, as I fish
for a match to hold under them, looking for passwords
to reclaim a thousand artists' souls— yours, too.

I'd like to think I would have been the one ingénue
of your unschooled, oh-so-wicked way to penetrate
and hold you fast, to steer you to the fast winds

eliminating the rowing toward God, and on green air
or water lilt and undulate, letting you seduce me
in a way that would offend no one, responding with psalms.

Instead, you would let me safely down. And I,
confused, took a twenty-year day job, writing on the sly,
and wondering, if I could have been with you then, would I?

Through all the pain, the poems sing back to me—
"So open the garage door, will you, hon?" And I do.
Black-and-white turns October technicolor, and every time

some Dorothy's pen treads paper, so do you.

SEA GRAPES

They clutch at the edge of the world
with gnarled, deep fingers.

Their fringes fall in toe-tips
from bluffs
and brims of caked sand,
feeling the flat freeway
of surf.

The surf would pull them in
with its lithe, foam grips
if it could, feeding the plump
berries to the ghosts of sharks
who no longer require blood.

I have not eaten sea grapes.

If you tell me, they are sweet
as pomegranates, as the voice
of Albanese in *Tosca.*
If you tell me, they are sour
as young lemons, or
the frisson of jealousy.

If you tell me, they are bitter
as lies, or salty
as tragedy.

And if you tell me they taste like
the fruit in purgatory, I might best
understand.

I do know the sea wants them.
And somehow, they appear to want the sea.

And if you tell me, I will trust you.

If you—

and only if you—
will trust

me.

SCOTT COUNTY

You see a crimson east
of Farley's corn and combines,
west, the fields are Sherman's fifty;
thumb at south, you trace
the damp dirt and grassy lines
to a wall of Schiller's barley.

The quiet here, even in rain
is the quiet aging David sought,
and through which prophets wailed
considering wheat and wet lilies;
alone the rusty cropduster's antiphon
assures a passover of locusts.

This is our life; this is our only life.

Silos poke this landscape.
From the air, they form
an image of the Lord
suspended on his nails;
from the ground, they
form nothing, except heaven.

NIAGARA

As if released from a Catholic's
cracked abyss, it flows
night to morning.

Iroquois angels string
in the latticework of mist,
the broad tongue of water
breaching the yaw of an Iroquois god,
unintimidated by missionaries.

Totems of aluminum and steel jut the surrounding,
humming in overflow, monotone chant
to the progress of false economies
leaching marrows to a stone-white dolor
as it has done for decades, the power
of this cold blue stream
devoid of fish, and otter.

Niagara greets young honeymooners
with a blind wave, too busy
to stop its roar, too real
for the fantasies of an hour.
Niagara has outlasted the Iroquois.
The turned spigot of an Ice Age
breaks off
in our tiny hands.
It rolls us over
in cold, translucent sleep, falling

falling to a Sheol of star-crossed
Iroquois lovers

and wets
the wings of several, sorry plovers
circling the boats
that cast their pennies
with wishes no one hears,
or could possibly
discover.

KITES

Snap the line
in hard wind trailing bright
bow-tails
or broken struts
of thoughtful, well-glued,
mildewed trust, on air
that speaks beneficence, then
wails on tight semi-
circles of grief
in skies' November rust—

take ladder to lindens
(lost without leaf)
to roofs of Leicestershire
to the Dover bluffs
to claim remains of a swoon,
a lust, the playmates
shake their heads, and head
to puddings on a piper's tune
forgetting, forgiving
making do,

impermanent as
box-kites, diamonds

the stringless moon.

CANTOS FROM FERNALD SCHOOL

You say we look alike, and don't we, reminders
of missed appointments you will keep eventually;

our eyes are round like Shintos, neck, thick,
muscular as Polyphemus, hands, limp as Michelangelo's
Adam on the ceiling, the dyes dried into plaster,
as permanently perfect as is this imperfect feeling

when you view the long trunks, as if gravity pulled us
harder to keep us here, restricting our ascension,
causing our loiter in amusement park lines, leaving
our number tethered to porches of old brick buildings

watching the joggers who lumber on our green byways,
short-cuts to the silvery clean of a good shower,
there but for the grace of Hades, guardian of the Styx
and of Persephone, whose offspring lose the lottery

of genetics and comfort of close friends like you
but who learn the secret of life before any white light
can shine a repentant ray upon them, who love
with an incandescence coiled in their kindred souls

their normal, normal souls so normally imbued
with something seeming far from you, the obvious—
to cheer with every laugh there is no tragedy,
that even you should never play King Lear—

we are, you see, quite happy to be here
to bring to you humility, to bleed your fear.

TRÄUMEREI

I embrace the brick enclosure of my youth in tears,
memories pulled like light-shafts from an unfull quiver
impossible to fire at the heart of my yearning, but I
can remember, when gay macaroni painted gold
on a cardboard candle holder was like filigree
to the crown of Clytemnestra, when the Ten Family lent me
a sugar cup and I returned happily with the difference,
when sky was at the top of the page, when the house was a box
with a pointy roof, when I was not swallowed by blue
or confused by angles, when war was unequivocal—
the standing or knocked over plastic men; when the smell
of paste was sweeter than chrysanthemums adorning
any soldier's grave, sticking doilies onto hearts—
and when attraction to a girl was the crinkle
of her nose, the sweetness of her being, worn on the face
without affectation, and I fought to be at her place
on the dancing circle, to marry in the momentary,
holding hands for real, in the church of children.

DUNKIRK SONG

Young, the white,
tumescent as sea-stones
played against dark
against black,
its tight shut mussels
easy to assume.

But age opens gray
like a monochrome
locker, a tomb
and varies its spectrum
like opposite lenses
turning in light,
like doom.

Sharkskin indifference
chafes a body's
battleship, turning
in water where
only weak winds and
one, worn wailing tug
have room.

The sea carves history.

Slate is betrayal, shale
excuse, bleeding gray oil
not ambergris,
from a broad, beached
whale's spume.

The cumulo-and-nimbus comes
to nimbus lone too soon—
thunderheads rat-tatting
the chop like nails of
invalidation, like machine
guns aimed at the moon.

The beach is filled with stone boats,
barrows, skiffs of cement, and Beckett stools.

Wait, the waiting. Gray, too.

Oh white, my prayerful Grotto virgins
black, my bootstrap
Waffen goons,
you mitigate yourselves with me
you leave my lack
my low distinction

quivering here at edge of land
unconquered,
wet, unrescued
but

still uniformed
and groomed.

AN INVENTORY, 1968

Homage to the U. S. Marine Corps, and the 26th Marines

The pogo pistons air; a yo-yo
yins and yangs its revolutions
in the year of the Walked Dog. The Slink
steps lightly on a Stepford stair; Superball
coils, coils, explodes past a milk truck
lending its ice (without collateral)
to thirsty boys in shirtsleeves.

The hula-hoop (and Kepler's law) say
"watch the edge, the edge" while Barbie,
too stiff for love, and Ken, too limp,
lie in the grass to the Indian music
coming from the west, from an upstairs window
above the kickball game, the hop-
scotchers, and the morning mailman.

500 pieces of the Civil War
from the back of a ten-cent *Junior Classic*
are missing in action or dead on the floor—
the kite's in the tree, the caps, in the Colt,
the pump of a Daisy that shot red dirt
shoots at the rubber-band balsawood Cessna
that falls in a spray of gardenias.

We play Parcheesi at the picnic table
trying to avoid being sent to hell,
or left an old maid, or without a chair
at a birthday party of a boy somewhere—

and at Christmastime we will light all the lights,
tie cones to a wreath, and talk of my brother,
Khe Sanh,
      and the meaning of peace.

(MAN ON THE) GREEN LINE

You roll on rails
in a golden train
to the promise
of a belligerent world
dissolving like beet
sugar in pekoe tea—

to go where concubines
align themselves in order
all sheered of pink and green,
their breasts, a music
out of ouds, only semi-seen;

to nightingales
that satisfy rumor with
a shrill song, and orchids
like the warm parts of goddesses
nectaring their love
for a dragonfly's tongue

then, down to the downy
quilts of trust
that wrap round snowfall
and seal a season,

arousing dreams of destination
the appointment of sighs
and welcome arms
of paradise, only to
wake, to inquire

and be advised
that by the next stop

you've gone too far,
and with no good reason.

YELLOW FLOWERS

A coursing inside, magnificent
and by invitation. The stick of blood,
the anther, virile, all strong felicity
blooms sideways, bends to a pistil

moan and shoots the breeze alive,
canceling appointments, the inevitable swerve
of sweet earth through the dark confluence
of balls and sun, the seconds incendiary,

the significance, sailing soft like cornsilk
in the nose of the day, becoming for some
a signature of pax, to others an allergen
incurable and itchy, yet enduring.

POSTSCRIPT

Saint Stephen awoke, a Hindu
in the body of no destiny—
a yogurt-maker, carting his wares
beside the Ganges in a long,
pink dawn forgetting, but knowing
there is no waste in life,
that a godhead shattered
rains stars for wise men,
and that every martyr, first and last
lives in the hand, a right hand
casting love, belief and courage
like pearls in ether,
like Cana jars, or light
in the corner of decision.

DORIA

Go to your station.

> Surrender your inhibitions now.
> Seal your soul-seams with tape
> and say what you mean.

Fasten your vest, sir.

> I have never been comfortable.
> I am a lingerer, chattel.

> And as estimable as lire.

Hold me, like this, like a baby.

Step forward. Forward please.

> I have always been drowning;
> the air to me was water
> and I was submerged.

> *Il dolce suono*
> *mi colpi di sua voce!... Ah quella voce*
> *m'è qui nel cor discesa!...*

There are biscuits in the boats.

> And I loved you as I loved
> my mother who let me breathe

you bastard.

Little Sal-lee Wa-ter.
Back— back. Let it go!

Oh my God my pearls my pearls
my pearls!
Let it go, baby! Let it go.

— and they have two boys
and they have two girls.

Hail Mary full of grace, the Lord is with thee.
Blessed art thou among women and blessed
is the fruit of thy womb Jesus.

I'll bet
during the Flood, the sea
was not salty like this.

It was more like tears.

Hail Mary full of Grace,
the Lord is with thee—

Alfin son tua, alfin sei mio,
A me ti dona un Dio...

I forgive you.
But I do not forgive me. That's

my penance; that,
and this

you see.

DALÍ: SMART BOMB
IN ANTHROPOMORPHIC ECHO

During the Baghdad assault
we came in numbers, all types,
some on foot, some taking the overnight bus from Basra
disguised as Jordanian donut concessionaires,
others assuming the shape of Queen Anne chairs,
end-tables, bedsteads and the like,
imported for colonels still in favor by the barber-
looking antichrist that validates our existence.

We had replaced the spies who were born in Iowa,
matriculated at the University of Chicago,
drugged themselves, dropped out, took a law degree
out of parental pressure, a bad marriage
out of loin stress and the last strands of religion,
applied to the Agency, left Northern Virginia
and all vestiges of family for Crete,
the Maldives, Iran, and Iraq.

Those missing fellows had provided
Cyrillic blueprints needed to mix the cake,
so to speak, and bake it. We thank them.

But we are the technology.

We are the secret mega-stingers,
the ironics, the ultravideo pie-in-the-face
surgical-strike night-time Ray-Ban
supper club comics, humming along to ourselves,
insurance men in sleek hats and pin-striped

flared metallic-look slacks straight out of Milan,
knocking at the stoop, waiting and whistling
like a Joujouka flute, waiting for a crack
in the door to say, "is Mahmoud in?" and,
sending him to Allah's standing-room only reception
in heaven, become a poof on the Master Cylinder's
wide-screen TV.

Armageddon, buffet-style.

Later, they send in reinforcements,
ice cream men who offer their cones
to apartment complexes, their contents
melting on the faces of children
who weren't supposed to be there.

Bad input. Sorry. But the God of the matrix forgives us.

Later, he will even appear to us,
in another generation of this system,
in the next theater of war
leaving no contrails certainly,
and hardly a whisper.

ELSBREE STREET

This weather—
without clemency.

Cold digs deep massage
in shoulders of December;
the blast of ill wind
stings a near-dead skin
that begins to remember
then forgets again, as
the car comes, and the fumbled umbrella
closes on some drip
of sin.

Rock-salt shrinks yesterday's
ice to vague impression
staining a black thoroughfare
once bright with our footsteps,
squirrels, a hare; everything was important
on those leafy walks— the cries
of us, adult in baby lives that grew
to cards at Christmas— Christmas lights, where?
Or is that just an ambulance? The one that took
your Gram away

                              her name was,

(stare)

— my once catapultingly industrious,
brilliant career—

I am counting out, without receipts
the three, or four, or five

of quite, five thousand times I must
have touched her there?

Her name was Claire.

The salt takes each event aside—
some great palls, some entertainments
of meek accommodation, some Mandarin
clowns
falling down stairs

takes each slippery magnitude and
dries it to a limp and lying
unlabeled year,
a casualty, a lining tear, to drop through pockets
keys to doors that since, it seems, lead
nowhere;

trees are scratching
at the mist, heads down, ashamed in their
alcohol bath, exposed
and bare.

Nothing is very important;

that first thing a child gains
becomes the last, light-lucid thing
you grab, get back, a golden pear
to take along,

in a rain that pours now, pours
as salt turns watery
echoes in a dark, deep drain

and frees the road
to casual travelers
every prayer,

                              and pain.

YOU NEED NOT FEAR THE CATHOLICS, MARIANNE

I know the wryness tips comport to the wind—
we are devils before you, Marianne. But cardinal
is not our color, it was Torquemada's,
and we are just as interested in your pendulum
and crossed cups as any irreligious squanderer
regardless of upbringing. I love your green agate,
your amethyst, your cockscomb and marigold,

they are better than the sameness of the host,
the wine that belittles in its dilution, the square
prance of the stations. But at our best, Marianne,
when the censer calls the smoke out of Purgatory,
when the nuns reach their highnotes, and the brother
scrapes a floor of humility, we approximate
your witch's list with a zealot's cast, kindred

to the last drawn hanged man, rune unwrapped
like a saint's rib-bone, the flames at Beltane
mirrored in bright novenas of other women.
We are together on the night-air of Protestant
conversion Marianne, tickling ourselves with delight
of the true miscreant, the made-men of Zoroaster,
corporals of a Jesus-king, we mystics, we maids

of May, the singing things mattering, sing
good goodness into a morning of missionaries
who forget their orders, drawn like martyrs, merry
to the orange celebration of sky and surrender,

to understanding of the general, end of the specific,
where cherries are sweet, the water cold, glass-pure
and where any number of sacraments flash, awonder.

FLOOD INSURANCE

Noah, build me an accommodation.

Take from the Negev
a set of hopping mice,
and serpents
whose issue can kill
the profligate Cleopatra.

Take grasshoppers
in their sleep
awaiting the plagues
across Africa;
then attend to the first things
first.

Take bees, for what is life
without candy
and organization.

I do not pretend you will
find elephants— in an emergency
you do what you can.
(I will make more later, on the sly.)
But the squirrels along the Jordan, take
two, and camels are a given.

Pay no attention to those
Semites. Look at them
and smile. They will suck in
a wet globe with

their nostrils, and
they will feed the fish
that feed you
absolution.

Make the beam broad enough
to ride a roll, because there
will be drama, and flat
enough to land
like the kiss on
a distant brow.

Your son greets the yew trees
with his spade;
your grandson brings pomegranates,
the women, wheat bales on their
strong heads. I will make them all fertile
and the seed of company
will explode among them, gardening
the generations. Pilgrims must
believe in gardening.

And later on, the rainbow I paint
will be my biggest,
made of blood sorrow,
sapphire sympathy, the solace
of new figs, orange for oranges' sake, purple
for the curtains of kings
I will send you, and
yellow for the wayward sun
that dries into
the stain of my robe

like passengers
to new land.

Obedience
(even to your heart)
is a virtue.
And for this,
this great idea
you so seem to comprehend

I promise to be real
some day.

THE APPARITION OF VICA

The Muscovite winter cries for glowing coals
demanding commitment, for tonight, tomorrow or as long
as two can stay together, safe and warm.

This, in a land of passing wars, night-starts
and cracked doors of governing or private mafias
securing lives and livings, collectively or alone.

According to the Revelations, it will become America;
Vica walks American streets as the Virgin,
rose at her feet, making love to abolish sin.

She could be Natalya, before or after the affair with Kuragin;
she can swallow Chomsky and flirt with a universal tongue,
she could settle in a suburb, or rise in a thunderstorm.

She is everything, nothing at her own commandment.
She is descent into animal delight, without regret.
She is golden flow from a samovar, sweet and wet.

Suspended in early morning, their faces alive
they contemplate the holy pictures on the wall—
they become orthodox in a spinning, surreal world.

Our Vica kisses her poet's ear, whispering
a tune beyond time and the River Niemen, balancing
her griefs with the heart of Providence's hope, and reason.

ÉTUDE IN E MAJOR, FINAL BAR

The very
last note
drops
like the last
drop of
water from
a crystal
bud vase, tipped

by the first
wind lick
of a summer
storm in
Paris

in 1829,

darkening
petals of the one
rose
it no longer
holds.

A gray goose
quill rests
in an ink pot
and

it begins

to rain.

A BIRTH SOMEWHERE, AFAR

I know; your tea is steeped,
and ready now.

The old have their separate wonder.
They own the codes, the secrets
leached into walled vaults in deep places,
gaining sights of young
and unshorn faces, as they pass
prayer beads and
sit, amid daily shows of predisposed laughter,
of bells ringing; they hear a seeped
and separate singing
of their song.

They repaint Seurats
with colors they've retained,
dulled by dust but innervated
with moments of lucid self,
and though they've forgot the coming,
and the pain,
they remember shoots of rain that slapped
the pier, and running
to the arms of one
who left them, but
who left them sane.

So don't pity, or profit from,
or profane them. They
are turning into angels—
learning the lyre and orange

guitar of the cherubim who
sit by the chair of God, or who return
with that music, saried and dotted
mid the drum and sarod
of Delhi's sunrise or yet, suburban
child, in a house with suburban
garage, not quite reincarnate,
but not quite mirage.

And at that,
I prepare my long goodbye, mother,
I prepare it now, and revel in
this passing of your passage
in every hour, losing to me your offerings
and your alphabet,

but gaining for me, soon enough
your stars.

PUBLIC SPEAKER

Good evening.

It's like...
I'm behind
that big snow-fort
of my ninth year—
warm in cold,
squinting pink
safe from icy bombs
a king of slippery pride

except that now—

I'm thirty-nine
and notice
all the snow
has melted and
has dried.

MONTICELLO, MAY

"I believe that Jesus Christ,
like Socrates, was a great man."

— from the writings

Strolling aimless
on the persimmoned
promenade, immersed
in the end of a first
long paragraph of
worthy declaration,
he trips on his young gardener,
a slave.

"Excuse me," he says
to the dark-eye man
named Hubert

Jefferson Clay.

Besides this fact,
small but indelible as indigo
ink on parchment paper, as
blood on hay

it also,
really

rained that day.

VEGAS

We've had our time.

Drunk to the punt
(on effervescent wine)
cashing in our chips
before midnight, in a bright house
where sin abuts virtue
at the eaves of old memory—
up the glass flue
to a swirl of bathwater,
trail of perfume,
a deft matching of sock and sock
as we pack for home
with a smile, a clue.

SOMETHING ABOUT ARYANS AND JEWS

Aren't we marvelous.

Fine cars, trappings gilded, hair in place,
with a breath of flowers
and bold belief in our own superior race.

We ascend the ramp, traverse the arch—
into the abattoir, stupid before stunning
we, the footnotes of history, cry
at once, at length,
our feet stuck,
our motors running.

CANTILENA: BRACELET OF SIMILES

(I've fished in the basket of words and phrases made
for you bright one, polishing the tips with rhyme
for a bracelet of similes that sing or somehow say—
"I offer a gift, for a fall day in ordinary time.")

No use for "useless as a turtle's wrist," replace—
(save it as comment for this, a daft endeavor)
nor, "like icicle stabs, melting without trace"—
this won't fit the fit emotion of love I treasure.

"Like a loose string, tuned by turns to a shimmering C,"
you grow in the grace notes touched, retouched, by me.
Better. "Like rain, easing into cisterns in Capri"
your laughter wells a clear, concrete polyphony

or "like plainchant, circling all the naves and vestries
of seven churches gilt with withheld mysteries."

Better, still better? Let me knife to the deep
"as the pearl fisher combs his sand in aqua illusion,"
emerging with the wonder of your eyes, erasing sleep
"like shells that open to their own light's bathing fusion."

But, where's *best* I'll find to give you now,
knowing raw gold collects with draw of days,
with the harrow of years, with a child's why and how,
with all the scars of blessing that cement our stay?

I've put one here, just near the fastening clasp;
it will open (fall days) in drift of our communion

"like spirits bound and spinning strands of glass"
that reach from God's hand to His endless ocean.

(The bracelet, incomplete, I leave with you—
as similes of image make us one, from two.)

LINES FROM *COMMUNION SONATA*

after Transcendental Etude No. 11,
"Harmonies du Soir," by Franz Liszt

Wild celebrant
in white and flashing red performs his mystic transference
of grain to flesh, grapes to blood
enchanting thirteen little penitents
whose crimes have had the time to stray
from chocolate theft
to giggling accords in a backyard of whispers.

About each golden-flecked
and collar-buttoned neck
and on each pair of shoulders, sets
a cotton strap of Christ's life sewn in multicolored thread—
from stable-birth
to the Walk of Palm and Olive, dead,
hung like meat upon a nail but changed,
in fortnights, to an elevated grail which would
"shake and almost crack the axis of this earth,"
so the rector said to his little lambs in the front pew and
anointed with their sweet, exhilarated breath announced:
"so much for death, so much, so much, for death."

The highest purpose flies
to the creation of effect.

A late arrival genuflects.

He gives them bread.
They bow their heads and turn
a little army flushing red
toward winking Sister Jacqueline who'd said

"Your souls will be as purely white as this—"
and taps, once more
a crooked finger
on her chest.

As fishers, we
who float on shimmering seas, each
servile to his Simon-self, to his own reach
hauling the twine of retrospective motion
the appalling grip-on-grip to find
beneath the sequined,
black-drawn drape of God's mind
a line that draws and ties
a small, paternally-created son
to one enormous
inevitable One;

through pain of progeny, the strain of labor,
it follows our ascendant wealth
(like kittens pawing walls of brittle paper)
and as fishers fall
amid the images of sackcloth, and some neighbors—
it can stain the warp and weft
of our collected,
frightened laughter yet remain
more tauntingly
along the border-stitch of Janie's
fifty-nine
cent

scapular, as lit
by a nine-
cent taper.

RITUAL INTERRUPTED

Here, fill out the grieving slate.
Sing a song to yourself while you wait.
A man will come to the door by and by,
shaking a tambourine.
Jump to your feet when you see him.
The long hall will smell of jasmine and memories
and you will be tired
but don't stop, even for those
who will hunker in the alcoves—
shadows of themselves, and others.

Stay near to his black shoulder, the man, and whisper
the seven words, over and over. You will be
offered a grape by a woman in white as you turn
to the veranda. She will say she is your mother
and she will be. Don't eat the grape.

In the veranda, you will notice the man,
the black man, will drop the tambourine.
Do not be startled. You are not a pigeon,
and he is nothing to be afraid of. He is
the last new friend you will remember.

You will be tempted by the water; it will look
like water, the cool water of your best thirst,
but it is not water. It is glass. Walk by, stay
to the black man's shoulder.

At the door of the Grande Maison, we call it
the Grande Maison, you will stop as if a soldier,

one, two. He will turn you around, and you will
try to count to ten, and you will not be able to.
Frustrated, you will turn around. Some don't turn
around for a long while. Turn around.

The door is etched with hyacinths and thorns. The knocker
has a hammer, huge and bronze. Lift it with all your might, and
let it fall down. Lift it again, and let it fall down.
Lift it, and let it fall down.

Pray. Lift it, and let it fall down.
Lift it
                                and let it fall down

ERNEST AND GLORIA

I have become accustomed to the emptiness of this room
faster than forty-nine years would have countenanced—
I must still take the pot off its boil and groom
the tiniest corners and cracks of our existence.
I leave often for Providence, the Cape, trips for the day,
they have filled my itinerary beyond your imagination—
see the kids Sundays, and the news at eleven, late,
my days enlarge in the penance of the seventh station.
Remember the lights at LaSalette, they burned
from our first Christmas to beyond the very last—
same reds and oranges and bright whites I'd earned
when you looked on me as somehow beautiful, and asked.
So I cry, you left your chair— but photographs
imply that then, and mostly everywhere, we laughed.

IN A ROOM, YEARS AGO, YESTERDAY

At times like these—
supine on the bed's
chenille spread
motionless

counting panels on
the ceiling

— there are still fourteen—

feeling
the waste, when I could have been
hauling the colors
to wave up smoking hills
or, dashing to damsels
who wrap
(like a Velazquez)
'round my feet, kneeling—

I see

it's almost time
for supper
here—

if not
Madrid

or Mongol plains

or on the dew-
dripped, minted
tea leaves licked
by katydids

in red
tomorrow morning's

sweet
Darjeeling.

ANT FARMS

It came for them as for us, straight
out of the box, requiring little construction.

On the kitchen table,
laminated with specks
and bordered in chrome
standing on aqua and blue-checked
linoleum, in a kitchen
enameled with Admiral
and Amana, ready as
a doll's house, too.

It was not big, but ready
to expand with life
after the waiting.
Finally, they poured in the
sand, pink sands
outside the Fontainebleau
as we from Aruba, hot flecks
from beyond the veils
of our first mornings.

It's a silly thing. Their
parents had one, too. But fun
to imagine, fun to do, fun
when the packet comes parcel post
and "fragile" it says, even though
we shake it like it
means to tell us, genie-like,
something we never knew.

Fancies scurry on the grains,
disappearing like dreams
into silica, setting up housekeeping
in the glass, according
to rules.

Did we, like you, seem to cast
aside such seeming boulders
ten times our weight, shoring balustrades
and hallways
with the busy business of such
young fools?

Or were they, the old ones as fascinating
on a night without cards,
with a model of a Windjammer
but no glue, to have watched it all go by
between the panes, the days
and hours, minutes only, known to the
nearly industrious few.

Now then, fleet ones, start anew.
Make your mistakes. Mingle
with genes that weren't cut
to carry bits of leaf in a long
latitude, but bits of a heart
bit clean in two.

Pull the dragonfly's wing
in opposite directions, let ambition
shiver as you ride it
in a drainbound deluge.

But first, enjoy
the symmetry of the glass,
hope's rainbow,
the still moment of freedom,
the invitation to dig, the doing
what the fresh June morning
of marriage means
you were meant to do.

Later, when
this wistful
pair of windows
falls
from the table, cracks
and leaks its intimate world
in sandy remonstration, or is emptied
in the yard of the busier world
and thrown to the barrel-men,
do not cry, you.

So it must. Accept the wrought wonder.
The amusement of toys.

The world is full of them.
The world makes more of them.

The happy world.
And the world fastidious,
fascinatingly
cruel.

AFTER, THE GUGGENHEIM

The art is in my bag.
A mobile of Miró,
linoleum from Klee,
big bright blocks for my patio,
the tears of Wyeth like two large
onions hung from the white-
washed window as seen from the outside—
scent and sight of Helga's undressed smiles
still nagging the reflection
of his long, crestfalling way.

The art is in my bag, surely as
Picasso's horse (in the stall of my neighbor)
talks a blue streak on the horror of war
and in my bag, the bluest Blue Boy, and the Alba
Madonna
on a barrelhead, her shoulders succulent
as breasts, the child beatific, blessed
as I adjust the halo.

The art is all mine,
mine, do you want my papers?
Fine, you Goya sentinel, smeared
with cobalt in the dying day
I have them in my coat,
which is on
the man that floats above rooftops,
on every man floating to the distant horizon
of hope, and the art that is in my bag

belongs to me, nope, nope—
let me go. I'll dry in hot shale sands
of New Mexico, a shamed head
reduced to calcium and smoke
but to the end, 'til an orchid of coral
and umbre through a socket pokes,
I'll claim this cache

as proof the sky is more
than meteors, the earth's perspective
something more for minds

to paint, or play
a joke.

SALINAS

Buses arrive in the Valley of the Sun King
dealing out Spanish paragraphs on tongues
of duty, dappled with light and a feeling
of the earth unwormed in dampness, reeling
from the past, but open to the epilogue
of new and late planting, of jugs unsealing.

Scallions bloom, smearing the day with their
pregnant smell and no sound; watermelons
belch so sweet, their pulp simmering in balls
so round around they roll with the kick of a foot
and speak themselves ready to spit their seed if left
just one more summery shower in the ground.

Artichokes organize; their rows are neat,
their hides, appropriately forbidding; they brim
a love of continuity, their good hearts beating
to the avocado's drum, it's green when done
unlike the unrouged peppers, just begun—
stragglers of the season, seasoning some.

All day the pickers move, bent this way
in the U of their existing, in the songs of May
that penetrate the furrows, tingle the roots
of sustaining, the *Santo* way, the animal, vegetable,
the sky and sway, the land gives, except
when it doesn't,
                              when it takes away.

MUNCHKINLAND
(12 poems of men and women without love)

I. THE LULLABY LEAGUE

LUTE (THE SPINSTER)

No one hears.

Head thrown back—
my nape is smooth,
my varnish warm
and belly round;

fine French filigree
forms a hollow where
comes no sharing sound
for this, or forty
other years.

Unregaled, the
strings unplucked,
unstrummed yet tightly wound
in musk of a closet's
silent sorrow—

sudden shrills, the lowest moan
await my stillborn,
still-deaf balladeer

tomorrow.

DIVA

She brings from the pit
a sacrificial moan
of saints, martyrs, Theresa,
Joan, the flush of griefs,
the quivering fire, flesh, and bone.

She's Andromache, counting laps
of Hector's corpse 'round
the ramparts of Troy

or she mounts

a Lincoln trunk in Dallas

picking up pieces
of her husband's memory
like parts of a broken toy.

She is Callas, Norma, Medea, Tosca,
all consumed.

She is beautiful too,
for a walking wound.

THE NAMING

What shall we call this tenth celebration of our love?
I do not normally speak this way because
I am illiterate as geese, as graceful as our sow
but I ask you, as I reveal another daughter

to the pleasure and praise of our so-special god,
the one who denies you males, who punishes you
for picking a Harrell girl over fair Demeter—
is it like the first, or was first like a second-prize cow?

I forget, won't you tell me, won't you play your guitar?
You retreat now, as always, to winter wheat, the plow.
Shall we call her Ariadne! Who waits for her lover
under gray and Grecian skies, only to surrender

her progeny to these tattered sheets, these baskets
of laundry, the dowage of her grandmother's mother?
Can she be no other? Be beautiful, be passionate and true?
Call her Emma, Emma. That, as you say, will do.

AND HIS LOVELY WIFE

Tongue slips into me.

What would you say—
would you be speechless
as this young man
who I'll happily pay
from the silver
lining of your capital gain,

clutching the sheets as
the last drop
of our attachment
clings to the blinded window—

dirty rain.

OTHER WOMEN

Persephone hugs her Hades' neck at tea
secure in dank Rubbermaid surroundings, her coming-
out notice and school plays trunked and mortified,
curling at the edges, the persistent hyacinth weeds

clipped from stoop and step to the ramp of the Lethe,
wellworn hands that dig with a suicide dagger,
with point lost (or clearly forgotten) just to keep
these walks of Forever very, very clean—

it's better to pocket sorrow, settle, agree—
query the widows who stumble on stubble-filled streets
out of Ilium, or she, half-mortal mother of a dead
bastard son, who'll say "This was my Achilles— *ask me.*"

THE BRIDES

Our engagement began in a smile
that froze us to our communion picture,
all white lace and prayer beads;

continued in the cloister of our Catholic schools
reinforced by lack of courtiers,
and committed like glue
to the tears of our parents,
the day we gave ourselves away.

We are the Sisters of Obedience.
We are the Marymounts, the Mercies.
We engage in the foreplay of lepers
on the south side of Pinotubo. We heave
as the waves do against Molokai.

We giggle to ourselves, patching up
frowns of beaten whores in São Paulo.
We are rammed, rammed, sideways and
down, cartwheeling off the road
in El Salvador.

We play cards at night, and say rosaries.
We know what the Virgin knew.

We are declining statistics. We are few.
We live our lives waiting,
dripping a soul-salve silkier
than sex.

We are the brides of Christ.

He comes for us separately
when He comes for you.

II. THE LOLLIPOP GUILD

GAUCHO

The sun drips
sunset frosting
on the pampas.

At a new fire,
he eats, as always
with his fingers.

He explains:

if you need a fork
you need a plate
so you need a table
to put it on
then a chair
to sit at the table
before long
you're living with a woman
and a batch of kids
and a dog
that kills your chickens.

ADAGIETTO

As a youth
Mahler was afraid
of photographers,
afraid
he would, by magic
be whisked into the camera
box and stuck
forever
to a cardboard matte

but if
he had, maybe
he would not
have written the fifth
symphony
and then I

having lost you

would not
be listening to
this adagietto
over and over
and would not
perhaps

be paralyzed and crying

even now.

AFTER A PARTY (OCCASION, FORGOTTEN)

Cling to you I,
pink balloon ballasted by
        static,
dusty favor
on a rueful afternoon.

You do not love me.

The chairs are put away.
The cake, swept into hands
and napkins, the cola capped.

And the ornaments.

Don't let me hang around,
bouncing my head at the ceiling
until time, really little time
lowers an unsolved self
to the cower of your knees

and floored in the silence
        like intact glass
unfeels
all feeling of inevitable fall, drunk
with amnesia of each
good-night
beneath our tall, our festive stars,
forever

wheeling.

AMONG THE GAS GIANTS

I'd read somewhere
that the seventh planet
spins backwards,
tilted on its side,
frozen deep away
from a pinprick sun
but seething, boiling
at the ulcerous core,
convulsions of sulphur
and selanate fouling all
its heaving ball of sea,
the waves roaring under
perpetual, poisoned fog
without a speck of land
for the drowning or undrowning
hand to grasp, relentless

yet I covet this, a dream
to wake only to wake
as it, my most elaborate
version of hell explodes

in the dullness of your eyes.

MISSION

Pretty boy, no horizontal bomber.
I am not prey for flack and old fighters.
I am your Stuka, dear.

I set my eagle sight in vertical dive
watching the wet, wan horror of your eyes,
I penetrate, I sear.

And then I pull away, alert, alive,
veer right or left, me whistling, you wise
beyond your tender year.

Of course I'll disappear, clearing clouds
leaving the hole, the carnage, trailing
mistrust, the scent of fear.

Rebuild the tress and trestles of your life,
cementing over whispers of
"remember I was here."

I am the way of war, the little crime
to be redressed in Desse or Dresden—

in some other year.

THE GARDEN

On a day before I die—

in dreams of drifting powder,
silky strands, and chocolate pie—
I remember
with no vesper of regret,
no recrimination or accounting of what's due,
no devil or incarnate,
no god and nothing borrowed, even blue—
the garden of our passion where
a wet, wide butterfly opened
to a stiff, pink pollen-
full stamen

and hyacinths grew.

§

FOR YOUR PENANCE

Step quietly at vespers.
Do not stir at the moment of blessing.
Build an asylum for your faith,
and live in it.
Wear the vestments of certainty
without stain or crease.
Dry-clean your mistakes
with Philippians and Timothy.
Walk among bees without fear.
God makes them buzz and swarm,
so listen.

For your penance, three rosaries
and the indulgence of your enemies.

Turn the light out as you leave.

SKYDIVER

You split the air my best girl,
attached to the stranger who companioned you
through altitudes I have not fallen,
but who saw you to my grateful
grounded X, and you fired a look, glint
in my glasses, love, that you loved me.

Why could I not have seen
attached to me in gravity, the grave
sameness of your years as wife
and mother, the adoration of plates,
photos, tolerance, the pains of babies
and known these loves were dual
and contracted, not of your private dreams,
your heaven of small solitudes, your
tart and still-sweet yet-adventures,
your possibility.

Can you forgive smug duty,
misplaced anger, that glum
look looking up at the sky, waiting
for sprouts that turn
to flowers, thinking
end was end and could not
be beginning
thinking sun awaited yet
another shower, and that I,

a fortune to be spent that just
hadn't been made, could turn
my dreams, and your dreams too

into everything we ever,
ever wanted, if

I could find my own way
cloudward, finding you
in each content you give with
freed or freeing smile, every turn
in wind, with every chance you take
and want me to be taking, sign of lovers
still invented, and with every shake,
so fortunate my daring, daring devil
girl, unshaking.

THE SEMANTIC OF GREATER KIND

Isn't it all about defining?
The walk, stuck of gravity
on this ballful of sin and rain on which
we conjugate and form ourselves—
appreciate the sun and smiles too,
the night-wane and the seldom
serious, opportune glue that means,
finds some binding
of a grammar known to many
though, perhaps, too
many few.

I'll leave the you but really,
how would I define me?

Loaded with entries.
Nouns that carry their weight like
mercury in a bucket. Quick,
silver, slippery but when contained—
a temperature of the masses
or poison of long standing.

Verbs that were action,
now *archaic.*

Idioms borrowed:
wish me luck (Br.),
don't take me lightly (Am.), mea culpa (L.)

Derivations from the Old
French, as in *ah* + *las,* wretched, or
aille, the act of.

I sit in the library that is my life,
poring over issue, dreaming new text
I will not have time to write.

I am your own to peruse,
to use in sentences.

In the end, as me for you, it's you
who defines me, bright or boiled,
you the subject, moved to who,
what, where, *why* me
into portals of shared history,
a good novel, handbook on husbandry,
a passion play

or maybe just one look of God-sent
wordless knowing that
might actually
divine me.

EPISTLE OF SAINT PAUL, ON RICE PAPER

The sensei
breaks concrete,
swimming
in the rocks.
The Christ,
tap dances on water—

you can hear the shocks.

THE CIRCLE

for John

Me, plot a point upon the board
a string stretched taut
and you, the chalk, the runner
running ever clockwise save
when someone might be looking
then, you walk.

Student, trace this arc
throughout your mileage and your talk;
stop and start, pass the lap
in mobs and solitude,
thicken its path with babies, blood, accolades,
bury your face in orchids and wisteria,
skate the late March ice and pull
your failures from the cracked channels,
fling yourself at honor.

Your geography will play and fade
in the full fast forward of six
by a thousand days— on the Mystery Ride
the doors blew black, remember,
to a stark, still brightness
on that painted track.

Is little Pip, or Edmond Dantes back?

The amusement park is closed and yes,
the hilly masterpiece of fieldstone

and spires gave way to the public Complex,
cold, so freeze a little in a wet-whipped wind
you forgot we accept here as expiation for sin
and check in at the door.

"What are you here for?" Pay the guard his homage.
Hold your copy of the cantos,
penned on derricks, held against the frieze
of a felled, gray column in a ruined breeze,
Cambodia and Camden, Portugal and the sea,
Aeneas to Troy City:

"Home, you see."

You return on the circle, in Shelley's place,
his burnt heart left on Leghorn's Beach,
to follow the natural curve of space—
has student come to learn, or teach?

Still plotting my pivots on the slate, me.
Can the new ones relate to Keats's pleurisy?
Can I make them dance in their own green bay?
I don't know, I still attempt, a little gray.

Here, hold the string taut, loosen me
in the fondness of this new memory;
oh, to be free-flown! this stoker stiff
as the statues of Hephaestus on Aegean cliffs,
let's circle on words, and geometry.

SONNET: JOHN HOLMES AS HAMLET

I saw my father's ghost laughing like hell
as I sought a memory that wasn't of yesterday,
or this morning (after the sun rose and swelled),
sought one romantic line, not white, not weighed.
My mother, set on a throne of love, spits blood;
I sit among concubines, unmoved, statuesque
like marble, member blessed in a black hood
under lights that illumine sonny-boy at his best.
My harem is rented. Ophelia to my left, she hums
the tune young women hum before the last act
leaves them wan, bereft, subtracting sums
to come or not to come, before they die, in fact.
I am the light of pestilence, the One.
I am you as you watch me, *and I am done.*

PRE-RAPHAELITES

Beauty clouds by accident and surprise
rendering malignant flaw from images benign
like the sliver in Fra Lippo Lippi's eye.

In tempera, forms the icon we surmise
awash with cherubs on a barrel-lid of brine—
beauty clouds by accident, and surprise.

Sculpting virgins out of marble, pieces fly,
the resolute and earnest strike resigns
like the sliver in Fra Lippo Lippi's eye.

A crease, a curve, soft to sight, it lies
somewhere between a rhythm and a rhyme—
beauty clouds by accident, and surprise.

But you, bright love, who set yourself astride,
my head within your hands, you drift in kind
like the sliver in Fra Lippo Lippi's eye.

You know, too well, an artist knows he dies
in increments of stone and paint, refined—
beauty clouds by accident, and surprise
like the sliver in Fra Lippo Lippi's eye.

ARIADNE OF NAXOS: A REPRODUCTION

She acquires a circle of men
dissolving, after a time to others, but always
men, reaching, souls extended
to unreachable flesh,
to a core of universes.

It goes on daily; it has for ages.

Her marble, rubbed and softened for the eye—
the eye of Theseus, of George and Fitzroy
(one, killer of a minotaur,
two, sweepers of a maze's floor)—
her tearless eye tearing from the inside
beholds a tribute of war, and wages.

She is you, and you are all
women of whatever consequence,
station, size, the object of conquest
and longing, the siren, the widow,
the nymph and whore, goddesses
of broad pantheon, all represented here.

Arcs of delicate symmetry stroke
the cheeks of white ardor, breasts enveloping,
small hollow before the mound, limbs
that climb from little feet to
junctions above, cool slopes,
warm valley,
inviting unrequited,

unrelenting
real

love.

STREETS OF FALL RIVER

This city opens
to the darkened east
in granite and somnolence,
the dawn behind it—
sloping its tenements to the green bridge
inviting Providence through
Swansea, coughing
itself awake, clearing
an everyday blear with coffee
and cream-cakes at the Terminal
Bakery on South Main Street,
a little before seven.

It is freezing in February.

The variety stores open
clutching bundles
of the *Herald News,* reshuffling
their sundries down to the last can
and candy bar you can find
on the next block, too.

These neat squares of Fall River,
a hundred of them,
same citadels beyond their
second century rise like
afterthoughts— they have seen
such birth and love, fight,
indifference, dying, they
are the same houses housing

the same names— Sousa, Suneson, Charette
that pass their generations under
new coats of paint or aluminum siding,
permanent as persistence,
still trying.

In the old days
the neighborhoods were parochial, hard
in their nationality—
parks had their bronze heroes,
churches saints, prayed
to in French, Portuguese, Polish;
their masses fed only familiar tongues
between the Latin.

Now, they don't assume
so much as a grandmother's stare
when they court and marry,
their bloods and festivals
mix and carry them together
like fitted rocks of Rock Street,
bound with trolley-tracks in a calendar's
concrete of chimed existence
until or if they crack
like any other coupling—
to tears and reminiscence.

This town was a cotton-weave,
a sewing machine,
the coat hanger of a nation;

Lizzie Borden walked its
ways the lonely figure of acquittal,
her lingering, off-put smile

printed on teeshirts; you can visit
the murder site, just down Second Street
from Middle.

Main came together at Pleasant,
at the heart of things; the garish
lemon of the Lloyd's sign you could see
farther than you could walk, the buses lined up;
McWhirr's and Cherry's
swung their furs and hatboxes
in promenade, Italian singers played the Durfee—
soft, these silver-belled walks
so swelled at Christmas, stripped in the seventies
for an inside mall, for one
closing after another— Woolworth's,
Newberry's, a mother with child
by the hand, all lost, all of them lost.

But the city goes on. The river
clings to the battleship
neath the bridge, considers ice
for water. Cars cross over
to a pink east of New Bedford
toward the empty Cape.

Through the day, commerce.
An economy of days; through
the night, early night, the deckers
and condos quietly fill, the streets
become a movie set, waiting
for scenes. Ninety thousand hive
and sleep, three-floored, three deep.

They are good
people; they work hard, they laugh,
at odd times, weep. I come here
as I can from far away, feeling
the drifter returning to monuments,
to some common, holy
or likely wholly lost
sense of all I see,
what I was and where I came from,
the everything I fear I know
too well, and yet, too often,
all I wish to be.

INSTRUCTIONS IN THE FAITH

(Our Prayer of Counterfeits, Prince of the Air)

Get the idea
of a prison planet.

Far enough away
from the traffic of this galaxy
to be squinting at a few sequins
in wonder.

Upon this planet
place the artists, the criminals,
the non-conformers, the perverts,
the Bolivars.

Make them believe in one life
forgetting the last one, like the cheap command
of a nightclub hypnotist.

Stir the pot, constantly.

Add flora, dumb fauna,
invisible plasms—
everything human aquaria need
to approximate drowned existence,
down to day-glow Christs and Buddhas
submerged in the mist.

Stir the pot, constantly.

Set standards for the sane. Fill the asylums,
and run them. Take toys from the children
according to decrees. Keep an underclass boiling.

Embellish violence with the King's English
and Sector 3 Logic. Put it in the papers
and on lively screens.

Get serious about national peril, per the schedule.
Reintroduce new fashions
of killing machines... demonstrate.

Get atomic, slowly, as if that hadn't happened before.
Have them scare each other with it.
(Don't make a mistake here, or you'll have to start over.)

Let them create, they HAVE to create, so let them—

pietas and sunflower scenes, with anarchists
to break off noses and slash petals
in random protest.

Beautiful robberies, well planned.

Rapes to calypso music.

Men in three-piece suits with large duck heads,
making statements.

Escalators of dolls in fedora hats,
our successes, fueling hives that generate
pharmaceuticals, tires, lipstick
and shiatsu massagers.

Allow them boats of various sizes, tied
to long quays.

Fan the insect urge for sex. Then
control it, like the honey-maker.

But whatever you do,
keep these little bleats from banding together,
except as a mob. (Assassinate, with panache.)

And don't EVER let them wake up.
Order new chemicals to numb them
or paint Picassos before their eyes.

Keep the keepers in charge.
Keep the keepers in charge.
Keep the keepers in charge, mister—
as if your lives depended on it.

Understand the task, always, better than they do.
And begin.

Perception is reality; the universe turns upon its pin...

in nomine
Patris, et Filii,
et Spiritus Sancti,
Amen.

A MAN FROM CALAIS

Dear
renowned
barflies
multilingual serviettes
      people who'd punch
      my face in
pretty nurses, poetasters,
pets—

is this on?

Come and love me now,
come place a bet.

I arrive at this noontide
filled with gall and comic
hubris, knowing
I have not only failed you,
but colored that failure
with an incandescent brush,
greasing my body with it
like some mime in a bathhouse,
and ready
      to plunge.

Bring me your mementos,
your betrayals, stupidities,
your lies
small as a thalidomide prescription,
big as an Edsel—
oh these brittle buoys of me!

I will sign in silver ink:

> Love and Kisses
> Loss and Cries
> anything you like

but here, you hold the pen
     it's time;
I steep
my too-wide feet inside
that cold blueness
     slapping the quay with its insistent
     scorn
and bear myself saltily from shore,
paddling champion
of the meek
father of salvation, going
     for the record
going for a streak—
     Kiss those chalky cliffs!
     (in French, the dots
     of all my paramours scream)

I'm swimming
swimming the Channel, me
swimming the Channel

out to sea.

YOU, CAPULET

In autumn streets of my demise
I believe I am still young,
barely shaven, not even muscled
into what I'll lose,
thoughtful flare of ideal June—
        a penny shined
and spinning in desire.

The world was against us,
it was forty arms' length to our selfish fire—
our parents were nagging statues,
the church made it legal—
and my best man was no closer
to me than Tybalt, red pools
of inconvenience on our way
wet, regal.

Yet I died that day
we parted; not of flesh, as poison
was too easy, don't you think,
and a dagger, comedy; it seemed I lived,
you lived at a lost address,
among old objects
an oblong box confesses.

I think of you. The dust
we raised, the desolate
insignificance in common
place of later days.

Some nights I tell me
you were nothing like
I fancy, first and not last,
        but comparing
for all its sport and happy science
reduces to apples and elephants
under any glass.

This I'll say—
filled of ale now, tracing
the blocks toward my shopworn number,
you had promised, you, more
than was delivered

        but you promised so much—
the sea was a brooklet,
smallest of rivers dying of source
in a silent mouth

and in this fine moment
of candor, of drouth
on a scene and to curtains riven,
        I prefer it all still
to the salt sameness
of stranding
in a swale of dead nevers— the oh that touch!
        but more, that kiss that in its such
and for its season seared,
and shivered.

Having died in my teens,
I should have forgotten
that bold, barely quiverless

man of men
and about the young woman—

well-known, winsome tragedy
a given.

TO THE POTTER'S FIELD

Gone now.
Soliloquy
grasps the concrete and evergreens,
spackled paint on vacant bench,
hushed words and subordinate clauses

of griefs and longings
cling to boughs and empty spaces
awaiting the night-freeze, the change
into crystals and shards

that fall in random, earless deafness
to the hard ground, tinkling
like the chimes of heaven.

NASHVILLE, ANSWERING MACHINE

AP 35— (Camden) A search is underway in West Tennessee for the missing private plane piloted by the manager of Grand Ole Opry star Patsy Cline. Miss Cline and two other Opry stars were believed aboard the plane.

At a corner booth
the receiver swings
to a listless tune.

On the steps of the Parthenon replica
three blocks from Music Row
Patsy's angel, coiffed and gold alights
sitting cross-legged
'neath a sultry moon.

                                        beep

Sorry I
missed you
not over you yet,
why don't you
call me
and
remind me
to
forget.

                                        click

Romance sings to
southern stars
unrehearsed and unheard; the fifth
of March, the anniversary,
thirty-first.

EQUINOX

Goldenrod flowers
explode in the Dresden air.
He rides in a rare open car
to the thrall of *Lohengrin* at Bayreuth.
Too late.

He has been murdered by these flowers
and doesn't know it—
they will, by afternoon
balloon his face into a turnip,
cloud the incisive mind (lined with lead)
that has kept him dancing on the globe like Colossus.

Frustrated, he'll order the defense of Calais.
Bewildered, he'll go to Wolfsschanze
instead of the mountains.
Dumbstruck, he'll allow a Catholic colonel with no hand
to blow the life from his arms and phallus, yes
piece by piece, and with every centimeter
it advances.

Even as Belsen obscures the smell of their blooms
with its own black musk.
Even as their shoots writhe in green
over dead corporals at Irtutsk.
Even as Eisenhower walks among
them with his mistress
it advances, like tanks of the previous summer.

Spring is here. Ozymandias crumbles in the desert.

And as always, it appears
to be an accident.

TWENTY-SEVEN WEEKS

At seven, I held it in my hand.
The sparrow baby
shorn from its egg,
abandoned by its mother
who was no songbird—

more like the successor
to archaeopteryx,
to a Jurassic past, cold
and culling out the small
and unfit heirs to a line of plasm
hurled through space and holding fast
to an earth just waiting
to release it, to oblivion
once again

and at last.

      *   *   *   *   *   *   *

I hold his tiny hand.

Evan, who at twenty-seven weeks
has no business out of a womb,
down and skin, angular bones and
the same big eyes with draped-
on lids, similarly transparent and
waiting, just waiting to be thrown
from the third floor of a warm space
to the cold and prickly grass,
except your mother, Evan

blanched of blood yet turning pink
with new blood from a flask, decides
you are better than the fittest,
you are hers, you are ours
and you answer in your thriving moments

every question every sparrow
or unthinking species
never even had

the chance
to ask.

LORCA'S DREAM

In summers of December

Christ returns
to His rocky beach
but no one's there,
alack.

He walks green water
in a stiff breeze
all the way
from the Tierra del Fuego
to the stones of Antarctica, and back.

Blindness!
                          The blindness!

This rumor
exists between shepherds,
among sheep.

From cliffs, the Señor, they pray to him
even as June comes cold

but now as then, before
(and when)
they have that old and awful knack

of humankind—
they fall

asleep.

ATLANTIC OUT A WINDOW, DESCENDING

From a mile up
water is a raiment
tight on a nubile world.

But to the distance
of an arrow flown, descending
it is scraped of dander,

shedding threads
of middle age.

Before you hit
it rips itself to bare skin
an aged bed-rider
dreaming
of wild tongues that lap
grey-green beyond

a mother's hand,
or two hundred
mothers' hands, a panoply
reliving all themselves
into death.

Splashes heard by egrets,
upset the cod
in their silver signature,
but a rain of accessories
does not think.

The sea yawns
among sparklers
then

redresses for dinner.

BENEATH MY RELIGION

for Gette

Beneath my religion I dare to worship, too
at virgin's feet, where youth and on was spent
upon the low and least spectacular of men, a fool
straining to understand (with head of damp cement)
how she could pass at lifetime's bright security
and cast her holy bread to pigeons of obscurity.

There are times I shake, I shudder, nearly cry—
despite dumb pride and predilection to be cruel,
mouthing wondrous nine-day novenas of why,
within our wet onenesses, or strewn across miles
I gaze, starving on her likeness, in bent cellophane—
miscreant who finds the Hope Diamond in his gruel.

However fixed, this lot I win, God smiles
at the straw man picked to ornament and gown her,
marvel at the beauty of her children, only to crown her
with mortgaged diadems of all my failures' pain—
but lit, by chrism of her kiss and candles' fire,
the mystery yet madly flickers, paling to explain.

THE WATER GOBLIN

In the Slovak highlands,
there is a story.

Beneath a lake lives a goblin.
He seduces a young woman
who is irresistibly drawn
to the water, although
her mother has warned her
not to go near the lake.

As she edges toward the lip
of the shore, the ground sinks
beneath her feet;
no turning back—
she is drawn to the bottom of the pool
where she becomes
the goblin's wife.

In the murk of her new living room
she grows sad, since
it is a gloomy place,
where the goblin holds the souls
of those who have drowned
in a cabinet with glass panes—
there, they can peer out only,
craving touch.

She sings a lament to her child
regretting what has happened.

When the goblin hears her,
he becomes angry and threatens
to change her into a trout
but is persuaded, after all
to allow her to return for a single day
to dry land—
while keeping the child
against her return.

The girl and her mother
are overjoyed that they are together
again. When the goblin
knocks at the door
he is turned away.

At this he raises a great storm
and something
is hurled
against the door of the house—

it is the child—
the head
cut from the body.

      *   *   *   *   *   *   *

Yes, it's an awful
story. The kind you
find in old fairytale books
with wonderful,
awful illustrations.

The story reminds me
of the Smith girl, the one in all the papers.
Yes, there are discrepancies. It is blurred, murky.

Not Slovakia, Carolina.
Two children.
Already a bad marriage.
Rich boy involved, hardly a prince.
Psychiatrists
and drugs, lending their own
wonderfully encapsuled
illustrations.

The mother only a cameo.
No flying head and torso.

Not nearly as sensational, really.

But the key
I think
is that the girl has indeed returned
for a long, lingering day
accepting a doom cast
by the one, inescapable similarity—
the water goblin.

While we each may view him differently,
and shake our heads, he lives.

Unindicted co-conspirator,

he lives.

THAT JANUARY

It's hard to decide
how a dead child feels.

Through the one west window
squinting at snow
in pink palsied wonder
appalled, adrift, ajar, asunder—
the bones of sockets are dry and aching now;
back we go, breaking the seal of yesterday's fall,
arriving with stiff burlap, clearing contents,
the white box appliquéed with daisies, emptied
of its laughter, the host of left-behinds,
the blue top, absent of spinning and string,
the cream-faced doll in party dress, prone and waiting,
and after her all manner of things,
with a sound, sound, and no sound.

Into dark, rough warmth, a final grace—
the clown face slides, its tiny filings align
in a bipolar field peculiar to planets
tilting on their axes in a void— shaping
the erasable smile that pulls a season
in slow, slow healing, yet retains
the yawn of the cherubim
along the ceiling, as the world lies still,
but still, still, speeding.

CONTINUUM

Dumb stone
rough and gray, barely round
cracked to reveal
the blast of majesty
the inner religion
Rouen and Chartres
pinnacles to an inner dome
of azurite and pinky-blue,
as curative, nexus for the waves
that amplify mute cries
from a dim ball
and cistern for replies beyond the sun
wastes its fire
in the morning light of the atrium,
on the red steps where
we left
the emissary.

PROGRESS IN EDEN

(The slug is a pest of horticulture.)

Not worth the time
he was counting on it
moving slow as he could
on a trail of self-made silver;

I watched him
an intruder
on verge of my next task
a mover of the earth, an important man.

Returned for a shower, for a morning cup
befitting the important, moving man—
I forget the talk as she poured,
the china was dull; there were revolutions in Africa—

out the door, beyond the wax apples, he'd disappeared,
no cracks in the walk, no bus to the grass savanna—
so quickly, was he all right? I am not a gardener.
No rake. No child to prod him.

He is not my enemy
and I'm glad if he's all right
and if he isn't, I'm unaware of the importance, but—
since I can still see the lines, I'll show you.

It'll only take a moment.

I know, I know.
But look, see.

The silver.

CHAIN LETTER

These letters.

Some received them just this week, yesterday.
I have no reports from today.

Some have received them in handfuls.

Many got their first while they were on vacation,
giving birth, turning bolts at the factory,
slashing sticky cane, or sleeping.

It is supposed to have gone on for years, now.
They come postmarked from Cyprus, from Indiana,
Beirut and Bethesda, the Bahamas, Boston, Butte.

They have proliferated, falling like
snowflakes to the hot Sunda Sea.
They are everywhere, going everywhere,
coming to you,
your acquaintances
and me.

They say:

> We are the truth and the light
> we are to embrace the song, we are
> to sing to the heavens and to our neighbors
> we are to be one, a globe of bees
> suspended in sweet honey from one tree
> a tree of Eden and Gethsemane

tree of Druids and Buddhists,
an embrace of bodies and without bodies
suspended in the emerald air.

At least, that is how I read it.
To you it might say:

Love somebody.

And in Portuguese, or Hindi, something else, a million
something elses, each to his own.

What it does NOT say is:

You will die tomorrow if you do not forward this.
Miss Mansfield of Beverly Hills
did not forward this, and she died headless
in a mink wrap, under a semi.

Mr. Kennedy of Hyannisport did not
forward this.

Mr. Smith of Omaha did, and he is now a
millionaire.

No.
It only says to make the contents known.
Like others, I am doing so.
Perhaps I am foolish. (Perhaps not, too.)

Who wrote it?
Was it you? No, you were with me all along.

As we walk, in common stride,
the orange edge of a new millennium in view—
I stop, again
to buy these stamps
and then again, to pray

to be

to have

to do.

AT THIS MOMENT

At this moment

a handshake; plans are concluded
for the conquest of a small country.

Camels yawn in the morning shadow of Cheops' tomb.
Thirty thousand herring lace like a helix
near a North Sea trawler.

A long, black wave laps new ice,
adding to the Antarctic shelf.

Marianna kisses Rodolfo, a long,
languorous kiss. He feels the light sting
of down above her lip, and is excited.

Mud slides into a stream, without witness.

The relief trucks continue their journey.
Dust flies across the road; they enter Mali.

At this moment, a paramecium splits in a dewdrop;
then another.

Two hundred-and-five million spermacytes crack their safes,
and enter the eggs.

Six hundred and two humans commence
the slow string quartet of God's creation.

Thousands of salamanders, too.

Otter and octopus, ocelots, and spiders.

(Some of the issue is immediately eaten
by marine creatures. More will become fodder
for hyenas, and medical doctors.)

But at this moment, what happens, does.

The second stanza of a great poem is revised.
It is in Italian. Garbage moves
under thrust of a bulldozer.

Children sing a psalm.
Others squeal, just born.

This could continue, on and on,
but should it?

It boggles minds; but it does not upset
the taproot of a eucalyptus.
Or the Cambrian rocks. Or Tasadays
who naked, share their breadfruit.

At this moment.

VERKERK'S PORTRAIT OF A ZOUAVE, 1860

Head askew, playing with lamplight,
scarf of lapis, the sky's hue at winter solstice
deeper than blue, a certain frost of reason,
certain *frisson comme*
une fièvre, non, pas de tout
just the maddening certainty
that comes of no particular aim
except to do what there is to do—
haul crates off the *Antwerp,*
offal and stink from the bedlam at St. Heroux,
devour hot chestnuts, a turnip,
the week's ragout, the odd job
and the odd sou that keeps alive
the women, three girls, a boy, and buys
an occasional bangle, lapis too,
hung from the ear like
a papal testimonial, like the medal
of St. Jean de la Croix de Toulouse et Cru—

Dutchman, the expatriate *voyeur*
etches with a pin the last
crease of windwear, the umbre stipple
of a hard sun, the glint of
simple certain truth, and pays the man
his promise.

Tonight! and for another week—
omelettes of Plessy sausage
to go with stew,
and kisses, kissed
from dried, dear lips

will press
their sweet like currant paste
and turn to damp,
like dew.

BARTO IN MOUNT DORA (II)

Barto— deep as Chinese roots
reclaims Lake County soil
rosed and ripe with spring rain—
a clever Jack returns, with beans.

Boys careen through orange trees
on aimless feet between the blackened
stains of yellow prime, retreat
to shards of shade behind a light

that dabs itself through scrub-oaks
and clefts a cloudy continence
in the cataracts of their lives—
never was he one of these.

Prokofiev had pierced the glassy
years before, and with such fire
as pennants streamed and died in rows
of venture upon foreign shores,

the Occident and Orient
of his chromatic rise, and falls;
black keys triad other senses
of a self, illumine traces.

*   *   *   *   *   *   *   *   *

Barto's home; he has shaken
the Musikverein and caressed Spoleto,
found a face in woman's eyes
and drowned his longing in a son,

put aside comparisons,
Kissin and Pogorelich,
the glove of aging Horowitz,
fingers of a Rosenthal—

all the newsprint metaphors
come sheaved as yen to purchase
wherewithal a kind of faith
that filters claret memory

into vessels of a small-town square,
where K. 311 winds its key,
the doors expel, windows see
that Barto's back, and plays for free.

HOLIDAY

The cay is memory.

Beneath my blithe, unswimming feet
I clamber for a sand flat
amid bumps of calcite tombs
and life, hand to the hand of this child,
pulling a blanket of warm turquoise
to his belly and my knees.

We catch the V of darting opals,
turtle in his sunbathed trance
but miss an anemone's show
of faux-flowers that would take
a dunking, the shadow
that was grouper big
as pigs on land,
the secret multitudes,

scallops dwelling in their dance
of insensate speed, siphoning water
like soup, algaeic and diademed, salty as a
pretzel loop and shimmering
with chance, to be stopped so soft
and short by the sucking glove of a star's
rough hand, popping the
shells like lazy lids, of already
opened, pretzel-cans.

We retreat, wet and somewhat red
to hot, soft silica that
sticks and brands our sandwich bread,

to shade, to home
and ultimately then, to bed.
With time, the shore remains the shore.
Lovely but,

there is too much happening
we do not see, and never see.

You check, little one,
the big bright calendar
of krill and cockles;
grow into next year.

Inland, we arrange our hope,
we dry with dread.
Spinning suns over no horizons
work the world
and alternate with artificial
light, the things in these aquaria

the living, the dead.

LIGHT BREAKFAST AT THE ALAMO

(Recollection of Captain Almeron Dickinson.)

It was cold. We ate stiff cornbread
and swilled coffee from McGregor's pot.
The lip of the sun swelled pink.

They came just then.

We had expected them tomorrow,
or maybe in the afternoon.
Half of us were still
sleeping
when they came, like mites
ripped from a dry-mound,
pincers glinting.

They meant it this time.
Blue mites at the South wall, white at the East.
Thousands. Halos on their hat-tops.
Death's angels.

My wife, I guess, pulled on the mission bell.
In thirteen minutes, the smoke had reached
the barber shop and livery at Bexar.
At the mission, we could not see.

I was gone early, a ball in the head, like Travis.
I floated above the scene, to the clouds
and down through the smoke again, spotting
Crockett and his Tennesseeans in the yard—
here was bravery in the form of madness.

Laughing at the absurd waves of blue, the tide,
the river swallowing the levee, tears that
precede the end of life, fear in the form
of urine staining buckskin—
all in the same man
at the same time.

Others ran like barnyard birds, in circles.
Many stumbled into the long barracks
to make their stand.

The flag came down.

Bowie shot one, then himself.
The bayonets are not palatable.

A baby wailed. (Farewell, Angelina.)
I tried to kiss my wife
but of course, I failed.
I stood near Susannah, here
there, there, comically
waiting for them to enter the chapel,
as if I was going to stop them from raping her.

Hell, I was still on the wall.

It went on for an another half-hour,
at the long barracks.

They turned our own cannons around,
and blew the barracks apart.

We were packed like Boston kippers.

Crockett and most of his Tennesseeans
were still alive when it ended.
No Mexican wanted to sacrifice himself
in the yard just then.
It seemed to be holy ground,
waiting for a vision.
The rage was gone. Crockett tipped over
his King, wishing to save the others.

He felt it was honorable.
Santa Anna did not feel this way.
He was honor-bound by the horns of the *Degüello*.
He could not give ground, even for burial.

Seven were disarmed and shot.
Their blood-spray in a gust of wind
baptized the wicked.

My wife was not raped.
Again, the funny honor.

My descendants keep the walks here clean,
and polish all the silver.

Next door,
where the dragoons
had poured through a breach
of wall along the riverbank
a cavernous hall
and dome the size of the Temple of Jerusalem
held thousands of people who cheered last night
as balls fell into baskets
and out their holes
again and again
until it ended.

Old Juan and I sit in the eaves sometimes
and watch.
(This time, the Texians won.)

The old church still stands.

In the morning, young peons
clean debris, and women say
their Spanish rosaries
asking the indulgence
of Our Lady of
Guadalupe.

Just
like
they always do.

Just
like they did

then.

WYETH PAINTS PICTURES OF MY FATHER

I. *Transition,* 1957
(Dusty blues, dark light, egg tempera.)

You will not withdraw.

Hero from conception's bed,
you sit with Mother on the old couch, carved of flowers,
your eyes earnest, making a promise.

At forty-three she has me.

We will head for the new house, all of us;
you forget six racks of empty beer bottles
near the oil drum.

Webster's Café will miss you.

II. *Showdown,* 1961
(Backlit, from below, drybrush.)

I am six.
You confront a drunken neighbor man
who threatens to poison our dog.

You do not strike
you do not threaten
you diffuse insanity

with the stare of Alan Ladd,
the kind that made Jack Palance flinch.

You are my god; you are my god.

III. *Blacktop,*
(Watercolors, image in distance.)

Atop a yellow monolith
moving off slow as sundew in summer heat,
you press hot asphalt to obsidian majesty
on our own Meridian Street.

I point out to Jesse, to his brother, Keith,
your shoulders turned, eyes fixed as if crowding the plate
that day, you're my Yastrzemski, or even Tony C.
and I would forget a dead pennant race—
forget it for almost a week.

IV. *Outside the Bar*, 1967
(Tempera. Brown.)

One day we go alone to the department store.

You buy my new glove.
Stiff, tanned, smelling of bright love and sure victories.

On the way home you stop. I wait in the car—
but I know more than the box scores, Pa.

You come back in an hour, smoking, smoking your cigar.

Tony C. takes a hard one to the temple.
The glove, I will never break in. Stiff it stays;
it cannot accept a ball without anticipating pain.

V. *Vigil,* 1967
(Tempera, borrowing the curtains of *Wind from the Sea.*)

The window screen smells of storms and strains
the figures of my face; the night breeze time
of August wafts against me.

I should savor a summer's splendor, but my brother
is in Vietnam and I must kneel at this sill and wait.

My father is very late. There will be trouble,
but beneath, another pale pair of lights breaks the hill
and makes me pray to Christian, Greek, and other gods
so one will slow as this one does, just now.

VI. *Saturday,* 1968
(Crumbly pastels, bright, for comedic effect.)

On the saddest day of my life
Bobby Kennedy's train passes by.
Children and veterans salute, and women cry;

some old friends swing on the porch
with Mother, as my father arrives.

It is suppertime. We eat embarrassment
like a tasty lash. That night they bury Bobby
under the Klieg lights. His thirteen year-old
stands by; I too, stand by.

VII. *Yule,* 1968
(Oils, uncharacteristic, thick oils.)

Christmas. Sitting atop the stair, a sentinel seraph
with faintest hint of facial hair, listens
for spells of quiet, drinking them like whiskey and ale—

a sober, so sober drunk unlike the one
downstairs who threatens my mother,
much like the man who would have poisoned our dog
that time, save for intervention of another—

the dog listens from his coop under cold stars and silence
as Old Kringle delivers his present, just for me.

VIII. *The Test,* 1974
(Tempera, brown and black, perspective from below.)

We meet on the basement stairs.

Mother in the middle.
He hurls a threat which,
like a bomb, misses my head.

She laughs, "Don't be a fool.
He's big enough now to fix you good."

It had never occurred to me to fix him good.
It never would.

Apparently, I had grown. Apparently, I think, he knew.

IX. *Goodbye,* 1975
(A close-up of his face, tempera eyes, robin's egg.)

On the day I leave, consumed of yearning,
turning to Jack's black road and the need to face

a life now tumbled into a duffel—
he meets me in the kitchen

no fight, one to another, the orphan, the cabin-boy
nods his head, his eyes clear, "take care, my son"

rings in my ears, in the tumult of buses, bus-stops,
women and thugs, canyons of sandstone
and cityscapes, big rivers, I remember one hug.

X. *Sentence,* 1978
(Pathetic sepias, drybrush.)

Years later, you have retired
and your body retires from drink.

But it lies like a moccasin in reeds to punish you.
During the Red Sox playoff game, which they lose,
your stroke strangles you.

It's a long way back, pressing the button
of the tape recorder, over and over, tears down
your face, searching for the eloquence of a mumble.

I wait, again, by the window of your eyes.

XI. *Recollecting,* 1982
(Bright color. Like his father's illustrations.)

It is not all bad. You recover enough
to slur with urgency the story of your sea days,
and you are fond of my wife.

You visit us in Florida, where New England
children go to show they are successful.

We play cards.
Eleven hands of rummy, like healing novenas,
arrange their kings and aces down to an orderly value
of four-three-twos, and common faces.

XII. *Goodbye, Part Two,* 1988
(Tempera, dark light, but lighter above.)

They have gone now. I stay behind
a moment, tracing your angel to a high corner of the room.
Below a toppled, cosmetic icon awaits encasement.

Mother will be all right. My sister,
who nursed your soul into the night
of her own peace, will be all right. My brothers, too.

And me, my Father, Me, talking to myself,
must face full-on our inevitable truth— indelible
as egg-yolk paint, I am, and I always will be, you.

REMEMBERING CLYDE BEATTY

Children sleep the dreams
of spells, impenetrable, we hope;
we lock ourselves
into circus-time.

It starts slowly,
cotton candy beside the grandstand,
a noodling of the band's lithe oboe
practicing the fanfare.

When we settle in, the
rings illuminate one by one
thrilling our seats, electric as—
what was that— these impermanent
planks moan and moan
our weight.

We imagine, we transition.

I am your Wallenda, riding my
groove-wheeled Schwinn along the wire,
height no concern,
a busy ant on a Parthenon step.

You respond spinning,
wet sequins whir
in your suspension, your
mouth fixed at the rope
and busy.

Ah ha, here I am!
and my rigging is fine—
there is no net, but my wrists
are a catcher's wrists, and
your curves at the moment
of the pike
inspire me.
Beat down the lion there
with your look, chair me
with only your sensual
fist, your irony.

Split the horses, silk
grey horses, round and again,
bob into hoops alight, tapping haunches
through an organdy veil, to come
where came to come
again, inflamed.

And I will, charged and channeled
at the stroke, stoke the air
aboom, projectile certain and improper
to a dowager's stare,
your perfect, caped, Commander
of Sighs,
your Fearless Debonair,

                              providing

we're not interrupted, we are
not made real by footsteps on the midway,
by a child's dream dropped just
too early, an early yawning
casting doors or canvas flaps aside

revealing us, the empty
stands and wrappers,

                            morning.

FOUR TRAVELOGUES

At the pole
on a cueball of curved ice
you fall in all directions
at once.

On the steps
of the Great Mosque of Timbuktu,
the air fly-thick with drought
you pay these baking porters
to carry urns and portmanteaus
so they won't turn into thieves
and kill you.

In a room
three blocks from the Place Pigalle
between the legs of an inspired woman
you reveal the secrets
of obsolete weaponry.

And you wake
in a tenement in Chelsea, knowing
it is possible to be nowhere at all
in a million places
at the same time.

LOS ANGELES RIVER (BY FIRELIGHT)

There they came to life and exulted,
the hurt mute.
The dust, as they say, settled.

— Gwendolyn Brooks, 1969

Through me.

A concrete gutter wide as the Jordan,
gorged with dry memories that stumble
on season to occasional dousing,
to the plugs, the planting. We have watched our stars
on old TVs three and four blocks
from Florence and Normandie,
eating our rice, our fried plantain but
tonight we walk, we walk on smoke,
on the rays of brilliant
Kliegs and shame
of our special day, our parade.

We burn toward the fashionable
climes, following the trough, the river
as mind, winding though flame— our snake
of the desert is the snake of the garden—
quixotic and cocksure
like bravery, like blame,
water to steam, like a thousand
teeshirts in faceless streets, like fame
it has flowed through our years here—

the hard and dusty hot, the filled with rain,
and hands upon the waterwheel are God's,
a god who will not judge tonight,
familiar with this game— our source
and single, caterwauling mouth remains
a hidden god in a city of lights,
of fires south, god of wild night, and of all pain

through me, the him who's it
in trinity seems to flow,
growing the guilt of inestimable grain,
his river drowns, his river is nowhere

everywhere, the same.

MAYFLIES

They, in their late spring lingerie
burn etches into a single day
and on the windscreens of the way
they Pollock, pointillize, and stay

so resolute, crave no caviar favor,
no hale, hint of the tamarind's flavor,
no cross to bear, no usual savior—
push their probes in an egg-sac savor

and fall like so many fairies, felled
by weight of hours, wished to well
in human teardrops, dawned and delled
to gloss a floor of heaven,
                              our hell.

TAOS (FOR MARJIE)

You are kindred.

You see no difference, though difference
is hurled at you like paint from a painted desert;

you absorb it, through the pores to the blood,
but it's the same blood, warm and human.

There are those who can neither see
the filament that glows and drives your chosen saint,
however slowly, to his source.
You are not one of those, of course.

At times your music's etched in Spanish inlay
thrummed from two strings singing unison,
or at the well of tears and untuned dirges
holds fractured notes in the clef of a stable calm.

You are kindred, frayed yet strung
as daughter/mother to father/son
as lovers hung on pins that trace
the map of Providence's face
from Brown to Banff, to Santa Fe.

Red clay beads the rain
and pours from the lip of the umbrella
meant for sun; I wait for you, for two in Taos
in my heart, my kindred heart.
Your kindred city.

SEVEN WONDERS

at Alexandria

The lighthouse stood
to seaward clouds,
highest of high and marblesque
when the world
was its own amusement park,
all flesh and horns
(before we came so gowned
and hazy blessed).

It winked across
a day of leagues
to biremes at Brindisium
where Phoenicians carted absinthe
out of port, and played their parallel
oars to a new moon
and Atlantis, heading west.

*   *   *   *   *   *

at Babylon

The gardens spilled their
greens and forsythia
between deep cakes of alabaster
and golden steps. The slaves
would never leave here,

fearing paradise
was better seen and felt,
than desert-missed
and wept.

Daniel, splayed on a terrace
sipped orange juice
spilling the stream
on a maid's breast, her skin
as brown as hazelnuts, delaying
his signatory madness,
his ungrateful, foreign
trust, for rest.

*   *   *   *   *   *

at Olympia

Gaudy this Zeus, crowned in olive leaves,
seated on cedarwood
hewn from forests by the Lethe—
Zeus the powerful,
profligate and mean, mocking,
majestic, chryselephantine

stared doubters down
from a height of twenty men,
ivory in arrogance, stiff of victory
his staff all ebony, engorged
with gilt seed and the blood
of athletes, sacrificed
to the yawn of need.

*   *   *   *   *   *

at Ephesus

Artemis, laid low by
a commandment, her house
by Goths, had dressed
herself from roof to floor
a block by block enchantment
full of fest, of flowing, late
Spring wine and roasting limbs
from fine
Ephesian flocks—

eleven naiads dancing round
the aqua of its font
passed with streamers through
the palisades, Ionic,
and through doors
without locks.

*   *   *   *   *   *

at Halicarnassus

Mausolus! What
missing lexicon without
your grand, galvanic shoebox—
sepulchre of statues set under
Scipia's chariot, horse

bound for twelve heavens
or eleven hells (after one
felled shot); your sister-soldier wife

who paid the artisans, placed
patterned gold in eyes and mouth,
cordoned the arch with roses
and forget-me-nots
then, fled her shining army
to the satins of your bed,
and died a slow-sung sadness
sentineled by ocelots.

*   *   *   *   *   *

at Rhodes

At Rhodes they stood you
like a tart to open ocean,
balancing act better than
any circus, the surreal pointing,
defiance comical and doomed
from the start, but for fifty-six years
they shivered for your shadow
in the glint—

my too tall and none
too fat Colossus, too soon
you departed, for
shook into the dull ground
you are sold by Muslims
to a jolly Jew

and carted to Emesa,
quarry stone again,
discounted art.

*　*　*　*　*　*

at Giza

All gone now, save the eldest
of the catalog, skinned by sand
but still it pins four points
to Ra— the Work, Wailing, Waste, Whim
surrounding and transfiguring an incest
that bore its isosceles sides
into stepping-stones of a god-king's kin—
the lion-pet, with head undone
lays lime before in shifting dunes
curious, yet moribund;

it knows the answer of our
monuments to nothing;
but it questions not the importunity of suns
caught in endless, blinding apogee
of edifice, grandees,
slaughter and erasure
as faceless hands that carve and lever
lean in long outlasting of these eras,

every one.

DOUBLE IN A DINER, AFTERNOON

Don't look now.

I've seen you often, lingering along lifetimes,
one of us, in turnstiles of the old stadium
only to be lost with a bat-crack and the dissembling crowd
or last on a passing lorry at the fall of Saigon
and once, just once when we were children, that was you,
that was me, and though we tried not to see, we knew.

A mirror mirrors us; we are more than synonyms,
than sameness, down to an aquiline nose, a smile,
the buzz of others' daft and dearest blather—
"you'd never believe, it was *you,* I mean *you*
as I live and breathe and I kick my dog, it's true!"
We avoid the felled dominoes of commingled eyes

as if spies who could feign no subtle signal, save
the comfort of peripheral view. But I wonder, as always
about you, about dullness and despair, clinging to a knife-edge,
precipitous longing, the momentary moments of truth—
did you laugh at every enemy who bested your best
or could you, unlike me, best them too?

You leave by the side-door; I order stew.

MAGIC MAN

From tinyprint ads
in a *Popular Science* I found
the great Heaney of Oshkosh—
(from the line of Houdini)
prestidigitator extraordinaire and
wholesale jobber of dreams.

I would wait by the flagged box
of my ten years and run
every so often to the house
with electric bills and a string-wrapped package
of Quumran scrolls, a small tidy grail
or a vial of the best ambergris
concealed in this sacred mail
postmarked, Wisconsin.

He would leave me notes in them—
not merely the formula, the patter
but notes that said "Here Al, you'll
really like this one! Yours sincerely,
Heaney." And I always did.

And I would practice them
in the upstairs Hippodrome,
waving purple silks
when the house was filled
with madness and
hope was gone, when Heaney's
Houdini himself
would come back from the ether

just to me,
and say "hold on."

There was the little
guillotine, that chopped the carrot
shard below your finger
but not your finger

the quarter Elizabeth
(whom you really loved) marked
with her blue Flair pen
then, popped in your pocket
would return in a second, in a box
choked with tight rubber bands
locked, in another box, and tied
inside a tiny felt satchel
you snatched from
the spectre who gave you this poem,
hoping that love would love you back
while showing her this one,
that one, that—

the plastic apparatus you
had to build as if it were the Revell
Titanic, the mystery body box
and the sleek plastic babe
without sequins, your stand-in
tied inside with more
rubber bands, as the hand
passed over with a great gloved
wand, like Heaney
and would disappear
to his Great, grand Beyond yes, "check it—
check it— here, I'll release the back"

let the walls hang down,
there is more to life, more true
than all this horrid,
hating sound

and when you grew,
lost track of Heaney
and Houdini's own great ghost
had retired, far from the reach
of every failed medium
and charlatan, too,
and you knew all the secrets
but lost the little guillotine,
coin box, satchel, and
Elizabeth, you—

lived your life the best
you could, devoid of horrible errors
that would close a show
and told your ten-year boy
in Magicland
your "Eric, this one's real good,
you'd really like this one, you—"
remember sheening silks
that flash

the majesty of moments,
the smell of glue.

THE CLOTHED WOMAN

There's an obscure tune, by Ellington.
It is fragmented, but sensual.
And beautiful.
I put it on.

Your painting, which the artist never titled
swings on a nail between the 23rd Psalm
and the Bhagavad Gita. I name it now
same as the song
and call it your legacy to me.

I refuse to remember
your body disintegrating from cancer.

I see instead you standing in an open space
steeling yourself against a gust of no source,
awaiting calm.

(Yes, in a satin raiment, like a love sheet.)
The piano plays on; it changes to a stride, to nostalgia.

Much is unresolved. But
I knew you. And you knew that my fingers were caught,
always, between
a triad and a blue
seven.

The picture will never betray you, you stunner
you
survivor.
In it your face is turned to a horizon of dust;

your hair is wild.
I admit it.

THIS was the you I could never have.
THIS was the you you always were.

        THIS
woman.

PASSION OF SAINT BERNADETTE

I.

In 1858, the dump at Massabielle
was visited.

Three girls, poor as mice
walked miles to gather sticks and bones;
without a fire, the late winter gripped
and clutched at the edges of their lives.

Massabielle, the place of rocks
grew from the land like a stout sore.

Barren, it mocked the sky with scabs
of granite and irregular, low temples
dotting the banks of La Gave, a stream
of liquid ice, the eleventh of February.

From there, the parish spire seemed far.
From there, in the French Pyrénees, Lourdes awoke
from the trance of normalcy, to rub its eyes
against the tail-flame of a single, shooting star.

II.

To Bernadette Soubirous, fourteen, asthmatic,
the image appeared from the stone
in luminous relief, with outstretched hands
calling the lame and stupid to its lap.
She would be the first, and willing.

Impervious to shards and pebbles thrown,
a girl and woman conversed on matters only known
in the dimension of saints and their opposite,
the burned sinners, a damned ecstasy
bridged by the fog of her intermittent breath, alone.
The other two, saw nothing.
(Faith is the act of seeing nothing.)

Among instructions, the hand-maid grasped her gratuity:

> *"I CANNOT PROMISE YOU HAPPINESS
> IN THIS LIFE, BUT IN THE NEXT."*

That would have to do.

III.

After the news
a woman rose from the street to slap Bernadette
for "telling tales out of school."

One wonders
if this woman
was sent by God to represent the singe of doubt
that paints our souls
with the fresco of Judas and other fools,
and if her progeny sold cakes and rosaries
by the side of the road
as a century moved to its all-too antipathetic close.

No matter.
In a few fortnights, the girl and two witnesses grew

to eight thousand, multiplying like fish in Matthew,
like the Mount of Olives, like the Catalan bullfights,
like *Aquèro* said.

IV.

Quick to grab the spade
or rifle for a fight, conscript or king
we file in duty to the yaw of Magog,
meat for an idols's fire.

But quicker still, thank God (and Christ)
we stop, dropping to our knees
at any evidence of something maybe more,
even the illiterate acolyte's story
of apparitions in a dung-heap,
rising to vigil at a tree of dead roses
waiting for the beginning
or the end of the world.

We are sick of the middle, and it, sick of us, retreats.

So from Paris, from Tours, all over France
in ox-carts and camions they came, carried lightly,
even slightly above their seats.

V.

There was nothing to see here.

Just a girl, wrapped in a beatitude
crawling on her petticoat, eating weeds,

digging the earth for beads
of penitence.

But within hours, her furrows
formed a spring of unlike water, unlike the elements
that formed it, the geology that contained it,
the chemist who strained to explain any vestige of it,
unlike the constabularies who would
fence and restrain it from eyes
that cried blindly for its invisibility,
from cankered throats who drank with glassy clarity
and cripples who rubbed that fond neutrality
on the withered limbs and minds
of a world, to make it whole again.

VI.

One day, after the sixteenth vision
almost as an afterthought—
reporting as the parish dean had sought
the name of the thing, the Lady, the *Aquèro,*
as if in incantation, she said:

> *"Que soy era*
> *immaculada*
> *councepciou. "*

> *"I AM THE IMMACULATE CONCEPTION. "*

One thousand Hiroshimas-to-be
could not obliterate what that brought.
As babies danced, and the fever

of lepers vaporized in one shot,
reforming their Rodin faces—
the girl would soon complete here mission here,
but not her lot.

VII.

You can today buy cheap glass balls
of Bernadette-in-the-Grotto,
showered with sparkles as the earth shakes
in the hands of children.

The faces pressed to glass
behold a special one, with the Special One,
not unlike the figure at Saint-Gildard,
who came in the spring of 1863
as prescribed by prelates, nurtured
by the dim prospects of alternative existence,
of that poor Lourdes life turned
tawdry by adoring masses—
and deemed as finally wise by a woman-child
who desired a bridehood of holy separateness

only to become, in convent, Marie-Bernard,
Sister, obedient spectacle of cardinals and kings.

VIII.

Little apothecary, apprentice to the infirm
when she wasn't herself
coughing blood mouthfuls and carried to bed,
to her white chapel—

prayed with the novices
who'd steal upstairs
asking for the story
the story, always story
and the official biographer
and the juries of Rome they asked, re-asked

for the story, and the story
was always the same—

while at Lourdes, a well-planned Carrara statue
of a too-old-looking vision, whose photo she shunned
won its place in the Grotto,
beckoning with slightly wrong hands.

IX.

She might herself have been the greatest
textbook case.

Ankylosis of knee. Lesion to the bone.
Tubercular, bed-sores
like monasteric tapestry
across the slight back—
but when asked, who better

than she should return to the water
of the spring to be reborn, she would say:

"It is not for me. I stay
 in my corner."

The miracle, she!
Did they not understand? Dear Zola, it was irony.

This miracle of
suffering

she.

X.

April 16, 1879. This was between her
and her Jesus.

Death was slow, like a dance
of stillness.

The sisters, seven magpies
awaited her, this most regal of creatures,
this little girl, now thirty-five
fixing her gaze on the crucified figure
transcendent as Bernhardt
at the Comédie Française,
as the Virgin soprano
at end of a well-done *Stabat mater.*

Quel denouement. Even Zola, miscreant had to say:
"she was beautiful in death, and the body,
  interred after three days, was still warm,
  lips red, and smelling sweet."

XI.

For other than Catholics, and constables,
this becomes a ghost story.

In 1909, the vault was opened.
They did not hunt ghouls. They searched for the chosen.
They knew what they would find
if she was one.

Inside the vault,
it was 1879. Again.
The body was perfect. No decay.
The habit was damp. The crucifix
in her grasp was green, devoured by rust.

Sister Marie-Bernard was redressed, replaced.
In 1919, the same procedure.

And the same result. The chill was now off the mystery.

She was, and she is,
Saint Bernadette of Lourdes.

XII.

She awaits her Prince, like Snow White,
in a gorgeous glass reliquary.

To the spring, they come in millions. Bees to the hive
immersing themselves in their own
dewy hexagon of faith.

Some do not believe. Zola saw two cures with his own eyes
and did not believe.

But to cure the blind, they must first
understand that they cannot see, and can be forgiving.

So, while we wait
the world turns, expecting new fission
as the restless Lady
chooses her alighting time
to once again wake the living.

I prepare my child. And I prepare myself.
Each bee to its own, and to her sweet commission.

MARY'S NOCTURNE

Blue expanse
blue as the invisible robe at Fatima,
blue as Galilee when you could
slide on the iceless waves, collecting fish
by their tails, feeding the landbound world
if you only believed,
believed in the expanse
as broad as time and the degrees
of the sextant, believed in the gaze of adoration,
the tilting of a globe of blue expanses
turning in a constellation of globes, and trances
liquid as life
luminous as silent nights
when blue turns black, but brilliant glinting
sky and water— one in the iris
of the Virgin's eye, where we stand
emoting one impenetrable devotion
in the Cova, the Grotto, or the shores
of any pilgrim's sand encasing subtle starlight,
and an ocean.

TRELAWNY (IN THE SECOND PERSON)

"Trelawny... had accomplished little, had no
specific aims except for dreams of being a
unique machismo character, and was seeking
attachment to solid eminences..."
                              — *Emily W. Sunstein*

You, who waved goodbye to Shelley's sloop,
swagger of Agamemnon in your port-clasped hand,
who dug the pit that burned his soupy heart
to ashes and incense in the Leghorn sand,

who tilted gin with Fitzgerald by the Neptune Pool
a gadfly metamorphosing, sucking on a plum,
you led the chorus, Greek and graven, drawn
from Hollywood opulence, and antebellum scum;

at the last reading, after Dylan's bellow blew
you lit a cigarette, talked the mob to truce,
"we forgive the excess, the alliterative addictions"
his decorum was what, "interrupted by the Muse?"

You who last disappeared off Papa's porch,
Studebaker backfiring down the mountain chute—
"we'd been regularly conferring with all his Mayo doctors"—
Trelawny, by any other name, is true;

your future's past, and classic, it recoils
to days of the blindman's tale, the catacomb's
review it's you, you who neutered Christ,
and killed the bold Achilles, over ale.

BOBBY FISCHER TEACHES CHESS

His way
Bobby enters the endgame—

                            knight takes pawn—

having invited us to gain the advantage
of his disappearance,
of his mirage on Hollywood Boulevard,
the rumors of insanity—

                           rook to King's bishop
three—

such a relative thing—
and we, now eager, swallow the poisoned pawn
waving like chiggers of complacency around the neons
of Chinatown, where he plays the ancients
a quarter a game
only to turn up in Belgrade—
to the rumble of field guns and mortars
in the distant hills on the other side,
like a universe in parallel, on the other side—

                           pawn to King five—

of the Danube, oblivious to politics
like Morphy in pursuit of his charlatan
Staunton, whose sculpted mementos
move in rapid succession
as Fischer dispatches Spassky again,

to the click of flashbulbs
and ping of satellites—

                        queen takes pawn—

with little practice
and a soul of ice
thumbing his disregard for American bureaucrats
with the élan of Capablanca,
cuffing our wagers as at baccarat
and stealing away, again in Alekhine's defense,
to Nice, to Monte Carlo
to the streets of Budapest
to a small café corner, unnoticed,
swilling black coffee and
swallowing an eclair,
playing both sides of the board—
while we, hope against hope,
in blundering normalcy,
wonder what we saw,
and if, when all is done
will Bobby, in a last act
of mercy, offer
Moloch, or even the Archangel Gabriel

a draw.

CHEYENNE REQUIEM

There is no trough or parapet to hide
from the end of life and laughter. We stand
on the broad plain, awaiting hints of yours
or mine, or any other vague hereafter.
A corporal, stripped to civilian resign—
the daggers in our tunics turn to salt;
we circle the slain, the quietly expired
counter-clockwise in mist of a dulcimer choir.
There's no time to the end of life and laughter
and place, due-west of one cloud-blessed mind
holds a vessel bare, and a barrow empty,
no marrow, no matter not in disrepair—
where's our driver gone, and on
what wind upon the end of life and laughter?
Is he a wind that hums this hymn
through the tiny bellows of a concertina,
the sprig that newly winds about the stair?
Is he dust for the sunflowers, rain for sunflowers,
is he the next seventh son that wails for air?
Does he walk again here— do we walk again, there?

ASPENSONG (WHEN I MOURN)

I've been told I should have mourned
you more, and better.

But I have mourned you—

in a space between seconds
infinite in its cosmos,
drowned in the diffidence
of small tears.

I have mourned you on Thursdays
and before I pray, when I shovel
geraniums; when I am almost
without you (but with you)
among larks, and showers.

The best place I mourned
you recently
was in a child's face, and the upturn
of a smile familiar as old psalms. I must
visit it again, on purpose, and bring
my reading.

I, too, sing you in the *Ave Maria;* I smell
the censer in other ceremonies
and wail when I walk
in wind. I mourn you.

There is no accounting
of this, I think, because
the world requires a schedule,

brittle and folded, that includes
even the smallest localities
and times, printed to the odd minute,
an organized debilitation.

Yes, I find it odd how I mourn you.
It hurts like birth, but then,
I don't remember it.

And when I do, mourn you
more and better than every
eleventh mouth of air, more
than aspen leaves along
the course of October,

I will raise this flag
to the assembly. It is
purple for pleasure,
red like beets for the embarrassment
of missed opportunity,
and the black sash
from corner to corner will stand
for the mysteries of death
that make us so dark on light days.

But in this mourning, as I do,
understand what is just for show,
and what is the true imprisonment
in those flecks of instance

where I really mourn,
where I really live,

where I celebrate your days
in the aliveness that you were,

breathing me.

RECONSIDERATION

The azure satin
bower bird of New
Guinea mixes charcoal
and berry juice, and
with a piece of
bark for a brush
paints
the inside of
its nest, blue.

So don't say we
can't handle this.

Not true.

SMITHSONIAN, 1975

(At nineteen, I left home
and landed here, holding
blueprints.)

The Hope Diamond is a doorknob
beyond reach.

My house
becomes a window box of Giza.
It is terraced for rain
that never comes. Palm trees
grant
perspective, shade
for a pen on papyrus.

(Across the Red Sea
an obelisk points
to a nimbus.

Beside the Mall
my impressionist paintings are arrayed
in columned vaults.) And on
one far and inside wall
I set my watch
to pinks and blues
of the Rouen Cathedral,
and the Waterloo Bridge.

I am not so permanent as these,
so "with foundation."

I tend to move.
With this baton
I swing the first
violins and violas into motion.

It is a sweet moan.
We could make love to this, in this.
This construction.

Grand as Venezia.
Common as Congo thatch, or Hopi clay.
Reflective as Versailles
or the whites of Mykonos.

Life flows in and out of doors,
these halls, and windows.

My own life waits, my destiny
of landmarks, my soul
in notes and paint.
Before I leave, west, not east
I rest on the Gallery steps;
like Alexander
at the lighthouse, I look,
and listen.

The philosopher says:
architecture is frozen music.

The poet says:

this
is a granite symphony.

NOT A GRECIAN URN

On the incline of its face
toward the neck
nude men ripe
with seed leap bulls;
they did not live long.

They swallowed wine
from this, sleeping on courtesans
who might
have writhed like figs in the sun.

It was a spoil. It came from
Crete with a slew of slaves
who spoke no Greek. It
was pisspot for a Roman,
target of another drunk Hun
who leaked from disease and died
without difference, or sum.

How it came to be here, encased
in my private library, dear
is quite a story.

Intrigue and malfeasance, bliss.

It is part of my own gymnastics. My bull was
inheritance, and I have jumped well, and I
have drunk until I swelled to this,
and in you I will rule the world
for thirty seconds, shaking my fist.

When I am dead, I will leave it
to you. It is a perfect example
of the period. It will pay for your afterlife,
it is priceless,

it is worth shit.

THE MARCH OF SCIENCE

God is missing? Jupiter should fall on an ant.

But we continue our research
into mutual voids,
systems, you might say, of God's marbles
spinning to the sound
of an organ's diapason,
probes hot-firing into cold space
burning out with momentum of millennia
and sun-wind, seeking voices.

Meanwhile,
looking for an excuse
the ancient buzz of a smart Egyptian
has launched a fleet of killing machines
that will burn out before they reach us
or will arrive after we're gone.

At the same time,
we adjust the little I Ching sticks
under the third eye
the micro-magic eye
serving up Mansons and Marys
with all the accuracy of the big wheel
at Harrah's, Lake Tahoe.

Finally,
we reach an apposite infinity—
still in marbles, spinning each
around the parent nucleus—
as simple as Hydrogen

with its only child, incendiary
'til it marries the Oxygen quantum
and turns
to tears—

complex as Uranium, stage name
of Milton's Angel,
conducting an immense traffic of irregular spheres
as if to say "probe me,
probe me, split
my worlds with your compelling fear
and assume
the expansion of heaven
(in melting Japanese
and singsong of Armageddon)"—

for now, though, sniff
at the confluence of compounds,
the incalculable cosmos
falling into harmony of bodies and breath
(minutes before supper)
careless of these crazy intimations
of immortal hope, or death—
to bounce and spin the red and hot-pink ball
into tiny hands of a two-year-old, instead.

Live and let live. Remember God.

God of the universe.
God of your universe.

And what
how wonderful, how terrible it all is.

Just ask the ants
who break beneath the ball,
blinded at the Creation,
trembling to forgive.

THE IRON RANGE

It starts with the divot of a pick-ax
and the need to fill armories.
It continues as a trough, itinerant Swedes
wheeling barrows in noonday light;

we sift red dirt
for Carnegie filings, dirt
that flies to a lodestone like the breath of God
into Adam's lungs, our red lungs, coughing.

It becomes a hole too deep for ladders, terraced
for new Nubians who cast Imhotep barges that
steam the cold Superior, carrying ore, and coffins.

Inverted, it expands like Giza,
its intent invisible, stealing the breath
of our descent, stealing our generations.

From Hibbing, to Virginia, to deaf bargemen
in Duluth, the cigaretted faces warm
to black, bitter coffee, blushing
unanemic truth.

We bleed so red for it. And it responds, taking
our sacrifice like fire to dry dogwood, exchanging
dirt for wind, growing through wars and wars
vanishing in the furnaces of Pittsburgh
making our magnificent, gorgeous,
gorgeous red gorge,

"the largest manmade
hole in the world," and growing
growing toward town until it takes the cemetery,
reclaiming its effigies, 'til it takes the Polacks,
chewing up their houses like bar-pretzels, feeding itself
like the wide-eyed beast of Revelation.

Yes, it teethes our children, who bite at its ring
but who are really we to question this
or even *anything* this big, *this* God,

this *king,* we dig.

PREPARE FOR LANDING

How am I? she asked.

I have been living lately
plane crash to plane crash
in a redeye stupor
jarred only by these
special reports, these
mystery baggage checks
the sky igniting, icy wings

ripple of swamp or hole
in the maple thicket,
the cries of the beloved,
fire and the water,
slide without wheels
(the cartwheel footage)—
sifting through shards for a black
box of happenstance

so that I may, again,
strapped into models
of this flight or that,
swimming in pink noise
and rewinding the frames
in order to deliver
to a full assembly

the final address
of our investigation—

I am fine I said.
Beholding the humanity,

the conflagration.

THE NATURAL ORDER

They attack the day
with a purposeful frenzy, insects
digesting pine and persimmon,
sexing themselves
in the long halls of darkness
leaving deaf collapse
of walls, and Gothic apse;

they screel, scrall
a vehemence of crows
in all their
multitudinous murder about
the stuffed men,
killing corn that falls,
redeeming them;

they paw the turf at night
seeing sepia outlines
of their future, pouncing
in pride upon them, jaws to the neck,
always the neck, after wives and cousins
have nipped, tripped the comic,
cloven feet for a handout
of sinew
and joints that are hard
to swallow;

they gaggle at pink suns
southward, graceful as prints
on a gin-glass, the formations

sound victory, but they
fall like clowns down
flights of imaginary stairs
to billsful of muck,
smelling sulphur;

they consume, they are consumed,
and they reveal nothing. We study
them for no reason but
to pass the time.

We are students of the natural order—

of the bangs and indentations of space
that presage life, draw forms on a map
but deliver
the decay of compost, the assembly
of claws and covetousness, talons
and betrayal, jaws, jewries
hair and whores, feathers, fortunes
hands and the ruby lips of prophets
pressed into humus, then to oil,
then the explosion
of stars,

and the sound of God,
plucking the string

of wonder.

THE INNOCENTS

Mary Surratt
guilty of innkeeping
fell
like a hundred pounds
of millet

through a hole in the universe,
her parlor undusted
in July heat

as the fight for Lincoln's body
raged in Springfield
and Mary Todd's
clairvoyant saw pigeons
roosting in a fat eave,
which meant to Mary

it was right to grieve
it was right to grieve

and while Samuel Mudd
boarded a skiff for the ride
to Tortuga, catching
a nail on his striped
sleeve

Edwin Booth
dodged rocks and turnips
on a Baltimore street

thinking of Lear, Prospero,
the Fates, and Corinth

under siege.

SUN, THE MOON, AND HERBS

The secret is always
the seasoning.

No matter the cut,
the richness of cream,
the searing on wood
that once held naiads,
straddled
as they sunned, naked
in the stream.

It is in the salt of our
better tears;
the tarragon of memory
more pungent with
the simmering,
the odd saffron that
stains the first and
last shame, cilantro
I detest, but endure.

Each dot of poppy-seed
is a day, and some days
catch an alcove in the
ivory, below the lip I kiss
regardless, as we sex after
eating.

Each dried leaf
is a regret that it was not fresh,

each use a reminder that we
were out of cayenne.

For balance,
pull something from
the garden. Radish-greens,
no, kale for a soup
of the Portuguese,

replacing the sonnet I did
not write to you
before you left
the jar empty.

The parsley is plentiful;
we will dress this offering
and pepper it as best
we can

tendering it
to dashes of curry,
of coriander, or the
sandy-looking dry, crushed
something

that forgets
in its forgiveness

one lemon, the zest
of epiphany

the thinking
we knew.

Love And Blues

(2008)

"To rage, to lust, to write to, to commend,
All is the purlieu of the god of love."

— John Donne, 1601

"... When the train, it left the station
with two lights on behind,
Well, the blue light was my blues
and the red light was my mind."

— Robert Johnson, 1937

for Gette

THE LAZARUS DREAM

We laid you down, Ma, in a garden
and I gathered narrow boards
to frame you among flowers.
There was no hole. You were like a geranium
or some other perennial expected to bloom
ornamentally in memory.

Others had left; it was dark
when you opened your eyes, just to me,
and I had to think on this: certainly you would
not live now, and if I left you alone
by morning your eyes would close and you
be as expected, a stone thing.

But it had begun to rain, the slanted rain
that comes with moods of gloom
and abandonment, and how could
I let it rain on you? I called you from your bed,
and as you rose I realized you were dressed,
not in a Stoker gown or the pink brocade
I recall from your real wake,
the one interred with you, but a charcoal
man's suit with stripes. You stepped
on the cuffs as you walked with me,
but at least the wool, I thought, would
keep you warm. Was it Pa's suit? That one?
And what would be the metaphor of that?
In any event, we reached the anteroom
where many were waiting.

They were startled of course.
Georgette, my light, was there and
called out "Allie!" with a look of
wonder at my triumph of raising. I was
very happy at this, as she never called
me Allie any more.

Just then, in the commotion, a dark-complected
woman sought to take your picture—
don't worry, I wheeled and motioned
with my hand as if I were a strong god
and hissed, "if you click that picture
I'll strike you down!" She started
to cry, and as my sister urged decorum,
someone else, just the back of someone,
shot a picture instead.

There.

So it will be
in all the papers of my dream,
and I will be famous as the man
who had everything, wanted nothing,
loved and lost two women,
fooled an assembly and stood, all night
in a garden of rain.

BUILDING THE TAJ
(TO LOVE LIKE THAT)

At our best moments—
Jahan finds
his princess in a flower stall
and carries her
a bride to the chambers of his adoration
and she, so inclined, becomes
as mirror to his sun
over a sacred river, running
years of wondrous by-and-bys
until she dies a fourteenth
mother of princes, spinning her Shah
into the grasp of memory.

And so he builds
among acacia and lindens
at the boulevard of the Ganj
an edifice for her resting grandeur,
dreaming the muezzins who call
their quota quintessential from her towers
echoing attachment like lavender
sequestered in the blooms
of eternal bowers.

We are the tourists
of a love like that.

Take us to the monument,
the terraced park and pools
appointed mosque to counter-mosque

about its center,
dome within a dome,
high minarets plumbed off
by degrees to shake, if shaken
and fall away from the majesty of embrace
where death misses its dominion—
desert sigh of radiant pink
at morning, snowy orb at light's midday,
blue at dusk, the lancets
of Guldastas jabbing skyward
in the haze— kiss deep this tribute
bound in fine-for-porcelain-
firing clay, the beveled, hewn
support of sandstone's age
and shelled in pristine marble,
marble laid in marble, black and white
where calligraphs importune
the gifts of God
and florals wind their small
neat knots of garnet, lapis in dimensions
of parade, of watered wiles to Paradise
and a thousand thousand geometries
carved with intricate sameness of days, dizzying
life out in small,
perfect (if unrecognized) ways
that stand us back

before these walls and spandreled arches
awed, amazed

we are the tourists of love
like that— wanton in our wanting
and refusing to accede 'til circumstance,

chance, and the long routine return us
to our lesser roof, its lesser eaves,
the house of our approximate affection
under linden leaves.

CAMPTON, NEW HAMPSHIRE, 8 AM

Five inches of white
cake the lattices of summer grapes
on a December morning.
All night
the storm released itself
to the ground determined
as a man talking
who knows he is going to die
and now, is dead.
It is a white
so devoid of color
the red of scarves
erupts against it.
All is white— even
the steelwool sky remains
dusted of it, although
nothing is falling, moving.
Death could be white
and not black. It
could have this peace,
and not melt away.
It could refuse
the tilt of the sun,
the coming of grapes,
stay just here.

This is the snow of forgetting
so remembered.
Beyond New Englands of the mind
we steel for the down

and dazzle of the nighttime
windshield, the aftermath,
the longing.

AT A CAFÉ, LONGING

What if the devil gave up.
Arranged to meet Jesus
at a sidewalk table and they jotted feverishly
on yellow pads, comparing notations
between sips of absinthe.

What if that is them, there
as we sit amid the honks of motorcars
our scones just arrived,
our tea steaming.
They get up; it is after a long while
and they embrace.
The world suddenly
seems to have more color—
green becomes kelly, simple red, crimson
and magenta, and brown
the autumn of your eyes.

Even if I am wrong— about it, them,
the man and the man,
there is still the day
and there are still, your eyes.

8

(LOVE AND BLUES)

Play it.

Stop the stopping.
End the end. These are things
of apparency, of dull earth and we,
so impermanently vesseled
yet are stranded in their cycles,
snips of it all, snips only.

The suicides are disappointed.

8, the perfect form
of the universe
is not anabolic, although it contains
bodies.
It is not *dia*bolic, although
there is God, and there is also
the devil. Without them
there are no clues.

And without clues,
there is the tap of the monotone,
and smell of burning.

The form is of a ribbon,
parabola, the mathematic infinite
tied to twist upon itself
looping into suns and mortar

and consideration,
and it is misunderstood.

Because of it, it is all right
if you never were a ballerina,
because we have stuck *never*
like a perch onto pointed stick,
and you pose, pliée upon a stage
as it flops, the fish, with feeling.

As a fish, *never* has been many fish,
perch and anchovy, and marlin;
it has been moss on a Spanish tree,
it has been stone, a pyramid,
a man who ordered a pyramid built
(king, he thought) and the man
who slaved to build it.

For *beginning* is obscured, then erased
as is the X on this paper I just erased
before you saw it, and the *end,*
it just poked from a seed.

The rhythm of the ribbon
tugs and pulls as on a pulley; people
come and go. Last time
my name was Desjardins.
I managed a chain of beauty parlors
in department stores like Kresge
and Hudson. Marine at Tarawa;
a trumpet player.

My wife and I cheated ourselves,
then each other. I was clearing

things up, a religious thing to do,
when my plane, a DC-6
blew up over Colorado, November, 1955.

(A bomb on the aircraft, wrapped
in a Christmas present for someone's
well-insured mother. They found out,
and he got the chair.)

And I got to be Al Rocheleau.

Because of this, I married
another, a wonderful girl. I forgive
and ask forgiveness, because
I remember. It is all change.

No stop no start. Change.
Time measures against it, only.
Not beginning not end.
Not never. Or ever.

Change is 8.
And 8 is all there is.
That, and the mystery of love.
And blues.

Love and blues.

ALMS

I am tripping over beggars, lately.
They are everywhere,
a shamble these empty tenants
but they walk on cellophane
careful not to wrinkle, and in the asking
try not to be almost there.

Yes, sometimes I swat them,
the affairs of the day.
Other times a wrinkled dollar
finds their sleight magician's hand
and burns away.
I do understand them.
You have made me understand them.

Supplication becomes its own religion.

It sets up chapels in the glade
of its apprehension, socials
with tea-cakes in the parlors
of its arbiters and bishops,
little girls dancing to polite applause.

Over the years, it builds.
The flying buttresses
of its new cathedral are impressive,
attract the faithful of neighboring shires,
and they sing like wrens
in its elaborate loft,
an inveterate choir.

I would lie if I said
I never found myself
an off-key tenor there,
uncomfortably in common
and terribly aware
that what I want, I want from you
and cannot ask except
in prayer, remains outside
the passersby, a missive not received
beyond a hardly
outstretched hand,

unpenetrating stare.

A SHEPHERD'S TOAST

From out a doorway
brilliant light, the hills,
cobbled street.

The bottles, large and drowning teardrops
basketed like chianti
rest in rows above the table;
a strollered baby yawns
amid the tinks of silverware.

You come maybe for *paella*
and to drink.
About the chatter
and the aromatic strains of *Zarzuella,*
dish and dance,
he, the baby sleeps.

There is a fable in Andalusia
about father and son.

A flask of wine that newly flows
will seem to last the night,
and just as heedless so, the child ignores
his father's blows, and every slight;
older, done by half, beyond the straw,
the boy endures the same;
later still, to reach the shoulder
of glass, he must resent these things;
and as the narrowness does quick
and quicken to the mouth
he regrets them all; with a last swallow

and without a mind,
he imitates.

So the father, seldom sorry and of age
walks unsprung his fields without a flock,
drunk of nothing, missing love
and lo! the son, now grown
uncorks an *abocado* fresh
and sweet to him, to all, except
his lambs, among.

THE ROADWIFE

before G.

I.

On a Greyhound out of Chicago
in 1977, the characterization violins
into mosaic of fluttery intentions
and sober claims.

The woman across from me
wears the journey on her sleeve;
she is a pretty blonde,
the kind men raise to icons
of their sexual imagination
with the speed of an electric train
careening off-track with gravity,
eclipsing the progress of this 60-seat theatre
of unshifting panes representing,
by the shoulder, Iowa.

Barely 20, I am immersed
in my road dream; she, not much older
becomes part of it,
part of the fabric of *War and Peace*
in the twenty-fifth chapter,
as Andrei prepares for battle and Pierre
ponders, as always, his existence. The book
is open on my lap, conspicuous as
a young writer can make it, saying
I am the sensitive type, the artist that would
revel in you and never own you,

the floater of iambs into the mist
of truckstop romance.

And then, without clocks,
Des Moines in retreat, it all flips back,
it is Pierre to the rescue of Natasha
from that scoundrel, Kuragin
and his thug, Dolohov. For Americans
it takes form in two Steinbeckian villains,
a perverse sort of George and Lennie,
inverted and black, the small man openly malevolent,
the larger calculating.

They have sensed the flaws
in my ingenue across the aisle
and work upon her, mile by mile by silo
and bale by bale of forage, pricking her
with suggestions and epithets
from a rear seat. Of course, in my world
of hurrahs and trumpets,
this cannot be.

I watch myself rise
like a thunderstorm, taking notes;
"LEAVE HER ALONE— NOW!!!" And I marvel
at my sudden posture and my basso affront,
all Achilles at the gates of Ilium. The little man
claims to want me bad, but shucks, his big friend
is in the way. The larger backs the duo
into their seats, "no trouble, no trouble"
with the covert smile
of a guillotine operator, but it's finished.
Somehow I've won.

And in snap
of a broken castanet
she is now beside me, a study
not yet nude but perfect for sonnets,
riding into Nebraska to the leaven
of the moon.

We hear the duo plotting their next move:
they will smuggle alcohol past
the driver at this forlorn outpost
near Platte; "I'll be right back,"
she says, a voice of soft bells.
I watch it unfold in uneven light;
the driver catches our boys like carp,
and they wave the bus goodbye
to a laughing justice.

And in the charcoaled west
of simmering denouement
she pulls from her satchel
a sealed bottle of wine,
and kisses me like
the last refuge of a long night,
the wet chablis of lips and tongue
a symphony.

II.

First it is me,
a hurried soul landscaping
across her slight body, clothed
yet opened to the sculpture
of hands, her breasts small

and rounded as damsons,
the core of her as sweet
moist earth.

To distant tunes of three Jamaicans,
we elevate each other.
By morning I want to frame her
a Botticelli in a small room
in Cheyenne; she hesitates,
not that her old man back in Sebastopol
would mind; but no,
it wasn't time.

We take turns
in our cushioned, steel chrysalis
revealing secrets;
mine are inconsequential,
cast in the sienna of
hopeful lies; but her magazine
lies open to the center, or
near the center, exposing
the bright credential of a courtesan,
a bed and her, yes her upon it
a Scheherazade, the spray
of melting men everywhere.

Cheri, February. $1.95.

The name she chose, Sandi.
Her special talent, fellatio
among small gods. Deep in another waxen
night, under a sweater, she shows me
what I could not understand

about morality and grace. Her mouth
nurtures in its quiet consonance;
I come for her aside the
outline of mesas.

In Winnemucca, the sidewalks
stretch with crap-table felt,
and she wants to stay. Now it is me
who delays, equivocates. From
long before Lovelock, to Sparks, to Truckee,
we have lived in each other's sweat
and touch and breath, compared our
lives for a grounding outside,

and failed to seize it. Yet we are married
into our hours, into their towns and dives,
reaching and withdrawing from each
other as shadows on the wrong
side of suns.

On the way into Oakland,
sand now down to a narrow thread,
she confesses her name
is Barbara Dean. Somewhere,
for years, I will keep her number.

I have read the book many times.
In the end, Pierre returns for Natasha.

In the end, all good reads
pine to be read again,
and persons drawn in the subtle
sentience of epic
find, alight onto hearts and minds

the library of selves
they have been.

Good life, Sandi. Barbara.
Wife. And friend.

A MARRIAGE

Sometimes what is said ends a season.

We are a threshed field
rolling to the boundary line.

The stubble writhes in winter wind
then sleeps beneath a warm
mantle of snow.

We're the picturesques
framed in the small parlor
of a farmer in the dell.

We put ourselves
through the misery of planting,
the want, the waiting, a hell.

And then, just as accounts
come due, the hour strikes
its ever-eleven
and the almanac portends

we grow into the subtle rain
and all is well.

THE NUNS FRET NOT

The nuns fret not;
their small quarters dance
the tapestry of silence,
the wedding night with Christ
extended to the knotted walk
of their later days,
their memories of service
washed unto prayer
in the misgivings of their children
who fly, fly away
(as children do) and carry off their names—
Patience, Mercy, Charity, Piety
to play in more broad lots
grassed and daffodiled with
the hopes of this world.

So I send mine;
and in between the temples
white with worry, wishing of a mind
that prayer make do, and they
that all the flesh expended
in this hillocked flock
I shepherded with not so much
a covenant or clue,
forgive the madness for the sorry
and save just something
for this true, sequestered me—
flowers on occasions,
little cards to bright and sentinel
a new, and narrow room.

GALATIANS TWO

Said somebody's Lord:

we are present among our sins,
guests of the dinner.

Nude maids dance
with castanets, the wine blurs,
the boar is cut.

So begins the pain.

Thou shall not covet—
it clings to the cells, taints
their cleave to a malformed destiny.
Pride nitres the nourishing halls
into blackness; gluttony
pools a Leviathan
in the gut. The slothing gait,
halved with each step
betrays any destination but a fall
(where the mouth of greed
yawns wide its aching, dry).

Anger surges along miles
of wire, doubling distance
to a static hum. Envy
penetrates in pinpoints,
then severs its serrated self.
No wonder the mind fails,
forgets, hallucinates truth
in pastels of blindness.

The heart hardens to a basaltic fist,
presses knotted breath.
The vanity is our smile, our blank faith.
And the slowness of its happening—

it creates new flesh.

Deep inside, the man elects
to grow another man, wildly rebellious;
this is cancer, *this man.*
We leave quickly enough,
sedated or screaming, bury it
before it grows limbs, and walks
as us, because it can.
If we stayed, all of us,
we would see the monsters,
marvel at them.

They would inherit the earth.

Fortunate or not
we die for our sins,
forgetting the crosses and covenants,
the cleansing in and out, our versions

of Him.

VENDOR (AND SON)

I grind my sadness
into sausage
and sell it to the passersby.
My stand is striped,
my stance unassuming,
the cuffs of my pants
rolled in homage.

"Mustard, sir?"

Twelve gulls
play a cribbage
of sound in the sky.

My son today, after Literature
asked his father,
a not very famous poet
what "The Hollow Men"
was all about.

The smile on my
headpiece struggled
to reply.

The stand is closed now;
winter is why.

SWANS OF TUONELA

They maintain. The birds
whose necks when brought to beaks
become a heart
prefer to swim in solitude.

Habitual figurines
paddling like mad beneath the calm—
reach for them,
they peck your eyes.

Instead we rent a large replica
and paddle in circles.

We remain; we hope
that our orchestral lives will find
just once, the arch of back,
the perfect lift, a turn on toes
in the majesty of silence
and sound, extending wing
to Finnish sky and settle
on a newer glass

not far
beyond the supple grass
of truer ground.

JACOB WRESTLES WITH GOD

And so Jacob sent his two wives
and eleven children on ahead
and stayed to wrestle with someone
he called God.

They agreed to one fall, no curfew.

Jacob was in a ram-skin,
barefooted
while God entered the ring in green sequins
and a gold-lamé headdress,
masked at the front.

He took the sequins off,
passing them to a valet who is unnamed
in the Holy Books, but could
have been Gabriel, since
he wore a bugle in a holster.

They circled each other
like Copernicus in his dirtiest
drawings,
and took hold. The headlock
of God wrenched Jacob
into new religion. His temples
throbbed like a man-root waiting
to explode the seed of succession,
but Jacob slipped away with
the good sweat of a parishioner
and flexed himself.

His leg-sweep of God recalled
Lucifer, the Prince of the Air, and
God tumbled to the dust like
a shiny mountain.

From there, Jacob applied
the half-nelson of vengeful Cain
in whose blood (along with Abel)
Jacob still swam. He rocked God
like a bad baby, squeezing
dispensations out of him, as the night
folded toward dawn.

God promised Jacob a place
in heaven, and Jacob let him
rise eastward with the pink orb
he had meant to ask him about, when God
pulled an old trick. A sneak
kick, to the round of Jacob's hip popped
that thing like a mutton-hind
in the mouth of fat Laban.

Jacob hopped, semi-paralyzed
but unpenitent screaming
"was that fair!" To which came the reply,
"I am what I am, and I could not beat you,
but of course, you could not beat me."

"Why?"

"There is too much story left to tell."

"Can I at least see your face?"

And God removed the mask. There was
a crescendo, somewhere.

Jacob's eyes widened like spittoons.
"Why, it is a man's face. Will we see the face again?
We will see it in men's faces?"

"You will see it soon."

"And your name. What is your name?"

God left with his entourage,
no bugle, and no more words.

Jacob limped toward the ford of the Jabbok,
and continued the verses.
To this day, we all limp round
with a queasy sciatica, because
of that kick.

THE FISHERS

Beyond the equatorial silence
of morning on Lake Tanganyika,
noonward rays pierce
the tensile skin of water
and shoot, spearlike
to the sandy bottom.

The fishers
parallel in their rosewood canoes
move like slothy caymans
atop warm glass,
stretch the twine between.

Strung beneath
are slats of banyan
like piano keys these men
would only tap to play; aligned, the pieces
shadow deep against the sun
their long trappings
of magic.

African perch and bluegill
back-fin warily as virgins,
slowly, hypnotically
into the shallows;
there they stand and dervish.

Sixteen women
scarved of green and fuchsia
knee-deep in the churn

bucket the entire school
in fifteen minutes.

A Lutheran
watches from shore.

LABRADOR

The stubbled road pencils to a brim,
pulls down a slate of sky.
At Coeur-de-Daigne the last Inuits
wave goodbye.

As far as the rocks are small
you roll to where you stop,
then pull the knapsacks on,
Sherpa of the horizontal.

At the end, a coast of terns.
In the distance, floes, and Baffin Island;
you follow with
your eyes until they bobble
true North.

This is the end of the world.
The one that was intended.
The one between the lines
that demarcate the soul
and the salvation.

Your confessor becomes the light
auroral at dusk; you tell it everything.
And if you can imagine, *imagine*
it sets you free.

Deliverer, it must.

ROOM 252

The woman, releasing
at moment of fire is a glass harp
cascading her quarter-tones
against the despondencies
of the day, swelling night air
with the unstrained highs, hushes
of her real instrument.

The man is in awe
at what he has done— he awes easily
since he is a silly thing, husband or adulterer,
more about bastions and balls
than a heart, and at this thousandth
accident he becomes again, Caesar
of seconds, the blind pleaser,
the lost and laughable
momentary king.

AND COLERIDGE SAID

The frustration
of your company is
that all the happinesses there
reside and cling to seconds,
then release.

I catch nectar in a sieve;
I live for you, honeyless of hope
among the hexagons
with nothing to re-live
as I live out me, not so much
a loved and loving man as just
a bumbler, a specimen
of big, dumb, bee.

JULY FOURTEENS

I accept.

I accept and commemorate
every pitch and syllable
that rains on me across spaces,
every catch of your form
arriving as planned
or surprising the gallery,
the scent of you smeared
among flowers and a dropped garment,
sung to me in arias no diva
rounds her O's upon to reach, reach
as climax to a swollen grace
the day you married mission into me
and became
my face.

LIFE SCIENCES

He is the baseball coach,
a blond and handsome Nazi
and Mr. Biology, too.

This is the class you remember
for its bouquet of formaldehyde,
its casual brutality
in the name of science.

His agenda is planned mayhem,
clinical and cold. Your A's
are for complicity, acquiescence to observations
you neither need nor want.
There are no doctors in your class,
no population planners,
not even a taxidermist.
But ah. Like Nuremberg under firelights,
or any summer camp in Poland,
there are statistics.

It starts easy, small clear vermin,
paramecia like bedroom slippers,
the green sheeny spots of euglena
ornamenting your microscope
window. Watch them feed on one-celled
things even smaller than themselves,
of a name forgotten, since what are you
if you are food for those who are
already next to nothing.

After the show, down the big drain
they go.

Planaria, they are interesting freaks.
With scalpel you cut the tiny wormhead
between its Chinese eyes, just the head,
a nice longitudinal slice.

In days, watch, as if by blackshirt
magic it grows two separate heads,
two sets of eyes, useless to itself
and no doubt retarded. Shower it
off yourself.

Speaking of worms, you graduate
from simple flats to the hermaphroditic
annelids, male and female
in one flesh-necklated package, shameless
and ready to be baited or slit.
(After all, they eat dirt, shit.)
In the stereoscope they are moist
as sex organs; follow their canals
into the toilet of memory.

I once pithed a frog, did you?
Humanly etherized
in a eugenic afternoon, you take the probe
and place it deftly through soft bone
behind the eyes, and give it a twist.
Death immediate, brisk.
You cut the T of its pathology,
find the fine intestine and the lung.

I alone in my class extracted
the pituitary intact.
But there was nothing to do with it.

You watch the lobsters hold forth
in their rectangle of mob mentality.
See the weak one, vilified in cartoons, put upon
by its Aryan brothers. They tear him
limb from limb, shell him, use him
as a spoon.

Fruit flies. You mate the vestigial
(of useless wing) with the virile ones
to render a race into extinction. They sex
as if nothing is wrong. And they
disappear before Easter.

Then the TURTLE. The big box one
we all place on its back shell
tilted forward on the nifty paper-cutter,
the kind for Christmas projects—

you! hold the head, you four!
be the bearers, and Mr. Biology
will snap the arm DOWN.
Its claws swim frantically
down the red river of vivisection
toward home, toward home.

Defenses sawed away
reveal the civilization,
the rooms of reptilian being
slamming shut their shop-windows

as I, much a fool as Parliament
massage the heart between thumb
and forefinger, thinking
of a risen Jesus.

You finish the season with sharks
wrapped in newspaper, shot with
latex so their organs won't return
to sludge, and label everything from
viscera to veins, to babies
hunched like packets of evil in the womb.

We are experts biologic.
We are college prep; we are, like him
and in those reluctant moments
masters of certain worlds.

It was a long time ago.

In the interim
I have split of two minds,
had two faces;
I have, headless, flapped
my disconcert of short arms
in the presence of betrayal;

I have lain there,
pulled out of joint, ripped
of love.
I have pithed myself
and found my glands lacking.
Resigned, no predators in my belly,
no sperm of consequence.

I am slipper and bangle,
fragile as these.
I have bred without wings
looking for fruit or carrion.

And I have met others like him,
the blond one, along this life.
So certain, so calm.

It's not me. I, like most,
many, more the *specimen of*
than *man among men,*
am encased in living trust
of someone else's glass but better in belief,
a God to somehow rather have

than be.

WETLAND

It has become an everglade.
We struggle among reeds,
the rustle of stiletto grasses
to the premonition of storm,
first loud thud of water
against palmetto.

Do we walk from
here, do it before darkness,
find, if there is one, the one road
east/west, leading out
of this almost quiet,
this nest of denizen reptiles
and pelicans, their mouths
full of feeding?

We were clearer about things
before the tropic,
a humid agreement
to withhold feeling.

I dream of dry, the Arizona
of early days, the cool of understanding,
the reliable faith of cacti
and pears that prick but when
you peel, bear eating.

Most of all I pray for love,
now and into the cricketeer's night
when such barely known, primeval marshes
of our circumstance

might seek some white and partly
civilized light again
and once redeemed
evaporate into meaning.

APOSTLE DOUBTS HIS ART

The poets of academia
screw themselves into the sacristy wall
and hang like Bruegels;
dust and dim light
negotiate detail.

The ones of the street
do no such thing.
They harbinger in costume
among throngs unrecognized;
they Rorschach, reel,
honk like Oberon's donkey.

I have been each,
usually striving for the other.

Eventually, stasis occurs
along the equator of broad yards and thoroughfares,
the ivy and the stench,
room for occasional stanzas for a lover,
snifters and sibilance, the eleventh
crushed-out butt.

And then I write something like this.
I care about it, it is rather good
I think.

So what.

THE LIMPING MAN WAS JESUS

A soft touch, you say.

When I was eight a man
appeared at the door. He leaned on a crutch;
he said he was selling magazines
to pay for his operation.
My mother slammed the door.

And the man limped away.
My mother phoned each
neighbor, quickly,
as if to warn of a firestorm.

I pleaded with her
to reconsider, to help the man.

"He's just after money."

In my head strings moaned
the beginning of a tragic song.
My protests were as tears on stone.
Why does she warn the neighbors?
Maybe they—

"Yes, headed down your driveway now."

From lace obscurity I watched
the man sink lower on his crutch
with each unanswered door,
the cracks of which strained the laughter

of Mike Douglas, the cackling Totie Fields,
or Lisa's cry as the world turned
from each TV.

With the last door before a long walk,
I saw him scream in silence
the oval of the Munch painting I would
associate with this in later years, and the music,
a sad Schubert quartet.

For days I could not forget the man at all;
for days he was Jesus to me, turned away,
and the stabs of the buzzers
were scourges, and long nails.
I examined my crucifix, the expression
of the form, the Munch-face there in miniature,
the minor chords in swell.

I forgave my mother, who was a woman
to be loved.

But I did not forgive myself who watched it,
the child aside the dolorous road
and the magazine man limping to Golgotha,
the cruelty of suspicion
burned in me as an old cigarette
into a glass tray

at three in the afternoon,
on an Easter vacation,
the Friday holiday.

ANNIVERSARY, PROBABLY 1994

"Al, you are everything to me.
You are all the happiness I need.
Your wife and best friend, Gette."

Such cards are without dates;
they anticipate others.
But to compare the message:

my blood, siphoned
into a font, still warm,
would be wanting.

My brightest lines read before
knowing throngs
that thrilled at each inflection
and cheered as I were Alexander
victorious at Antioch,
would beg a single listener.

The best of silken, savory,
unabashed encounters
among unfettered souls that was sworn to
or lied about by a score of suitors
more accomplished than I
would become stories
of mechanics, and variations
in temperature.

And if I could strand
time atop this promontory
of professed love, feel the sun
on my face, deliver song to a happy God,

weave silver into
the lattices of your grace
and stay there as in this drawer
forever, I might then find
some way to thank you,

to embrace you still, to lean against
the meaning of this tiny,
tawdry life
and then at last, at last
to lever.

UNDER LIFE'S RAY, KNEELING

When you came to me, the amulets spun
sunlit lights, lingering into lattices
of promise, tipped back tilt of day
to soft hurrahs, the graceful arch of healing,
turned a scatter into image, icon,
place where it was comfortable to pray.

And you remained in light, and I shined;
dull black still I shined, as sea-stones
give themselves to smile of children's eyes,
believe there is no gray, no love withheld
in pockets of the night when subtle waves
belie a passion's wax upon the moon.

You left in dark, a dark as closet grim
and clothes yet hung, conspiring the scents
of years you took and wore me from within,
provoked the heavy cries of birth again,
a kind deaf angels sing, and even set
the worst barrage of memory aside.

But when, or when erasing, if, it dawns
you to return, to play as fire through window-
blinds my slivered hope, recall for life
one shiver in the madness of this shivering
want and warm us both, that blessing end
of God's redeeming kiss, a new begin.

ANOPHELES

She follows my breath,
sweet with carbon,
my skin emanates banana and mint;
I'm so hopeless.

She lights as the lightest kiss,
a duplicitous fairy.

She licks me down
with opiate, strokes me
as a boy until I don't even know
I'm numb.

The lancet, small as the smallest deliverer
pierces the cells with spit,
an overwhelming
divider of worlds.

As she sucks, she dissolves
every attempt at closing the wound,
invisible to eye but under a scope
the red spreads everywhere.

She lets it fill her belly.

Behind she leaves first that itch,
the knowledge that something is wrong,
the stupid, stupid self-denial.
The coils of parasite course
like a gathered family
beyond the light.

You sweat it.
The head pounds.
Villages are leveled by it.

Too weak
to sever your tie
and dancing with memories
you lie, waiting,
so close to the quinine
of infinite divorce.

Meanwhile,
the bloodmeal
courts and enriches
a thousandfold,

product of another mating.

"RESCUED FROM DEATH BY FORCE, THOUGH PALE AND FAINT... "

after *Methought I Saw ...*

So what about
my own espousèd saint
fired of porcelain and placed
in curio among
the treasures of my fate?

Can she return
the woman I forgot to love
in momentary nodes
of natural self-hate,
and ring the ground
with quiet footsteps round
the kneelèd altar
where I wait?

Can the face
blossom into cheer again,
a pink carnation
expurgate
the sins of earth
to scent and send one lover's loss
into erasure by its grace?

Milton, blind and willful
yet reclaimed
a wife in reverie
beside the penitential gate—

so who am I, by force
of love alone to not forgive
myself and her

before it is too late.

SAINT ALBERT OF THE ASSES

You had come to call me Saint Albert
during one of many recent discussions
about the trouble in June.
You meant it lovingly
enough I know, but I have decided
that is what I am. And a martyr, too.

I have lived among
the wild asses west of Genoa
and far from Assisi. I have picked olives
and carted them on these animals
and each olive, ripe and plump
and oily to the touch, represents
a failed purpose squashed beyond
our virgin basket
into memory.

I am poor and have helped the poor
help themselves to me
so that feeling sorry for myself
rises to the level of vision.

I see Horsemen. You cannot
come out of the sun on asses
and dictate to anyone. I was hit
by a truck and lived. But my miracles
are one step in front of the other
and the love of you.

My arms are wide. A willing target,
a place for vines.

ACCORDING TO O. HENRY

We are stuck in our paradoxes.

I would do anything
to sleep behind the warm bars
of your authority.

You would pay anyone
to unburden the child I've become,
red-chiefed in petulance
and doubt.

You offer me the watch-fob.
I offer you the comb.

We are storied in our volume,
the beautiful and simple swindles
of contact and release, silence
and a comic serendipity,
love beyond graft and grifters
set upon a hearthstone
of singular peace, that clicks
our literature so sound and commonplace,
characters who find each other
in each other's need.

EINSTEIN'S COROLLARY

(The Theory of Loneliness)

When you stop in the hall
stranded
because the person you face
moves left when you do
right when you do
then left
right
again, again
it is like
the line that shoots off into space
seeming not to meet
another skewed
beneath it

but, as
space is curved

and one of you in the hall
will relent

the lines will meet
an eternity from now
when the hall is quite empty

unless

of course

it was a hall
of mirrors

and you stayed, awaiting

a new

proof.

ANNILISE SHOPS FOR GOD

The perfumed escalator
occasions a falling upward,
exchanging love for want of love
as purchasing new clothes
with a blank currency,
vivitar of glitter, damask on dead souls
bought and sold
in the opalesque rialto of tears,
tears that run like stabbed women
down sidewalks
to inevitable end, to silence
of a downturned smile
on a mannequin.

LOVE THAT IS DARK AND DEEP

you can find
in the casual morel
that springs to a Pisan tower,
a nose uprooting truffles
at splay of an oak,
mossy things, mold and wort,
mistletoes daft with sleepy belladonna
      (the hallucinate of minutes)
      dilating the eye with pleasure
in forests of our secret life
browned into silence of a smile,
the trust, musty, succulent
      delicacy of different light.

NEWTON'S LAMENT

The fortunate are acted on
by the small magnets of love.
The pull merely tingles,
creates a smile,
a tide in the blood.

To gaze on one beloved
spins a compass
against the judgment of its stone,
makes one useless to wayfarers,
erects an effigy of air
as if it were bone.

Sad to say
such polar force can be measured best
by its absence, in the essence
of equators,

and being alone.

CHINESE APPLE

When cracked, spilled
the pomegranate
disgorges its seeds, so many;
one of them, a true believer
is encouraged by his company.

And yet that number spread throughout the lonely world,
would seem as nothing. Sweet, sour,
something of a forgotten fruit of a forgotten tree,
of so many.

Until, until
one must remember
(if he is one)
to wish and yearn his planting
among the currant
and the palm,
and in the season
of the coming of the pomegranate

come
of plenty.

FOLLOWER

The ant sustains on tiny air,
hung beyond gravity,
sifting clear blood.
You can pinch him, throw
him a mile by his senses, bounce
him off a papered wall;
he continues.

Like him I am a good worker;
and I too sniff the small air,
mocking these accordion lungs, walk on ceilings
until the concussion,
paint the stairs red.

Fifty thousand ants
pulling together could make
the figure of a man, but fifty thousand men
wouldn't amount to an ant
in any aspect of trust or valor.

Look, I'm not accusing,
certainly not you.
I'm the one
any rubber ball could break, curl fetal
to speck a giant's eye.

But you know, I could be organized.

I could sacrifice myself.
I could carry my own weight and more.
Yes, I love sweets too well.

And I do tickle, slightly.

All the same I'll join you
on your next crusade, I promise.
I'll try to be that noble, that mindless.
Leave your signals on the walk today.

I'll follow.

REVELATION

"I understand a fury in your words. But not the words"

— to Othello

The world is jaundiced today.

School buses careen toward
destinations.

The caution light is misunderstood.

The sun butters everything, glares
with subdural heat.

Dandelions choke Bermuda grass.

The pollen count is high.
Pollen is everywhere, my nose
my ears, my life. My fingers
go saffron with it.

Cowards win the day.
Their spoils golden, golden
haul themselves away.

I think these are magic glasses
to see only yellow.

And when I take them off,
I am found to be blind.

Poor thing me.
Poor fellow.

RECOMMENDING, OF THE BOOKS, *ARIEL*

What a thrill—
My thumb instead of an onion.

   "Cut" by Sylvia Plath, 1962

When opened
and her words, viewed
the pages fly to the corners
of the room.

When she died,
her kitchen a Treblinka,
one finch sang on a branch
opposite the storm window.

At the camps it was like this too.

Art in the air;
on the ground

too much to do.

BOMBING THE MUSES

I am sick of answering to clichés.
Of awaiting the uninevitable.
These are after all, not
the women you marry.
One carries asps in her purse.
Another folds the arsenic
into raisin bread, and butters.
Her sister lays perfect spikes
under a slip of gardenias;
another wrinkles the mind.
When the hollow one laughs at you
you're too embarrassed
not to laugh back.
The dancer will not trace your instep
or help you when you fall.
These are the coveted apparencies
that perform tricks
when well fed,
that pretend to scream of satisfaction
but after, they fish the wallet
for cards and open accounts.
The muse you keep is the one you love,
more than yourself, and not finding her
you break into the sorority
after midnight,
and crush them all with lamps.

ITINERARY

Each dawn I die to the miserable reveille,
slide down the banister of blades into pails
of well-meaning iodine and poultice of nurses
who've seen men naked before, and seen better.

Each day I tell my story to a debutante;
I imagine she imagines me younger and her older
and in my convolutions of wit and wagging esprit
marry and divorce her in a bright Vegas of memory.

Each afternoon my siesta, like tamarind taffy
lengthens in the window of a Daytona Beach giftshop
and when I revive the world seems new again
for fifteen seconds, about the time of a bus stop.

Each supper should be serviced by apostles
and waiters, but I too often settle for a silver tin,
the inscrutable Swanson, brownie of burnt edges,
ration of regrets and really green peas.

Each night my prayers mean more to the wall;
I ring my R's like Gielgud, or Pound in his vehemence
or Fields, thumbing the Bible for loopholes,
sipping antacids like the balm of Saint Boniface.

And in my sleep, each sleep, I leaf the catalog
of lives, my own many and as bit player of others,
my dreams dusting the hedges as dirigibles
drifting to nineteen soft landings of hopeful youth.

And in the waxed black hours of early waking
your face comes clear again, ornament for taking
from the pine-bough of covenant, before you broke it—
exited without instructions, shaking the tinsel down.

And each dawn I die, each death a realization
that life, as mass or mystery cures itself
of particular revelation— rather, its majestic routine
courts the eyeglass of surrender, and loves waiting.

MURMUR OF THE HEART

Sand ribbons ornament
the edge of reason; the sea
promises the land
what it can't deliver.

Undulants, pink noise,
spikes of occasional turbulence
on the paper day, the hush, hush
of backwater.

The core of us longs
for immersion in a saline peace.
Longs for love, the end
of separation, the woman and the man
that have carried, carried each other
to finally fall into one, secret shore
of utter release.

It is the idea
that fixes the heart.

Small crustaceans pulled from
the cradles of their silica
dig again for home,
want only the damp, dark saltiness
of their way. Children stress
them to their ends
only in the natural acts
of discovery, of play—
scarabs to them, amulets

between ill-formed castles
and the shiver of spray.

You can live with this condition.
Check it every few years.
Assure the valves that
force and filter everything
do not further decay.

The prescription.
Spend time on beaches,
watch the blast of sunsets
fall into the sky
of starry crosses, thankful
for a tenuous union
of body and soul, and for these arms
around what you can't fully have,
and from which
you can't fully get away.

RETURN TO MUNCHKINLAND

Once I was a reporter on this beat,
and wrote a series of commiserations
on the subject of men and women without love.
I called it *Munchkinland.*

Then one night
I found myself shorter in the mirror,
squat, and fat;
my clothes turned to primary colors,
my belt to suspenders,
buttons, bright orange sprouting like mushrooms,
and so did my nose.
When I spoke
to myself as lonely people do,
the sound was pinched
as a drunk in a cop's full-nelson,
and my tears were as pearls.

I had neglected to notice, I decided,
that my wife was short and fat also,
though lovely; my children,
hatched from eggs, rubbed their eyes
with fortune, awaiting instructions;
my street was bumpy, yellow.

People here
in each holiday cookie house
live in fear,
fear that it will not get better.

I was right about that.

But since Dorothy came,
we pray to her: *Hail Dorothy,*
not so small and meek, blessed are you
among our separate squeaks,
please do not surrender.
Be true to yourself, your friends,
your one exceptional lover.

Remember the secret.
The secret is water.

Deliver us from a hell of technicolor,
remove our makeup, each secret ill;
it was all a dream, tell us,
and there IS a place like home,

there always was,
there always will.

NIGHT AUDITOR

He emerges from Hopper's oils
amid solid eggshell, taupe, planes of brown
parallel, perpendicular
and pierced by the hot-red exit sign
above silk flowers.
The single figure is magnified
by perspective; you are
looking down at him, at his head-crown
and a smudge of nose.
There is furniture, nondescript modern,
an orange couch, coffee table,
bare floor stretching left—
he is uncentered
and he is looking
without eyes you can see
at an unringing phone.
Outside the twin glass doors, oversized,
a blank stoop under bad light
that could use a crimson prostitute
and beyond, just black—
as the memory of birth.
No one checks in; no one checks out.
No sounds here,
even though TVs and
sex-cries should be just a walk away.

Reading Dante,
matching Pinsky's and Ciardi's
terza rima would be a funny
thing to do.

Following Fischer's 900 games,
move by move.

The man is married
(although it doesn't say)
to a woman, sleeping now
who will rise at morning, open
the door to a lapping ocean,
nude.

There is another world
that waves like yellow silk
in between seconds, and our other selves
live in it, in a kind of
concordance
captured by artists too often misunderstood,
and by the lonely, too.

ARMY OF THE POTOMAC AT THE LOVE BAR

Lo, the inconsequence of humanity.

Pretty girls sidle and stare,
arcing like red cellos to be played
with physicality and depth.

But the dare.

Batteries of Bud, Cuervo maunder.
Men are posturing when they could mate.
Flanks are exposed, they smell of gardenia,
look back with pimento lips,
parted.

My stasis is voluntary;
in the excitement of the order, "March
south at 2100" I see my issue, the watch
and compass, are without arms.
I am married anyway, more of a correspondent.
But these boys are regulars,
full of self and saltpeter
and plenty of flints; yet they are decisive
as clams. The field defines itself,
arranges flags; nothing.

Like McClellan,
they await further instructions.
Like him, they consolidate,
confer, assess the endgame
and forget to begin.

"War is hell," they shy;
disappointment in the offing,
so is sin.

THE MOON THAT COMBS THE SEA

Brightens to a knob
turned of knuckles in the night,
peels itself across a month
of mourning,
raises starfish to that stone
of periwinkle height,
only to be let down.

On Surrey streets
the howlers turn their bocks,
their bottles, up
to a dark heaven illumined by fright
and wipe their eyes
in its mirror, the mad and mortifying
deliverance.

The moon that combs the sea
appoints the sextant
and its sailors, each Phoenician,
Basque, or Barbary black
that rolls off centuries in the spray,
the gondoliers on glass canals,
the shrimping souls
who tie their nets unto the wake
in knots assured and tight
worship in its grave
a dollop of hope, the coin
that shines a shill upon black felt
to flip and disappear
within its own magnetic sleight

and pull upon the rope
a blue veil of dawn,
obscuring in unfettered sight
the blindness of everything,
a writhe of eels, the apology of earth—
a bound and spinning slave
of its own satellite.

POET GAME

Making Not the Case if Poetry Matters

We come to play
shaking our pieces out—
Scotties, howitzers, Potemkins
and Hupmobiles,
thimbles, flatirons, Homburgs, lead versions
of red wheelbarrows,
and the boots of a long day's journey.

We tap these squares
of no horizon on Oz-feet, traipsing
to music, trapped
in a clockwise tour
toward clocks that tick
our duration.

We are the poet, the serious thing.

The portfolio begins
and ends with death, our villa.
These wrecked hotels are easiest to
acquire, you need only two,
neoned purple as unpulsed arteries—
one to die in alive (with a pool),
and one to die in dead.

They are on deserts but we name
them after vibrant seas, as is our licence.

We collect nothing in them,
but we own them
because they are cheap, tawdry,
you can write by
the bathroom lights,
dishevel heavy spreads, forgetful while
the high sills drop
occasional frescoes into sidewalk cement—
the suicide side-effect
of psychiatric meds.

And so the bones careen
as indeterminate as inspiration.

Sex; in search of powder-blue
love is nonetheless sex
and it's everywhere—
it simmers out of
New England cottages,
shanty rows, sex like dogs in April
or pretty as a robin's-egg
triolet of need, of orchids and anthers,
fine poundings of the pistillate,
pearly strands and the cries
of bel cantos from
twigs in the foreground
maples.

Three steps on
to the madness of saints,
religion and irreligion coming in cascade
of violet Gitas on avenues of God,
of tumbling Lucifers and
droning Oms, the phallus of Osiris,

position of missionaries,
the baths of milk, the perfect psalm—
dualities, trinities, floods
of righteous wrongs,
crucifixion by lot, dervishes and deities
in machina of Olympian
thrust, intrigues and
unexplained incest, some kind
of deliverance, a from and to,
of idols in dust.

Ride the Reading, however you pronounce it.

We hold those railroad deeds
because they provide steady income;
we work as switchmen or ticket-takers
or prostitutes in the Pullmans,
though these cards are the first we mortgage to
our failed dreams.

Slip-slide on nature's tongue
to the tan dunes of Sandover, sifting
a hundred-hundred greenslate
seas, scaped into scansion;
sandalwood harboring a thrush,
succulents breaking to release
themselves to thirsty wanderers
of an elemental trust; the s of sidewinders
signing their silicate names
to an endless erasure of wind,
winding down azurite canyons, carved
by a river within,
river of urges,

urging the words "it is beautiful"
not because
we say it, but because it is.

The poet—
in spirit of a troubadour-thief
is paid for services at weddings
or a far funeral, providing toast
or elegy that sounds
as Greek but is mellifluous
in its sibilance and bell-like rings—
everyone's Pindar of the fleeting hour,
blacksheep
with a laurel wreath.

And flung, to a deft pirouette
among the red lights of cause
and fervor, broadside the world
with an often irrelevant polemic,
the dark comedies of war
pestled into penniless stations,
attitudes of open doors moving masses
to the streets, a lot of to-do
in our lines of provocation, pushing
out what had just settled in
before, and the knowledge that revolution
always starts with a poem,
passes to prayer
yet ends with the gore
of an obvious solution.

The poet is assessed
for his various constructions
by narrow-eyed peers

over Arabica beans
and French cigarettes.

Me. Me. Yellow me.
Castigate or cower
the world must have
our heartwrenched, dripping sleeve.
The pain of love (invert),
the love of pain, confessional as Bosch
to the inquisitor's rats,
the elegant sarcoma of the dance,
self-pitiful honeywell
of spasmed slights,
rapes and near-rapes, back-hands
and the killing ennui; we creak
the scaffolds with our blame,
tear and stain and swing, swing
off life's seemingly uneven
and eventful chain.

The poet goes to jail
or to college or to bed;
free him with three rolls,
or files in the bread.

Did I mention death?

Or its antidote, *nostalgia!* Yes!
The striving greenly paradise of
recolored yesterdays, hillocks
chlorophylled to emerald
by new memory's rain,
the wood-top spinning

a gay equilibrium and love's
scent, lemon, summering shadow
to a fine hope we share,
Samaritans into evensong
of whippoor-willed decision—
I, writer of these
shall author a smiling sanity into
worlds of derision— take me
home, take me *home*—

even if you are a vision.

The ultimate reveling
(with or without revelation)
of man's itch for art, for transcending
includes of course
the notions that we brew, poems
of the poetry, the state and struggle
circular that circling, renews;
we labor in the workshops
like bruised elves
striving to these stellar properties
of deep, deep blue,
the place of our achieving,
the walk of any recognizing, too—
we cross our legs at readings
of our number Chanced or Chested
into magnitude well known to us
but somehow
known to few, since plumbers
and their helpers
have a metaphor
for what they also do—

artists made essential by a broad
and better comprehended
truth.

It goes on, these laps;
we wile, exalt the air,
we sail and sometimes, sin.
We think we have it, pass
back into our round of glory only
to be taxed again.

We never give up. From
picnic table children
to the parlors of colicky return
we flap, unflap the board, arrange the bank,
shuffle Nostradamus at our whim.
Some games you don't
outgrow, but grow in.

Your turn, my darling;
double-six will bring you safe,
eight, ten, eleven
wears you thin. The poet dies
most often in his sleep, line breaks
broke and a meter sprung within
that leaves a marvelous, counterfeit paper,
its wondrous colors
whirling the world among numbers
of wondering kin.

Goodnight, goodnight, sweet ladies.
And green-bay gentlemen.

All right, the night ascending—
You win. You win. You win.

THE HOUSE OF ME

This mansion of myself, come of bricks,
a portico, pick-up sticks, heavy misfortunes,
carpeted up-and-down stairwells of hope,
coats of blather and intrigue, intricate dormers
pointed to heaven, to the sullen hawk's relief
(the eyed carrion or soon-to-be), windows
clear as birth-light, of oncoming calamity
and shuttered for such storms as can be seen,
touched, felt like muslin or stiff canvas
on a hammock tree, divided from a world
by exterior glacial stones, Norse runes,
Indian epitaphs, wind-chime's leeward lean
leading to the open door, a sometime life's
wiped-foot anteroom, its portraited halls.

In one wing a nursery, emptied of importances,
the tears of pneumonia, the bruised eloquence
of late, encumbered appearance on a mother,
the darlingness of sister who painted the child
a lipsticked gypsy girl for his first Hallow'een,
and a room tiered with bars for rolling sleep,
to stop the monster of a bed's underneath—
the packages, packs of soldiers fighting wars
across a floor of silence, struck with points
appended to issues swabbed of alcohol,
the ice-daggers in their melting madness
sweated to the awful drone of Friday nights,
the older ones fleeing to their head-lights,
ballroom chandelier swinging like a gallows.

I grew into it, and additions were startling;
the conservatory filled with Lydian modes
and scales, rock and ragas, blues, Basie;
in basement den I'd countenance Thomas Wolfe
and plan my sojourn on the road of crazies,
wrapped the road round me only to return
like unopened mail, to the bed of no roses,
womb of worst hurts, carved daisies,
a mailbox number on a less traveled road,
waiting to escort you on my run of luck
into this domain, mistress of it and of me,
salve in the broad bath of a redeeming,
beauty that expounds its quiet grace,
the sorrow of a battered face, leaving.

Years of children sculpt into softest marble—
relief is everywhere, sheen on the railings,
song in the garden of asters, symmetry of slate,
walks of ever-afters in our reverie,
the years of a refurbishing cast from image
to a real, live estate this breathing building,
this generation assured of its corrections,
drywall's fall that frees all buried-alive
to love, to sleep among the brass and blooms
in bedroom of our dawns, delivering decades,
patrician and deliberate days released
like sighs into screens of a summer veranda,
the swinging lilt of permanence all but assured
and then, comes calling, the collector's answer.

The address accounts to forlorn corridors
where emanates the Department of Lost Chances.
Children, older, file down the driveway;
you surrender, and I close off the sanctuary

of our adoration, the finest of all rooms
within my heart and perfect as a tomb
sealed with wax and wisteria, and move
the metaphor to a place on another street,
where vendors hawk and smoke of card games flows
from upstairs windows, where the evening paper
folds to that column-inch of arrived future:
    House for Sale, choice location, spacious
    and priced for acquisition, fine for such
    as know their craft's ambition— call for details.

A WINDOW SEAT

The box on box,
the pencil-like spires,
palmy brocade and broccoli of oaks,
stripes of gray
assumed by toy motorcars
moving slowly
as I descend, helpless baby of the silver line
that promises timely delivery down
to any illusion or tiny town and yet
     disturbs
       not a person, one,
across and down
arrayed in this helpless amusement.

All disregard the tattooed bird
or Aztec legend as if it were transparent
as the air that couches it to soft landing,
defying the beliefs of the uneducated.
     I am among them—
the physics of this escapes me.
What I wanted to do was get
to a certain address, to conduct some business
that will later appear to me and its subject
as not consequential and here,
     as many times before
be given to the board and accessories
already assembled to play, with and amongst
the more important avenues
of an aging mind,
and wanting the little pools
     like lapis to be lapis

that I could pick up as jewels and hand
to my mother (long since dead),
move the little figures
onto some slight glory, some colossal transfer
of imagination so often forgotten
as loose change, and become
one of them.

Upon a touchdown, everything's big,
apparent only as walls, facades, angles,
faces, busily businesslike and melted
into today and tomorrow, mindless
as a plastic man in a bowler, one holding a shovel,
     one standing at a light,
     then

come back to the planes
silver as temptation
and wait
to be born again.

FUNNY ADONIS

The vanity of men
knows no excess to which
it would retreat, even unto destruction.

Knowing this
I imagine me again
as Anne (Gray Harvey Sexton)'s lover,
her student in all ways
wild and frilly and stiff with meaning,
and her
upon a chariot of swans
writing this bit of an unfinished poem:

> *You were the glass I broke*
> *that weekend fire,*
> *you put me out to smoke, hon*
> *not a bad lover*
> *for a good liar.*

While I'm at it
why not climb stairs
beyond Victorian shrubbery
(chance the boar!)
amid Wedgwood and pallor
to make an Emily
scream with oboes of quenched desire,
offer me Proper nouns
in a slew of new lyrics,
turned at the point of departure
on tunes of harpsichord wires—
no.

I doubt I would change
the woman's face of verse
with manly arts or equities,
        my gimble, my gyre.
More likely me to march reverse,
pen the night with edited manners,
mumble and retire.

BODY POEM OF PITHECANTHROPUS

In the shadow of a stone
he paints the image of horrid things
in elderberries and blood,
to scare the others.

He cries at the smoke
of first fire
and fear of freezing.
He cradles a son.

The meat he tears,
sinew from thighbone
raked the bare land
with its tusk and foot,
only to find his lance
and screaming.

He will die
without a calendar.
Erect,
he mounts behind.
Prone,
he sleeps in the mortar
of a thousand centuries, and guttural consonants
that rhyme with lore and love
beseech the kindness
of radiant carbon,
the thanks
of a genetic line,
the changing song of animals
to a soft and animate dreaming,

the society of his company
kept in the finest museums
as proof the future's dawn
is past, the timepiece
gleaming.

THIS THIRST

There was the time
we skipped to Tansey School
to listen to a symphony
of oboes, violas, bassoons
and walked back parched,
and I, a droughted reed
stumbled to the fountain
penitent before a water-god, entranced
by the cross-eyed gush
of what we called, in New England,
the bubbler.

Or at North Park
where we baked among crowds
like tarts on the concrete bleachers
of August, and with all I could afford—
two quarters out of the lining, bit
into the cold core of a softy-cone
trying to conquer it.

One time I blew
a high school tennis match
for the gulp of stinging foam
and knew I would always
fold under just the right torture.

Now, this thirst.
Tantalus was a Greek;
I am French, but in the dead ghost
of a salt sea, of this our misadventure
I might as well be dust itself,

waiting to smoke with the first hit
of a raindrop

that never comes.

LES QUÉBÉCOIS À LA CABANE À SUCRE

(Quebequers at the Sugar Shack)

In February
north of Montreal
at confluence of three rivers
(where Cartier had smoked his pipe
among Hurons and *voyageurs*
that smelled of otter), the trees
bleed their centuries sweet.

Caught in drab, hung buckets
neath the wound of each confecting maple
drips hold true to the patience
of elders, to the half-full
impiousness of youth.

We boil and boil to a sticky thinness
between *quadrilles,* like prelude
to the conjugal of French and Indian gods,
the pacts of which are found
in naïve bumps
on all our noses.

We celebrate a fetal Spring
kicking
in the womb of our laughter
at long tables, the disappearance of crêpes,
the beer on beer to a pinnacle
of brown glass stacked to the cornices
of afternoon, because men are this way,
and women understand.

Outside a trough
of new snow catches the red-hot run
that drops and hardens into twisted *tire*
on flatwood sticks.
Children lick and chew beneath
their bright red *toques* as spectres
of the nascent Huron did,
passing one to Cartier,

predicting this.

SOME PEOPLE

Some people shine in the air
above their graves.
They go home in the blood
of the living, having lived
aflame.

Some collected, seem to be alive
but live as dust.
They move about a corporal
slave, blank and unforgiving.
Blow on them; they dissolve
into the matter
of the world, a shadow,
very still, unclaimed.

ORANGE BLOSSOM TRAIL

The past two years of weekends
(on the graveyard, bound)
I drive the shambled avenue that blights
Orlando's outskirts at the hem—
what a cavalcade.

The whiskey store
with drive-thru window,
bailbondsmen, check-cashers,
pawnshops and Punjabis
(who pray the gun won't be loaded),
cheesesteaks caged
in a sub-shop window.

The whores, as pop-art mannequins
mostly black, and skinned
into dresses drawn
with fuchsias of imagination
say how now, afraid,
they suck on only condoms—
safe and not-so-sorry
in their similar refrains.

Dope is corner currency;
baggies tight with distillates
of coca leaves and poppies
fall from Oz
onto a rash of dreams.

Sheriffs in white sedans
lurk on sidestreets, missing the obvious
like wrestling referees;
sometimes they tail my nondescript Dodge,
one blown taillight away
from a parade of colors.

At *Parliament House*
the Disney dancers, airline boys,
disaffected flamboyantes
two-step along the lines of truth
exchanging numbers,
valentines; they tongue the air
with dry vermouth.

Someone we have met
(who would guess?)
moonlights at *Le Cabaret*,
where silicone beneath the nipples
feeds a cute, blind little girl
she drops at school.

Shopping-cart Man arranges
right and left, an overflow of soda cans
that seem to have rained
from a disposable sky; he balances them
like cargo on a freight-deck,
each ball-bearing
of his Winn-Dixie wheels
dear as diamonds.

While in the haunt of morning
at *Soup-Mission-of-the-Lord,*
figures looking for bread and sausage

gather like unused alphabet letters,
spelling nothing new,
or caused.

One drunk a month
is crushed crossing the bridge of sighs he sees
that no one sees
and bounces, same as spaniels
in a dead-dog reverie,
mourned by one or other crows along
the long and teemed merengue—

twenty roaring, silent blocks
where no one goes and no one stays
yet always of its number, ready
for Baptist rapture, to halfway levitate
and fall in pools that drown
such absolution in

the Orange Blossom way.

EATING SALT

(after Yeats)

All that is personal soon rots;
it must be packed in ice or salt
as promise removed
to an audience dwindling,
must last its melting
onto generations leapt
to where no photos endure
     and there is only
the faint echo of words.

My children, I know
will not be me, nor theirs.
My wife is me, only, and I her
     in the flash of climax
when identity blurs between;
you cannot survive so much as nourish
the idea of it in dreams.

But there is love,
and there is honor here;
     eat these as the salty things,
and through another's kind of happening
     hope to hide some piece of day
to live,
to live and breathe.

EVE'S APOLOGY

It was as yours;
it flowered at the mouth, baby's-breath-like
and gained sustenance
as the rainforest orchid
clings to high mahogany
out of darkness, drinking offered light.

It accommodated. She said:
Here, do the same, make an O and bite—
I will not forswear betrayal if you do
because it's sweet, so sweet
the gay cajole, the juice of flatter,
the blind search for motivation,
the falling.

I cannot blame
because I am as you, clay of clay
and not immune to calling.

What is God to us now.
What are we to each other.

The desperate hours counted out of paradise
spell miseries of such distinctive feeling
a soul cannot deny its destiny
in husband, wife, or brother.

Forgiveness is a future thing,
so come!

Come with me your clutch into the perfect
penitential night
my love, my lover.

METAPHOR

The act precedes eating,
sleep, and likely breathing.
The convulse of genetic eternity
from grasshopper to the marmoset,
to man in his own induced, inducing feeling
marshals up the hundred million selves
in a spoonful of silk,
(doubled by stress and a fear of losing),
that can populate a continent from Madras
to the steps of far Darjeeling, yet fall
on foreign roadsides
so one alone might reach transfiguration
in face of a new God, leaving
wrecked battalions, wiped
of swords and scarves of tribute,
dead, and kneeling.

A DIARY

Fool to think I am your diary,
quill and indigo etched in arcs
and staccatos on a mind,
pricks of feeling on a soul.

I have here your wedding eyes
berylled on me in sacrament
to be one woman for one man,
controversial over time.

Each new day particular,
happy tides, travel and larks,
or tragedy that pulled your face
unto a putty, dripped of tears.

Every other page left blank
for you, for saucers full of secrets
not divulged to me within their hurt
but good, good as wounds and salt.

Here and there, some pages few
I've carefully ripped apart in folds
of all their misery, sailing them
as hopeless cranes in dead calm.

Speaking of death, I do promise
this diary, the real gist of it
remains at last between us, love,
becomes, to us a book of leaves

to scatter madly in our trust,
to dissolve amongst themselves
as so much grave and golden dust
like the cuneiforms decayed,

the day I fail to revive
in your last kiss, when moon calls roll
and sends your lent biography
to waning light of its unlearning.

WHO IS JONES VERY?

"In September of 1838, Very... had a mystical experience; he told his students..."

Jones Very, tutor of Greek
above the Harvard Yard
made his case to clatter and tumult
among the desks;
some laughed and some, as young do,
rudely disbelieved; others
thralled to his obvious transcendence.

Presented with the Holy Spirit
banging as insistent as a Cuban drum
he demystified the end of the world
with the aged and newborn
clarity of rum.

Thrown out,
his prospect letters burned in a censer
he sonnetized to a dark asylum's raff-and-wrung
with his vision of "The Dead"
and "The Lost," then went into hiding.

Folded slimly in the *Norton*
between Browning and Lear he was, at last
declared at least as sane as William Blake
if not so very taught or ever much revered
except perhaps, to certain
barnswallows on a heath,
his champion Mr. Winters, and here.

Jones Very.

FOUR FROM MARCO POLO

fragments of stories told to a friar and
a Bedouin who spoke Turkic, over tea

I.

At Pem, when a woman's husband
leaves her to go on a journey
of longer than 20 days, as soon as he has left
she takes another husband
and this she is fully entitled to do
by local usage; and the men, wherever they go
take wives in the same way. *What if this*
happened in the Christian world!

II.

Clement the Pope received
a cloth of asbestos, gift from the Khan;
to clean it, you throw it in the fire!
In return, at Khan's request, he offered
drops of oil from the Holy Sepulchre
of Jerusalem. To avoid confusion
regarding hell, the Pope secreted the cloth
away. The Khan, his vial of separate heaven
unrevealed, did likewise.

III.

During the Great Khan's
ceremonial, anyone fortunate enough
to encounter the funeral cortège
was put to death
to serve their lord in the next world—
Mangu Khan's corpse scoring over twenty
thousand victims, fortunes
being relative to the beholder.

IV.

The Pleasure Dome of Shang-du is real,
and it is portable, like a circus;
the walls beyond their exquisite marbles
are made of cane, supported by 200 silk cords,
and alongside, a stud of ten thousand speckless
white horses, whose milk is reserved
for the family, and fermented into
something like wine.

At dawn next day, sandstorm clear,
a train of camels loaded with carpets, raw sienna,
plates and spices headed due-west
toward Kashgar.

FLOOD PLAIN

It used to be, or least it seemed
that happiness was grant of breathing
constant as the metronomic heart,
a simple calculus of being.

Tears were scarce, desert drink
to sate the occasional man-and-hump
en route to some auroral speck
of green, oasis of every well.

Now, it's tipped like the axial earth
upset in its leaning; the desert flood
bewilders in its retribution,
the sin of every calm turned inward.

At last it is, or least it seems
we swim this stagger of ourselves,
striving toward the small reliefs,
sorry stones that smile, redeeming.

GOOSEBERRY ISLAND

for D. W., who urges me to reveal

I.

Above the Cape, one broad scythe
of sand sweeps the Atlantic
and commerces with stray humans on its strand
from Andy's Shack to the Head of Westport
north of Horseneck, past pink shanties
and across a little quahog bay, landing
by a borrowed skiff and up three quays
to the Town Beach that trapped me
in October dark with my thirty-four
year-old employer, tossed
from her tenement by a husband who drank—
casting Lana Turner
to the nets of my seventeen sympathies,
turning me abob on buoys
of opportunity, rash
as sin that can age the young
(like spars of Bedford ash)
and quicken in the mist, soon moonless
in dunes of panic, clambering back to parking's lot
and light where I could
have, or not, among caress
and open kisses, that slip
into the shell of her as some invading
mollusk might, without a man's regard
for such significance as this.

II.

And I stood at shambled
shoals of glacier rock and calcium sand
separated from the diffidence
of mainland by an after-thought
causeway— Gooseberry Island,
a scab of brambles
bitter bitten of its pointillized fruit
and with one good stretch
of leeward beach
beyond the towered Nike missile site—
the Tarot tower, overgrown and strewn
with the halos of old rubbers, their
guts dried in stains like men-o-war
off waves of illicit wanting
decade after decade, displaced commas,
semi-colons in the
preponderant sentences of lives, an island
where I met in afternoon kismet
of the next July
her husband and their daughter
mid the wading children
of some Portuguese wives,
and I tried to be polite—
the girl was fourteen and fully
bloomed as an Italian starlet
might etch her curves upon the air
and carve into the sheen of her pink
swimsuit; I stumbled to small-talk, walking
the discarded glass of old suspicion
and my new guilt, tying themselves
to me like an endowment, pulling

rotten chains of seaweed in and back
from a salty shore and learning
how to ask, and not receive
from the cold, green quilt
an absolution for this world
without absolutes,
so filled with yearning.

THE CARDINAL REMAINS WITH THE SNOW

Through the shimmer
of storm window and on a few
bright, cold occasions of my life
he's reddened my faith.

Unlike the dozen tanagers,
three orangebelly orioles and nuthatch
at the repeated thicket
of my wasted years,
who shared my
well-imagined apple-bits
hauled down from laden boughs
and hopped in mad
song-sodden certainty
that went away
one by two by one
with October blows.

My champion-rouge
defies the crystal hexagons
flopped like icy lace
on grasses embalmed with the weeks
of loss for a sticky wormhead
heaved into March thaw.
Here and there
he claps upon my sill
an audience for a canceled
performance, a reverie.

Real friends are hard to find.

The summer embraces all
with abundance of bright acquaintance, pledged
affinities that seem like
thick, black lacquer on the limbs, only
to dry as nothing
with the ghost of rain.

Such flocks of chum and buddy,
confidant. They come always to parade
on a new warmth, faux-frosted
colors fleeting.

This is brittle loyalty, to sun
and stale bread.
But the cardinal bird—
independent, steadfast
beats my heart.

If I were him, I too would pity
the likes of parakeets and me, empaned
within these
unshorn lonely days,
similarly unseasonal,
shook of inevitable betrayal
and trying to be brave.

DECISIONS OF THE EDITORIAL BOARD ARE FINAL, OR POOR SOLOMON

Between the Benedictine
and the snuff,
they fought over minutiae
like terriers over
a baby goat—
words as dust-specks, clauses as dust
for dusty sermons that equivocate
the Church of England's standing
as a Church you can count on,
the one you trust;

and so they came, these learned
men, collared by and for
an upper crust and a King's commission
to the Seventh Song of Solomon,
and there they stopped.

In the old books, rolled
and hammered the I AM did not
have his draughtsmen mince, his
actors walk around soliloquy
like pious clods— they bled
as martyrs, lived
of coursing blood
and to this end, Solomon took a wife
and being a poet of some standing
and King of Many Parts
as deeded him, commenced
to describing his beloved,

nude from toenail-painted toe to head,
those objects of his inner world,
his outlined sheet-warm circular bed
with metaphors
so laden as the stamen waits
for a warm, stiff wind.

The clerics chewed
these lines over and over
as cud, or caulk and catalyst
of shivers, clucks
and quizzical grins.

The feet, all right, the legs,
dissenting, thighs an outright argument
that lasted seven hours, canceling
vespers and a lamb
with condiments, but of all of it
a prelude to the heart, the gist
of this, the unfathomable burden.

He refers, they agree, plainly
to the core of a woman, and grants
the King's compliment
to her so-gobleted accouterment,
always wet and full.

But yet, to *call* it!

The Hebrew is obvious, right to left.
In Greek, from *Kunthus*. Latin,
of the labial, vulval or deeper, a sheath,
a vaginate lip, while just down
lamplit Lancashire Street

from the parsonage to the Boar's Face Inn
the tawdries, singing, toss their heads
to quips of cuns and quims.

There is an uproar. The Abbot
of Kent pounds his little fists. The deputy
archbishop recoils, rebounds at each
suggestion, lithe or literate. Ballots
round the roundtable one and twenty
times until the tapers cry as
stubs that have to be refit into the yawn
of another morning.

Ideas drop like lines of piped
grenadiers in some miasmic mist
until the last
one breaks the sleepy tie and compromise
unveils

NAVEL
as the orifice that's it!

Her *navel* full of wine.

Thus did God and Solomon
fall to the commerce of committee
dismissed toward heaven,
then of course, to the bindings of forever—
this, the year of our Lord
sixteen hundred and eleven.

THE SENSES ALL CONFESSING

*Synesthesia (Greek, syn = together + aisthesis = perception) is
the involuntary physical experience of cross-sensing. That is, the
stimulation of one sense reliably causes a perception in one or more
different senses. It is, in fact, a normal process of aesthetic cognition
that is prematurely displayed to consciousness in some individuals.
One interesting phenomenon reported as common in this population
is the existence of a "palette" of colors unique to each subject,
claimed to fire or impress upon the physical view or imaging of
specific letters, numbers, and other symbols.*

Scriabin saw purples coming from the piano
like sprigs of violets, or a sheet of indigo wash;
Messiaen could taste the bitter dissonances,
coffee in F minor, cocoa in a diminished fourth;
Dalí's morphing echoes were in bas-relief
and brayed like fine foghorns off Barcelona,
while Nabokov complained to Mum that the blocks
were all wrong, the A wasn't red, it was blue;

and yet, it's yellow in my alphabet
the B, a charcoal Brooks Brothers suit—
you can feel its wool; the greens are E,
dark emerald, and P darker like the Argonne,
S's are sweet, lips bathing in a Venus rose;
the D's, all tan like café-au-lait, N's
are hazelnuts and then, the Arabic numerals—
1 is a peppermint stick without stripes

tangerine is 2, as smooth as scythes,
a 3, enrouged, unpointed breaking heart,
the saffron 7, coronation robe of 9
combining into sums, the letters into *words!*

what punch of hues and flavors, trebles, drones
of plucked sarods and songs of simple birds
more difficult than dander to explain
except in what is seen, and felt, and heard.

It's why a poet tries himself in tears;
a too-afflicted painter sells his brushes
to repay some bit of human rent
that's fallen to arrears, takes up drawing
only clowns with bells above the ears,
why composers tumble to a jingle-
song of sighs, as wayward metaphors
reduce such selves to simile of lies

and why— I pledge a world for just your smile,
upon the curves that figly arc like cellos
over winds, your kiss a Jordan almond,
voice, a choice of orchids, eyes, like quavers
of Sibelius where the shiver meets
the sound, and every consonance of chords
repeats the outline, look, the strange élan
of you who reach me colorful, feelful, found.

THE END OF THE HUMAN XYLOPHONE

What we fancy we can become.

The accolade
of hands, whistles in the loge.
A billing that rises from the anti-climax
of dyed-green poodles
popping through hoops
to the curtain-calls
of a vaudeville reality.

Once you tapped my bones,
double-tapped and trilled me
cheek and chest like hollow stone
or blocks of human mahogany
tuned to magnificent memory,
thighs like bands, the teeth
as white keys shining
to the smile of scales.

Sweet Sue, it's true
a Chopin étude
and *Why Don't You Love Me*
Like You Used to Do?

Played me and I played for you,
mastered the body into symphony—
I amazed in the reflection
of your admiring glance, melted you
into duet, and danced.

What we achieve we can lose.

The joints have swelled,
the stomach, E flat falters
in its roundness, comes bass from cello
an octave split in two;
the evident metronome clicks
to a monotone of appointments
and apology, fists through walls,
acts of fools.

There is always the comeback.
Perhaps a firewalk, the spinning of china
on sticks, a soft-shoe to exhaustion,
or the ungraceful exit of
a fan-dancer's valet.

And I was top-drawer, too.

In my day, recall the feet were quicksilver,
hands divined as mallets or
tines, the music matched the majesty
of you, my audience and pay,
the novelty act of prayer
creating yet to footlights dark
a dawn to each and every day.

Now, it only says, appearing.
Now appearing.

Now away.

CROSSOVER LULLABY

Sitting across from Kenny Rogers
at Wolfgang Puck's in the MGM Grand Hotel
I am tempted not to tell him—
but I do.

Kenny, you don't know
but "Lady" turned out to be
the soundtrack to a suicide.

Actually I don't know Kenny Rogers,
and I wasn't in Las Vegas.
But life is so often a lie.

Beneath my wife and I
in the subterrain of a second floor
of a three-story tenement in March, '81
a young woman washed in and out of our lives.

She was nineteen, with a two year-old girl
and a marriage built on kindling. We woke
those nights to a shamble of screams,
slammed doors, and the song.

"Lady, I'm your knight in shining armor
and I love you..." it went.

My Gette, a pretty dumpling plump with Julie
had left the same record under our tree for me;
and as millions did, we made Kenny's tip money.
But below, stuck and drugged
on automatic repeat, a needle lapped

the hours of bad Merlot, of hope consigned
to a suppressed hysteria, the kind
that finally shoots men
and drowns children.

In winter drear
some, as she, choose The Bridge, the vast
green span over the Taunton River,
a long plummet to hard water, big headlines
in a small daily.

Rumors of adultery. Misconception.
Wrong fruit on feeble vines.

How bad luck loves the country song!
papering walls of foregone minds,
moving unnecessary furniture,
lingering longer than the face
we couldn't sketch from memory
shadowed in the simple words,
notes on a stave, four/four time.

Lionel Richie's crossover hit.
Kenny Rogers' valentine.

PARADOX

The best poems are never written.
They are regretted, half-awake,
vague snapshots
of radium on aluminum foil
glowing in the long
half-night of their being,
degradable as Christ,
impossible to place on paper
that wouldn't become dust
in the persistent glow,
separating themselves
from this popular art as some daily
repast from the ritual meal of saints,
and the full disappointment
of knowing the existence—

without the revelation.

TO HELEN

Unseen, and silent, from the train she moves,
Led by the goddess of the Smiles and Loves.

—**The Iliad,** tr. Alexander Pope

Every woman
is in the curve of your hip
as it turns; your lips rest wet
on other lips, outing
the sweet exhale
of propriety.

I marshal every royal thought
from every kingdom of heroic memory
to come after you.
The ships are laden
with goats and gold,
the plumes of helmets
filled with Nubian feathers.

Parts of me
expect a quick campaign,
the senses rectified, forgiveness
falling as wine-grapes
at those bare feet that yet
excite and moisten the night.
Other parts know better;
they sharpen blades
to shave a thousand beards.

The casualties of honor
burn bright upon the pyres,
prove the power of women
is godlike, Zeus himself
a loinless boy in its thrall. And me,
cuckold of silver
ministered by conscripts
to a cause unelected by its master—
I shine, shiver in this wind,
knowing that victory carries you back
into my arms, but to a meaning
stripped of sinew in the brightness
of your smile,
the smoke of you,
the prize.

LILY AND PIERRE

(from the pages of *True Story*)

She and I
married to others
perceive the same French kiss
the same way.

We have never met
but our bond
is of music.

We are the ones
talked of fondly
and yet
so forgotten in a paired embrace,
the kind repeated
in the aftermath of felled monuments,
the shivering, disgrace.

Hello I say.
Hello she says.

And though
we never meet, aside the grand
duet pianos of the rainy night

we play.

A TULIP SYSTEM

I subscribe to it.

Since a child
drawing green stalks
under orange cups
and red
cups
like
maraschino
and blue cups, too
serrated at the edge,
permanent as the next paper.

So we talk of Amsterdam
and the Spring of Flowers,
of colors like hope
before the bringing of heat,
the X's in the wind,
the cancellation,
talk of dry bulbs in summer

     I will write—

and young Brinker,
skating for the prize
and his father's operation—
the spring will come again.

I conduct my life
according to this;

cycles pass
along canals of strangers

again and again.

Again and again.

SOMETIMES

I want to be in you
so deep I penetrate the core of universes;
stars wreathe my brow
and I become the red G clef
of our symphony—

more, much more
than a marshalling metaphor,
than Miller and all who transmute apples
onto babies' arms,
than afterthoughts lost
in flesh elastic as a pastoral lyre
thrummed magnificent,
and full of balm—

I want to wear your form
upon the wire of my soul
and in your throes of orbit
and of smile, become the sound
of satisfaction, the ninth
elevation of calm.

And becoming you, *you*
I would be everything then—
a thimbleful of God's breath,
the expanding element
into vacuum, and know that
the reason for entering ten thousand times
(man to woman, beyond a man)
was chance, the flash of forever
planned as chord between scales

a hope against heaven
that eternity dawns within, without
these hands.

THE STILL, DANCING

When the body tips to horizontal
and empties itself of self, of soul caught whispering
near the top of the room,
it becomes more than still.

It is a relief
carved of a universe in which we play
at dramas and comedies,
costumed.

That world is super-solid, anchored
into the core of itself with the chains of blast
and commandment, the work
of one unfathomable, busy day.

The cheek becomes faux-marble,
the breast a mine of carbon,
the legs, petrified.

The dizzying thing of wakes
and water-launchings is the movement,
all the movement vortexed round the effigy,
torsos like battleships turning
yet the tiniest fan of eyelash is noted,
the wriggled ear of nervous laughter,
the heave of moaning.

Look at what the self pretended,
that form half-boxed as a new doll,
then look away.

Look back.
There is no change.

Away. Back.

At that moment you see the difference
of life and death,
the gorgeous, frightening stillness
more than stillness.

Such parting gift!

Secret seminar
of what the living lack.

LAST VALLEY

Long left, the valley of my birth
has forfeited memory.

And I, afoot or saddle borne
on rocky roads and rills
ripe with thunder came to this place,
grown old in its renew
as I were first a poplar
to the wind of it.

So I came forth to hew
and frame
a home from cedar and from stone,
my heart pinned to the mantel
of purpose, yours alone.

I could have done as others,
a lone rider backed by black sun
dipped in hell's shine, shodding
down the trail and out again,
rumor of self-betrayal
nights behind.

But in you, and of this valley
felled of juniper and plaintive wails,
green as grenadine is red and three
times bright, a scent and signature
of breath became my object of avail,
scaped the land with legacy

and stayed me to the twenty
years of blinding

in a majesty of light.

THE FAT CHILDREN OF LOUISIANA

Why the precious yield of Louisiana?
Three times fat beyond an average child
toddling Seattle and Duluth.

We get that question all the time, now
some alecky-smart TV man has sugared it
over the screen, raised it like king cakes.

Is it all that butter n' lard, soft sizzle
of pigmeat, andouille in the starchy rice
of our ways? Or a love affair with gravity,

the daring to adhere to earth unless, until
our angels pull us as light as red balloons
to holy height of our reward— but who

would kill a child anyway? Leave
Ti' Jean Delhomme alone, B'lin Landreaux
not even seven with those *jambon* legs—

the Lord, he syncopates her waddle down
the coquille walk aside a short, fat dog
to fully fit the snapshot of communion,

stuffs the boy, enseasoned in his girth
to priest a faithful felled in Opa-luse
or call the women down Canal Street.

In heav'n we are equal, vegetaires
of air, slim as eels, in onion, pepper,
celery of trinity's redemption

under oil and anointed at the rail,
leaving all our proper grief at stairs
of merry monuments atop flood plains

the while we live, as red ants on beignets,
like everything not Lent's before or after,
drowning in a grace of life's great grail.

NOW, VOYAGER

There is a non-geography
and it is where I stand
on a rill, beholding savannas
of a tropic misgiven.

I am accompanied by natives
of burgeoning population, who smile
on all possibilities, even sadness.
We track the great Cape buffalo
to pools of a mind littered
by predators, and
the legacy of drought.

I leave by
twin-engine plane; it whines
and coughs me all the way
to mountains named after symbols, only;
where the trees stop,
my staff leans into the lightheadedness
of snow and failure.

In the place where oxygen
comes from woodwinds,
rain-ripped canopies of mahogany and sweat,
I count the colors of gay frogs
marooned in their sanity,
marvel at the beauty of poison,
chug of a blow-gun,
the paralysis of pain.

The desert I have not
yet invented.

Ventured, I will entreat you to follow,
but I will know the locations
of water, and keep the promise,
against all hope,
that things may grow.

This panoply could fill a book,
or two. Slides and lectures
available for garden clubs,
a lunchtime show.

All about humanity, maps and globes,
and the urge to go.

EIGHT POINTS

original study for the poem, "Voyeur"

The eight points, paired of velvet on horn
bow in the awful risk of long, cold drink
in glassy Athabaska; November borne
among late shadow of the water's brink

the shot, instant, wheels him to run
and does not fell him. He is dead, though,
forgetting the protocol, tail to the lip of sun
he flails two-footed, two-footed in early snow,

a dance of reddening royalty on the way
of this peculiar coronation prize,
king of all these followed footsteps, gay
and awfully dead themselves, too dull for whys.

VOYEUR

I saw Diana bathe
in the still water
wearing that shined sheet
 of wet like a coming-out
gift from her father,
hair atangle and every
curve drawing centrifugal
tongues of wanting, deep
into crease and cleft—
enough to die for
and for mortals, that's something;
 her opalescent view, afire
spelled me into bodies
of repetitive stags, staggering
through history, drunk
of her pool and sighted
by the hunter's smile, dead
upon running, running still,
 into the myth
of the dogs,
their cold eyes.

PERCY GRAINGER

"People like me ought to be burned at the stake."
        — P.G.

He had an obsession
with blue eyes,
ate only rice, tinned peaches
and stale bread,
hated Jews, Blacks, Latins,
anything not of Nordic, pale flesh;
had violent childhood relations
with his mother
(she whipped him regularly)
so he grew to be a sadist
and a masochist
whose greatest pleasure lay
in giving and receiving
intense pain.
He wanted to have children
(had none, fortunately)
so that he could beat them.

And yet

he wrote hundreds
of the dreamiest transcriptions of the masters—
Bach, Debussy, plainsong and chorales,
the handbook of English centuries,
its landings airy,
languid, sentimental
as a thrush on sweet-pea; his "Danny Boy" alone

provoked weeping from
usurers, the deft piano
evoking crestfalls
of Irish rainbows, Scotch heather,
the breakers
of the Northern reef.

So how can it be
that cornflowers
and chrysanthemums grow
from the shit of humanity,
the smell of sweet hope
shined and rinsed
on pointed staves of
a saned and manicured
insanity?

Play on. Aaaaah.
Worry of it all tomorrow
in the parlors, playrooms,
conceptions of
our vanity.

HOMELESS MAN WITH VUITTON SHIRT

He strikes against the sun an untoward Apollo
dipped in lavender sheen of his Louis Vuitton
shirt, distinctive lines that almost fit
a wasted frame idling the library steps.
Instead of musing the death of the dollar
you chose to surrender, eyes drop fixed
on that sleek, pearly-buttoned vestment—
is this the resplendence of a suicide stockbroker?
Did it fall from a truck, tossed in the hijack run
or handed out from a deep, deep carton of excess
flood donations from a fashionable slum, by nuns
who'd left their youthful habits' broken hearts
for the charity of dressing the undone?
The image echoes at a light lunch, that *chemise*
of the heeled and pretenders, not of slippery dung
beneath the feet, not of down-on-the-lucks,
or rummies or flotsam-men, yet when you see
the rich, too rich and overflowing with it
don't you see, once sated of remaining reach
a commonality of these, of everything and nothing—
tottering satisfaction that must fall to a question
whether to linger, laugh, or just release
to the aimlessness of destination, Prague
or Pimlico for the one, Libby Street's lonely
shrub-shade or berth of rat's alley the other,
an apathy and lovelessness that sticks both ends
like a needle's sharpful of drifting lidocaine
leaving us middle-sorts sorting importances
of things, our dreams, our spitlick lusts,
a want and ever-wantoning that populates

the massive belly-undulate of our statistic,
our moving, measured humanity, homeward on
past those who pass the time, who dimly stand
simplistic in their trend, too distant from us
nearly to extend an empty, friendly hand
to one we fear, and one we like commend
as both lie lying in an unmarked, upright grave
of freedom's vacuum, bound with every breath
clouding definitions of master and slave,
the index of economies, the shibboleth of saints
who occupy culverts, verandas, stoics in the nave
of our fortunate lives, dying of pity, or praise.

GLIDING

You would say this to the other
starting out, and the metaphor may not work entirely,
be unconvincing in another's eyes, but mine, I see it,
wings like Orville or Icarus attached to me, running to edge
of the cliff they might call a wedding
with just one intent, for any other would fail me of life,
snap, like that, spent.

A belief in her, under God,
in God, as God must be absolute
as the smile of her eyes you covenant with every calendar
not yet printed, every baby's life and cry, every empty pocket,
every sin admitted without alibi.

Do this, and the countryside
emerges under your flight
a panorama majestic as heaven, the breezes
flung at last from dreams of that beginning
you have no need to reclaim, to a destination the wind
harbingers
aside a pink sun.

You stay aloft for hours,
for decades, for multiple versions of Hindu lives.
Commitment binds the air to mission,
to magic, to spirals of the higher kind,
and the faraway landing
for which you were, you pray
predestined to arrive.

TWENTY VIEWS OF THE BABY JESUS

(based on Messaien's *Vingt Regards sur L'Enfant Jésus*)

1.

Asleep
he is a slipper
in a winter closet
that smells of straw.

2.

A woman's hand
traces his brow
to the button nose—
lips go to fingertip;
good perhaps, that he looks
like his mother.

3.

He bleats as he turns, almost silent,
but he starts the lambs
who melt from figurines
into realness.

4.

He awakes in glassy beneficence.
Already looks a king.

5.

Basks in the cradled light;
the cool night does not reach him
or his glow.

6.

Hungry, he yawns
the O of imitating cherubim.

7.

He takes her breast
in umber of the moon
and begins
to grow into his cross.

8.

Seems at home to this
father's presentment to guests;
he appreciates the favor,
returns the adoration.

9.

He sniffs
at hint of frankincense
and sneezes;
Galilee lifts a wave.

10.

The purple genuflect
of an Oriental
keeps the star
out of his eyes.

11.

He whispers to that man
through strands of mind
"listen, listen
to your dream tonight."

12.

He, the baby, lies in wattles
wrapped about his unwrapped
gifts, foundation
of the multiplying.

13.

And he really does
smile at the drummer.

14.

Enjoys his little rest,
the drinking of its ale,
knows it has come
all at the beginning.

15.

He stares beatific
through the roofbeams
of the nave,
planning the long tomorrow.

16.

On his specks of nails are
the ten commands he will distill
into fists of essence.

17.

His arm
unhinged of attitude
casts the air with miracle—

cattle that were lowing
to their shepherds, speak.

18.

He hides for a moment
beneath the homespun,
as if consulting.

19.

The crown of fire about his head
is hallucination. He causes these already.

20.

When he goes back
into his dream, the sleep
all babies sleep
we follow, maybe unredeemed
until the last, but every year
about this time, we take his view
of things, of what
we simply can't resist,
that seeming of belonging

that we borrow.

OUR BAGHDAD

The last act, last scene,
handful of lines that will define us
are not reached by this bit of black dialogue,
flintily Arab, meant
for the dustbin's coffee-stain.

So why entertain it.

Every great love
is strewn with barricades
and shrapnel, cries for first aid.

Is the alternative a tyranny
of loneliness so long held
you become its satyr, concubine,
respect its trench
till you walk the road
of startled refugees, too numb
to recognize a flag?

Love comes wounded
and iodine is scarce;
you make do with mud
and a sewing needle, and in
the absence of oil
and roof, you huddle
by twos among stars.

The epic is all around you.

War and peace
spin themselves a blurred streamer
on this axis, the me and you
multiplied by billions,
the universe of the earth,
the oft-played history
back-lit in the brightened eye
of a shattered muse.

REACTION

The iron nail
placed in a jar of vinegar and pennies
bubbles as the sour sea
turns blue.

Across dull time
excited ions dance;
the nail specks with brown
and shine.

The still solution
once aquamarine, goes golden,
then like tea, finally
coffee, very black.
Smells like pennies, too.

Each day the nail coats, counts,
forces itself to accept conditions
to which it is not immune.

The boy and I record results;
we've come to understand the silent,
acid bath, what it can do.

We plate the hours copper

missing you.

IT IS NOT ONLY

It is not only
my being within you, between you.

Your voice is hemmed
into the cloak of the air,
the bright surplice of years.

Your footfalls tap
precedence before an opening door.

When you're not,
I imagine you there.

Your counsel comes down
to which way to turn the steering wheel,
to turn my life.

Across the tiled mall
your figure grows larger, my smile
an apostrophe of advancing age, warming
to the soonness of livelong days
when I can play the guitar of memory
unto rest at the soft whistle of your sleep,
and the scent, a lure that whets to the majesty
of knowing that a wife I keep
has kept me—

against a house of odds
and the spin of dizzy prayer
she has, you have, kept me.

WATUPPA POND; THE ICE HOUSE

I am not a Wampanoag;
in fact, they are almost all gone,
come as whisper, outlines in the oaks,
legend distilled to street signs
in an old town.

But I as they, having latticed the broad water
with formations of celebrant canoes,
cross seasons to when blue turned white
their own potential and my dreams.

On the eastern shore, what they call Copicut,
place of trees that had descended from the sponging
of a glacial age left its cold, transparent gold
each winter. The industrious Yankee and Canuck
gravitated to its promise,
hauled the fieldstone and mortar
to a cleared notch,
and raised the monument.

A Copicut castle, both edifice
and device, stored its cache in solitude,
block on block cut from the lake
as it stalled to a frozen stupor,
each ton stacked and weighed on stone sleepers
separated by clean straw,
added from subtraction every
chill January through March,
keeping meat good for the well-to-do
of Bristol County;

skaters and sleigh-parties
cut their figures, jingling at the Bedford lip
while Irish pick-axed
the opposite rim, filling the cold
thick masonry
to its four mortised brims.

New ice could even last three years
within.

Today, the tired fortress and
machine, obsolete as an Indian
is reclaimed by boughs of huge oak,
maple, birch, swallowing its ruin.

Nothing is preserved.
The seasons pass;
and in spring winds

Watuppa waves.

T. S. ELIOT

"Say hello to Valerie, say hello to Vivien,
give her all my salary on the waters of Oblivion."
— Bob Dylan

Why explain his *Waste Land?*
It would have been shit without Pound's
razor and wand.

His Vivy rode her coastering
hormones to a wild whip,
a mudder at Ascot.
And he put her away.

She once gave in to Bertie Russell
                family friend
                that wicked old roué
but *he* got even in *the Cathedral.*

The Anglican Church
accepts the literate semi-anti-Semite.
                Bleistein was retired.

His second wife
donated all the manuscripts to worthy institutions.
Her name also began with a V.

Yes, for me he is the greatest poet
since the other Pope
and here I am playing with him so.

But what's to say that hasn't been said.
What's important, really important

is the night
he and Vivien
                    after the moon fell
spat
into Monty Shearman's
letterbox at the Adelphi
Hotel.

So much for all the cisterns
and exhausted wells.

CASTING FOR PUCCINI

In the opera house
of this particular existence
coloraturas reach for the filigree
of notes like wrens
        soaring
and falling in the vagaries
of capture and release.

The baritones
fattened of age, pass
old pictures, make allusions
to woody years of good port,
        poured in the one glass
of a set not shattered.

They are the best, the mark—
stoic, pillars of duty, basalt
and old bark;
        betrayed
in the third act they strike
        at beauty like blind Oedipus
        in the hall of his discovery
like Samson caving in.

Jealousy strands their blood
in octaves, blocked and orchestrated
to pulse, pulse.

The chorus reveals everyone
lost in life, from childhood acolytes

to somebody's concept of
a perfect wife—

it swells between the arias
among the awful cellos
strong, indicting.

And ah! the tenors
(to whom they flock)—
fresh from triumphs at Caserta,
Amalfi, young tones slipstreamed
and elastic, virile as silk from spiders
        or stallion stock—
claim their legacy of felled heroines,
preen themselves
as I watch the clock.

Sing to me now in laugh
and longing, close the audition.

Arrange another
sick affair on stepped-on, sticky playbills
        of La Scala, the Garden
or any stance of happening,
tragedy in sorry lanes
among songbirds,
        suitors, pigeon-filled walks
of distant parks, the moans
of the newly, inevitably shot
and to a sforzando
the deft glee of shooters,

the web, the rock.

CHRISTMAS SONG

I remember the aluminum tree,
the turquoise teardrop balls,
twin color-wheels embering orb, fleck,
the cast of wax-or-waning discs
in aqua, violet, ambergris
as shadow on the ceiling light.

And I remember that
peace is not anesthesia,
and that the joy I found in you
and drank till drunk,
I drank before in child's eyes like this.

So leave me my carol of the mind.
I watch the tree.

And all I miss.

THREE SECONDS AFTER, TEL AVIV

What kind of a crawl
or suck of a god
asks this.

The bistro of young lovers
smirched red
with a dead promise,
the legs of chairs
and fellows strewn,
the deliverer
undelivered.

The voice you hear
young snot or old miscreant,
saracen or crusader
is your own gurgling
dispossessed soul
dancing to a drum without skin,
choked, the throated reed,
a black silence siphoned
of meaning
and reserved for sin.

SHOOTING CARDS

To the temple of Topps,
the recessed basement windows
silled of granite and cut into the brick
we came with packs of antiphons,
samadhis of devotion
at five cents for five,
compounded in the weeks
of first and fourth terms.
The cards carried the only history
important to us. And only
Leviticus and the Vedas carried
as many jangling names.

Minnie Minoso. Felix Mantilla.
Bobby Knopp. Tom Tresh.

The representations, our currency
are mostly lost to dustbins now,
but their occasional remnants
light the rectangles of memory
and like ours, their bent corners telltale,
their faces too young,
carefree to last.

Gods, lesser gods, half-mortals
they spun on their axes
like showers of Pleiades
igniting an elementary sky.
It was a caste system;
the homely Dick Hoaks and J.C. Martins
would pummel the wall,

break their edges in constant servitude
to the glamorous Mantles and Clementes
who'd hide within the palm
as Madras virgins,
the gum mark intact
as expectation.

The cards would lean
and wait to be courted, popped;
kissed
they would lie down.

The ring would fill
with suitors; each shot
over and over, attempting that impossible touch
of brick so slivered in its infinite gap
that the silk on a bumblebee's leg
could not separate it.

You had to be that close,
or you had on the miracle of air
to land standing and so
see the rampart fall to you
or to another, bested as benign,
bested again, your band
of characters dissolving
like childhood absolution for
childhood sin, emptying or fortifying
in the ways unknown
to the subtler sex that jumped
and rhymed across the yellow line
of appropriation— we are men! Men!

What do they know these girls
of mission, starved of energy
at the ten o'clock bell, the noontide's
triumph of comeuppance, singular
experience of Krishna's heaven
or some scimitared, deft centrifugal
of hell, the lost face,
the blurring name, missing statistic,
the shore of our growing that shifts
on Red legs, Indian sands

to the adult deliberation
of how sad to be here, how
great to be there, the files check-listed
of quaint recollection, quietly sentient
and very, very swell.

GEMSTONE

Unearthed by a simpleton
at the Crater of Diamonds
like the famous Kahn Canary,
uncut and settled into gold
a triangular, pillow-shaped
diaconate of light—
so I accept the casual brilliance,
the always potential of your fire.

It is better than the orderly prisms
of hammered expectation, appointed
to a Harry Winston window
so well-appraised.
They can keep the pears,
bright baguettes, their round
duplicities; the amber
of your allegiance to a dull,
devoted eye
cries me into my long nights
of celebration
and witless wonder.

The flaw that matters is me,
and yet you adorn, adorn
a dedicated expenditure to the break
of every dawn, married into servitude
to set me free,
the absurdly rich man
scrabbling acres of volcanic pipe
searching, beyond you
for a reason to be.

GOD'S VERSION OF A CÉZANNE CHARCOAL

Make believe it is Day Six.
We are cylinders, ellipses, eggs.
The spheres of us roll like billiards;
cones intend shadows
to a black wall. Block by block
fix us into the perspective of an eye,
but don't portray yourself.
Keep something for imagining.

Come and soften us now; smudge
the sides into diffusion.
Capture light.

Sign my name.

Forgive yourself the dazzling
illusion.

PEDESTRIAN ACCIDENT

When it hits you
there's no feeling— perhaps
a warm knife through butter;
as you fly you smell gardenias
that flower electric aside your eyes
and tumble
in your big, bony bag
of letters and sighs.

And to live or die,
the raiment half-off the soul, anyway
you must decide.

Always the provider.

Decide to scream,
after disappointed seraphim
fat as pincushions
have fumbled to hand you a script—
there it is, after the prayer,
line five.

Now the pain,
delicious as raspberries.
To the ambulance man
you are "Partner, doin' fine Partner;"
to the radio waves
you're "Trauma, Brain."

In the hospital hall
you line up behind
a minor figure in the drug trade,
a heart attack,
a drip, drip, drip-drip;
nightingales, gray-white
and songless bob under ceiling lamps.
One scolds my Partner
for that signature on the floor—
my elbow torn,
still-steady red rain.

She says
among electrodes:
"You have to stop shaking,"
so I tell the bag or its apparency,
"stop shaking" and it does.
I imagine it walks to the corner,
waits outside, lights
a Newport while technicians,
yawning like artisans, preside.

And here's my wife.

The leg is broken.
Pages of memory turn
to airplanes.

But I do recover.
The limp almost indistinguishable.
Archipelago of scars.

I remember that you always recover
what you can. What's left

can even thrive.

What can't leaves a stain.
But leaves you alive.

THE DIVORCE OF ANONYMOUS RHYMES

I'm leaving my cockhorse
parked by the cross of your misgiving—
all Banbury tells of my largesse, the gold
and tinkling finery
on your hands and toes, your mount, the chorus
to follow you till Tuesday.

Yes, you are a beautiful thing—
but I've come to my senses now, have sung
good sing with the milkmaid milking,
with pussy in the well,
pat-a-caked nights of our forgetting

and rung the ding-dong bell.

TRILOBITES

At the Rock and Gem Show,
a table of fossilized trilobites
squeezes into the strata
between amethyst and quartz cure-alls,
turquoise belt-buckles, and
a Sno-cone maker.

Used to be these characters
with backs like hand-carved Jell-O molds
too fast to catch, too small to ride
dominated the land when it was the sea,
excited in their feed and breeding.
They acted like they owned the place,
and their lease
was for two hundred
million years.

While we seem to be a yawn, comparing
and look to make ashtrays of their
sandstone impressions,
they are pulled from the cracks
of that once opalescent salt-soup
of rolling fathoms that was
Colorado, looking like
yesterday.

They reassure us of our nowness
if not our longevity, but what if we, too
could be strip-mined from the even
deeper stone primeval, showing

a self not apelike but enlightened,
setting aside our anthropols
and carbon-dating
as so much posture and speculation.

Here's why.

In the Sahara, the dunes
blow back whisk-broomed
to reveal green glass, the peculiar obsidian
left only from nuclear explosions,
the kind
men dream and wake from screaming.
Such glass exists in the Southern Sinai,
in Algeria, in Mali.

What if beneath, we take
the tungsten bits
of boiling mass-machines to turn
and heave up sixty-six sub-ancient
documents, the keys to locks,
credit-looking cards, the tailfin
of an airliner and what must be
the basilisk-like talisman
of some minor god, caught
between floods and species.

Did we yet proliferate, articulate
once before upon this old, old rock
the verbs those trilobites of saucer mouths
could not, the ones like *love, betray,*
supplicate, *pray, elevate* and *dismiss,*
prosper, decay, and fall with a sort
of degradable recall to convulsion, meteor,

missile or the dynamo of some great
de-aspiration of race, and the race itself,
the march upon eons pressed like baubles
into patterns of single,
passing day.

Until the trilobites return
themselves to play, we set
their shadows on the coffee-table,
converse of sports, of happenstance
and sink, the inch-by-ever-inch
in mantle of our minute-minds, a hubris
of uncalculating clay.

THE NEAR OCCASIONS OF SIN

I am drunk with them.
The bar stool spins
and my eyes fly from azimuth
to apogee, moons
and mariners spread far and wide.

I am heartily sorry.
What I have done will not prevent
what I will do to you,
devastate most
with what you don't, won't know,
and what I won't own up to.

The same with you.
Oh, my Christ, the same with you.

The duality bonds us even as it cleaves,
wide open, the terminal wound,
the laughing
maw of separation.

To detest our sins, ourselves
and pull from embrace
in order to save the other
from our viciousness,
is a virtue meant for asylums
missing benediction.

I await the help of somebody's grace;
but I long for you.
In that, my resolve is hard like

the face of the cliff the diver sees,
descending.

He hopes for the best,
penetrates the water of his absolution,
(not too near the rocks!)
to reclaim the birth of all his reveries,
or the damning.

THE SALT HARVEST

He urges us along this stubble
beyond the far, low walls,
a valley's fire-corona at our back—
in heat comes mourning the intransigence
of men, fickle curiosity of women,
the striving toward that little town
he's promised us, leaving
all those sculptures on the way,
pretty forms unlikely to decay until
they're cracked and ground as a preserver
of flesh, condiment-waker
of the bland lives, pious
in our pursuit and waiting for dinner—
obdurate and fast they stand, strewn
a lean, unliving litter
as the backlit errors of our path

— don't look now, my love!—

the heavy heads, smooth lips,
shoulders round, the folds of hard cloak
like schists on a cliff,
no feel for the hammer's dash
upon their paler selves and shiny,
shaken grains
in grainy light that ever thirst
the pitied, lone survivors
of their memory

at our empty wells.

THIS IS THE SHORE

This is the shore
where the dead are transported,
where the fickled husbands await their mates
and dreams dew-dripped are yet aborted
to the wink of the moon.

The sea gives and takes,
disinterested panderer of tenants,
guileless passengers on barks
run parallel to an advent
and a blessing moored.

This is the shore
of our disappointment, a cache, a rook
of turtles flipped a flashlit way
of us and all that we mistook
for want of feeling.

And this is cause—
for lanterns and clapping hands
this shore, this sea, this air and embers
smoldered in a dozen reprimands
upon the wrecks of you and me.

This is the shore; this is the sea.

BARRETT VARIATIONS

It is perhaps too famous a poem,
their story too pat,
then and now, overused.
      People are fools.

To count the ways
really, is to lose count,
the fingers of stadiums of hands,
multiplying.

Depth, breadth, height?
Twenty years of skipping down steps
      in that hollow to a Chinese day,
wide as to catch the horizon
in its nap and sew the seam
straight onto linings of the cloak
        of God,
and height, well He Himself
looks down in air, but barely.

Ideal grace comes in round tones
of infant-cry stilled by your breast,
the arm around my tears
insular to the ice of failing,
the turn in the night to realize against
the sameness of Sundays a delirious flash
of my life's purpose
in your place of breathing.

So forgiveness goes,
a bag of golden coins exchanged

for the currency of old griefs
and salvageable admiration.
My lost saints were arrow-pierced,
sung in grottos, rogues that cried among lambs
for salvation.

Yes, you saved me.

To love better after death
        is no specious argument,
not one for cloisters and shuttered rooms;
having died in the seconds strung
like black beads in minutes, hours,
days of any parting, death
is a dull synonym
for calendars unemblazoned
with your name.

And if to say,
within this yearly world,
beneath the scepter of scars
there is yet a call for pretty sonnets
        read by pert, pink maids
to throngs at weddings just like ours,
mantled in bright Junes,
commissioned among stars,
then bring these Bobs and Barretts
back to broken stands
and kiss me long, and hard.

AND STILL

This is how it is.
The inadequacy.

There could be a room, a large room
with a long table, all its leaves intact
and I could write I LOVE YOU
on a piece of paper, folded once, and place
it on the table.

And I could write I LOVE YOU on another piece of paper,
folded, and place it on the table.

And I could write I LOVE YOU on a piece of paper
in bigger letters, and put it also on the table.

I could write the same on a tablet of brilliant white paper,
over and again, and place each sheet upon
the table, a bivouac of tents.

(A tablet of a hundred sheets.)

And I could light a cigarette, two, and fill another
tablet, also of a hundred, and place each sheet
upon the table. And the table fills, and some

drop off. So I begin to stack them atop
the others like tenements, or Angkor Wat.
Flocks of doves of them, with I LOVE YOU
inside.

I carve it on a brick, two bricks, and place
these at corners of the table.
Twelve bricks.

I could bring a cake of orange marzipan,
the words in your favorite color, red, and push
it onto the table, watching the doves descend.

And I could commission a Klimt or Chagall
to pastel I LOVE YOU as vapor on the far wall—
and I do. It is so pretty.

School children come by to sing of it, do re mi—
it is emblazoned on their collars as they smile.

I continue to write, and give up smoking.
The children are gone, but I have taught
a mynah bird to say it. He is black, with
a crimson sash of which you would approve.

I continue writing it, in charcoal,
crayon, red crayon, on the flyleaves of books
I will never read, stacked in the corner.
More paper, more writing,
more sound, more nonsense.

The room fills with everything those
words can see, can say. Thousands, millions,
of I LOVE YOUs large as the ceiling, small
as carnival grains of rice, etched with a pin, one for every
second I felt this way, back years, years
to when I first imagined it.

And just now, it all burns. It burns.
The walls cave in, the room keels and inverts
as a worn sock on someone's floor,
eruptions melt rock over us, the world
as we know it explodes.

All the I LOVE YOUs, gone.
These symbols, gone. This poem gone.
Me, you.

And still.

Flying Machine

(2013)

"The freethinking of one age
is the common sense of the next."

— Matthew Arnold

for my mother

A BOX OF MOON

From my knees,
head angled as penitent
at the age of eleven,
I spied the moon full in a window-frame
and boxed it,
softball-sized and glowing
into a four-dimensioned cube
that admitted time
in casual suspension.

There it remained
a magic prop I could carry
to agitate oceans,
light the halls of old churches
and fascinate young girls (like you)
who suckled romance
as if it were siphoned
from an orchid.

I, for my fortune of capture,
sacrificed the sensible life
even though I pretended, danced
alone in an eave among wardrobes
long discarded, defied
the ultimate discretion.

I would often grab a piece of the world
by its length-line, its width,
the colors that filled its borders,
and design a concurrent scene

stripped of the usual artifice,
to brim with feeling.

But the moon in the box,
caught amid others' madnesses
was my greatest
prize. It will be yours, love, on the day
you find it, beyond the curtain
of this mind and when you do,
promise not to fold it up
or drown it, or pull me from
that window, at eleven, where
I leave myself
behind.

PASTORAL

So many times we've arrived here
      shined round or beveled,
nimbly found in the business of fingers,
holes in our teardrops,
blind girl under a tree
stringing beads.

We know the covet
of starlings, share their blackness,
pretend to ignore a seasoned hop,
the escape, silk flown to the bungalow
of their monogamy, crystals
among seeds.

We cannot be swallowed,
so we shine
in the dryness of reeds,
in hallowed crest of limbs,
shine for the blind girl,

shine for Thee.

MUSIC FOR STRINGS, PERCUSSION, AND CELESTA

We are enamored of the wrong universes—
the ones glinting, glued to domes of sky
no more significant than pigs to Circe.

With feign to one sun for its power to blind
the weak imitations of eyes, these strings unstrung
in hollow puppet heads called yours and mine

yet dare to orbit a billion-fold places
in the peppered air surrounding our breaths,
a business of immortality in painted faces.

The sky is nothing except to be considered
or discarded; so, my viewpoint on skies to you.
But where edges of an envelope have withered

comes the internal answer to your question—
we are twin suns gathering gravity, giving off dust,
stray gods convening in contrary genuflection.

Laughter and mathematics can come of this:
your circle invades, intersects the horizon
and I am flattered enough to love your kiss,

to hold your radiance and trust and mortify
us both in the becomingness of something,
in games majestic, common with malady.

Such go the satisfacting novas of acquaintance,
their plan's light drifting so far from source,
extinguished names of dead celestial dance.

So many of them— dramatic lens of life
where put upon these orbs' single selves
commingling like billiards— husband, wife,

children spun like satellites cold or seething;
employer, collector, adulterer, agile thief,
personae of quantum spaces, solar breathing.

The distances deceive— how far can prayer travel
unmolested, without a landing? The closeness
of powered numbers causes compasses to unravel,

equations to erase, the foreign probe to fail
and at end of no beginning, where we fall
in the astronomy of our days, only days prevail.

STELAE

To articulate love is to mend a shadow
with symbols;
Cervantes and Shakespeare fail
and fall into a horse-trough
joined by Keats, by the Barrett Brownings
of our estimation of it.

It is like explaining religion to a dove.

It is not, it cannot be
a verb, but a wavelength
to split in minusculed perfect hue
upon a canvas
untouched even by DaVinci's eyes,
that makes faith as solid as ebony,
a key that slakes the famous *Liebstod*
chord only in approximation,
a little fan of overtones
toasting a ghost.

We approach it in metaphor,
we know it is more real than us,
we capture it only in transfiguration,
the chrysalis to wing,
a dead Christ to everything.

Idol in a jungle, overgrown
with the impatience of it,
it settles into the landscape
a harborer of random aspiration,
a blind receiver of the poetry of man

who will see it finally, finally,
when the kiss and throe
and sacrifice of words
and paint and sound— and promise
curl into a strand of magnificent
empty space, and its equation
comes to us, like the face of a woman,
                    in dream.

WHALING SEASON

So here we are, Leviathan
on a rebounding main,
rotund pariah cast of our romantic rejection,
floating on our back,
waiting for hookblade-
style harpoons
cast by drunks in this direction,
grabbing one fast between flippers
and ramming
it into our abiding heart.

Don't take us home to nurse
as if a calf.
We will U-turn onto the beach
of our hurt to the accompaniment
of flies.

We know this Ahab; we lived
for him or her we told ourselves, among our lies.
Finish it, we brave! Finish it!
But rather many, stupefied
will corral to the pleasure
of cardboard tourists, see an orange hoop,
pirouette on the waterline
like a big, inevitable Jesus
with nowhere to hide,
and take
the fulsome dangle of fish
or Jonah, with his open hand
inside.

FIRST CHILD

There is a girl and two boys,
sweet, wonderful as raisins; they save
our lives regularly
by breathing.

But they did not know our first child.

Effigy of ideas and straw,
he was not a child
we filled ourselves with, too selfish;
we made him each time
we tied our sinew into bows,
when we matched, happily
and erupted pearls.

In gay serene
we rocked our silly thing
down lanterned vias
somnambulant in the night,
bathed him with the pink oils of knowing.
Child, lark, dandy in his red
suspenders, his blue-blue cap,
his alphabet of scrabbles
that stand for love.

He was a good boy,
all respect and trust and honest
tears of care at such tender age;
he looked at us, we looked at him;

ventriloquist, he spoke through us
the vows we spoke again.

We didn't tell them, our new prides.
They keep us, after all, from being
gray statues on a mantel somewhere,
twin and saltic in our shames—
but there is no, no shame
among our lot for *him.*

He left us between seconds, and beyond years.

Was he lost under truck wheels,
the cough of cranes? Turned back a doll
who borrowed an aspiring from the living?
Or did he just leave,
a bus token we forget
to remember.

I look at you, you look at me.

We look ever by our shoulder
to see the screen door swing
and there! Come and meet him children, see!
All grown to a strapping, marvelous
wish, this moving tribute to the everything of us,
a writ of forgiveness on your bright behalves,
emotion on a sleeve
and a calling to account
every syllable the sacrament can bring.

There's no way to turn again,
deny, even if it's crazy.
Welcome to our world, you three—

realities. Consider as you grow,
a maybe.

It's why, when lights are down,
doors closed,
and even after shrill of our misgivings
we can answer
to his outstretched hands
and call each other

something warm,
like baby.

TIDINGS

With you away these days
I must do clothes as a profession;
I have become a good Chinaman,
if not a good you; I labor as if it were a song,
monotonous, but a song.

The heaps of textile
stripped of three men
and what is left of you this week
is enough to set the clock an hour.
Each piece uninspired, separate to its pile,
socks like shedded annelids
carrying their dirt, the haul of yards
and locker rooms.

My shirt is nondescript. Would you,
in my absence, take it to your face
and remember me fondly, some trace
of something you needed? I can
extend amongst the tent of my fingers
a silk piece of you and I do—
I immerse myself in the small bouquet
of flowers and must; I swim through it
toward you, think of keeping it in a drawer,
but know the scent will ghost itself
shortly and there it will lie, still to do.

I toss it—

in like the last conscript
of a ship bound for swells

and distant occupation. The water
is dark; the tide rising.

Come home to me.
I am writing poems about laundry.
Come home to me.

DISH OF LEARNING

So, my last son,
we circumvent the sty
of bullies that has become
an American school as if
it were the Cape of Storms
and teach each other.

For the sculpt of hours
whiled in the soft wood
of my fiftieth year
and the good clay of your twelfth,
I try to be something I'm not
or haven't been, or could have been
but went the road of pearls,
picked them and lost my way,
only to be gifted with your star.

Where do we begin today?
The idea of the negative?
Pulled through and beyond an equal sign
to make something of it, something
positive, lasting, an answer.

You know the capitals of Middle Asia,
can recite them and their strange phonology
and you should visit two or three someday,
in the sidecar of a motorbike
shaking hands
and snapping your camera.

Your father had his times,
calls them to color
in and around the decade of Khe Sanh and Hue,
how the imperial nature of man
is hoisted in weakness,
a rich catch for a poor hand,
Spanish, English, too-white Afrikaan
according to their century,
how all are duty-bound and brave
or less than brave, all of it
hard to understand.

We have the pictures back! Of you
and the Wampanoag at Plymouth
in the house of three fires,
you between John's and Priscilla's graves
in Duxbury, at the hilltop fort in the minister's pulpit
extending your hands, you with the knitting ladies,
with me shivering on the *Mayflower.* Your report is due
next week, or if we want,
whenever we can.

Look. In the bookstore.
These Happy Golden Years, I like the title, you?
The year we graduate the other
from the other, I will look upon it all
like that, and you will cement the ceremony,
smart I hope but better in heart than head,
with a smile into my grateful tears.

Do you want Mozart or Bill Evans?
Listen to his left hand.
What shall you paint in these last minutes?

Those straw-held pears?
Yellow and the flecks are brown, the basket
oblong sort of, not quite round.

Remember this maybe, in my borrowed wisdom:
the important things
are the ones that are true for you.

Over ice cream we discuss
the significance of the chemical earth,
and whether this, here and now is solid or liquid
or in-between, to the slow, slow
falling of our spoons.

TWO VAGRANTS IN SORRENTO

You say, of flip assurance
in the philodendrons of your mathematics:

one equals one

      and of a philosopher's bent I ask
           one what,
and curl the red moustache
I've grown among these mornings
as you cough your cough-drop up and rasp
one apple equals one apple.

      So I, reclining on the bad hammock
      that pulls to the right as if to dump
           its corpse into hell
      reply, ah well, a large bright Golden
      and a Red Delicious? and you say,

no, the same kind
      (is that some faint, seaweed smell?)
the very identical fruit of one
incestuous parent
      and I ask you to be a microscope
      and count the cells, and you say
identical I said! mirror-image, equal
as the dreams of Marxist fairies
but I'll do you better, one apple
equals itself!—

yes, it's seaweed... but I shall relent to the strain
of this ripe, ovarian protest
and fix an unpocketed sum— don't get up and stretch,

or yet walk to the piazza for such
fresh orbs as God and Eve extend—

yes, my dearest oldest friend,
one apple equals
the totality of itself,
so long as you don't ask

the one divine, dissembling question:

when?

POEM HAVING TO DO WITH WATER

The young man drowns
off the shoal of his disappointments,
pulled into the sloop
bloated and marked
of a hundred mouths.
He cries at his condition—
mails himself home
a corpus of self-pity
and persistent memory.

The older man
confronts the wave
wested into his face
attached to a woman's name;
he rails at the wind of it,
silenced by the howl
of so perfect a squall,
a nodding statistic.

Older still
he merely rolls in the dew
of it until it disappears
in a sun
of ticks and cicadas,
resigned to the afternoon.

And when he dies
of these seemingly
unconnected events,
sallow and leathered

into a small bag
of insignificance,
regret is a dry salvage,
the storm an invention,
wetness wish,
the sea a gravel,
the night, beholder.

AND COUNTING

We rush to the penny-candy of our blood,
engorge ourselves from the stiff paper bag,
its contents strewn like years upon a table
set for supper, stealing our appetites away.
I am one, legion, example, epidemic.
Mellitus, drum-major of the children's crusade
grown into the inevitability of denial,
of lengthening foreshadow, diagnosis, schedule.

The hours it robs it does not save, I am sure of it.
I am its footman, boosting it into carriages,
walking its dog, arriving for appointments,
holding its other hand through the lecture.
I am sick to death of it; annoyance is worse
than pain, pain that is sweet in its certainty
of now, not then, not when. If it weren't for you,
I'd let it go, loves, and laugh at my ignorance.

The shimmer in my sugar-addled eyes,
the broad clay feet, swelled and secure
in their infirmity, the heave of heart
that shudders in the place of breathing, falls
all down me now, downfall slow and sick
and teasing, strafing pretty calendars
with marks of no appeal, smiling back
resign upon a looking-glass, annealing.

CRUSADE

It is eloquent to die for what you know,
not always for what you believe.

The broken sepulchre trods the night
down separate dawns
to separate understandings,
apostolates based on tilted alphabets,
their calculations pinned
to separate moons.

The children march divinely.
The bestial part of a proposition
intersects them in some diameter
of a circle calculated to stop hurrahs.

I will tell you the reason for all this.
First we will sample claret, and dance
with the ignorant belles. It is a difficulty,
but when it is resolved, all will
be in order, peaceful as the dinner table
readied with yams.

TIME MACHINE

History is an old map
strewn with death and calendars,
but it sends an invitation. The car is outside;
the driver has dark glasses.
In the confusion that is past and present
we are all together, inside of it, this
celebration of flash-fire,
ecstatic breath and tears, jumping
in and out of costumes,
drawing drama, less often,
comedy. Don't worry.
If we didn't come back to play
each time, the world would be full of ghosts.
We'd be tripping on them, saying I'm sorry.

So I will be the great betrayer now
and you be precious; the villain is always
more interesting, gets to wear wilder colors
and snarl and rub his hands together.
Before I cried too much, too much.

The penitents protest their old deeds;
they are sheep, and grass,
and the worst
have turned to rocks in the ground beneath.

What is to be said for virtue
is it's the real definition of heaven
that misses the dictionary by leagues;
but it seems when offered, offered

and transfigured
it so often tries and fatigues.

The funny thing is always what
is missing or exaggerated. Repeated and
repeated, it would become obvious if
we weren't so good at forgetting.
Pull over at the next corner.

Hordes shall move beyond the mountains
of continents. A box of cigarettes
we will share along with concepts
of duty and dishonor, and their burning shall be
the measure of persistence.

SMALL PROPHET

If I could cast a satellite
far above the social graces,
catching the outline of succubus or cheat
before their consummations
      as one can see the image
      of Eden, yet faintly immortalized
      on the sphere—
I would be that walking God
I worshipped in his sleeping
and I would thresh and separate
good wheat in all the gardens
of the earth.

But I can only throw this stone
up where I can see it fall
arcing to the lake

in the gravity
of it all.

SALISBURY

Buses let out
along this shimmered ground
of patchy green
a modern pornography
mixing dialogue among stones.
      Who can unleaven risen grain,
reverse the withered vine and leaf,
the purple ferment of their globes?
Can silver a stream through ruins,
the perfect chattering ducts
to a cracked gutter, betray a dead pool
that merely pocks the landscape now
with drybrushed groan?
      Briton, Roman, Pict,
Saxon and Norman bred their blood
into the holy ground,
pinioned light off a high spire, dolmen,
assorted crowns.

Wiccan and Catholic parade
in the Avalon shadow of conglomerate rock,
not far from the tall double-circle
of granite sentinels arranged
      like finite stone pi's
to the sun's dagger every solstice and equinox,
the dial of day predestined as
a thousand spinning clocks.

The tourists volley snap-
shots, unaware of the real

history, written of invisible ink
bound in the magnificence
of astrology and ancient astronauts,
the call of armies of night,
ancestors ignorant and profane
who marched in formation or, enlightened,
    floated over thatchy rooftops,
    released from a nape of chains
to spell this desolate landscape
dashed of war with a modicum of deliverance,
    the hope of grails
drunk of prayer as prayed
by later Lancelots.

Go home, you people. There is hallowness here.
    It trails the gone moon
and every pence you paid to sever
sameness for a hour;
it is the place where mystery conjures
morning, memory fails to attune,
but roses flower.

NOTE TO THE OTHER SIDE OF MYSELF

He speaks, but I
am indisposed;

I see, clear as leaded glass
your now-denuded thigh, bent to the light
and kiss the arcing arch of your foot
up to the toes; clearer still
this concept bends religion
into art, turns me into a bad
broken cast of David,
eyed similarly insecurely
by him who doesn't speak again,
but waits for speaking.

ARTUSI ATTACKS MODERN MUSIC

"A wop bop a lu bop ba lop bam boom."
— *Richard Penniman, 1955*

I, Master Giovanni, composer
and musical theoretician,
canon-in-ordinary at the Church
of San Salvatore,
standing as buttress and defender
of all that is decent under God, hear
His harmony of voices, wind
and strings as if among
the cherubim who spread their wings
to fan a holy breath into the day
and say, beware the onslaught
of Monteverdi and his kin,
who rock the world with secular shocks
in the cause of innovation,
who poison postulant minds
against the highest of religious incantation
for the sake of feeling!
Here, entering our new century
and all by His will— return to worth
in hearth and home the four-part song,
decora of the humble canzonette.
It is not too late to lie as lambs
in the order of recanting,
not too late to clothe the nude
in staves of prayer
and write another
safe motet.   — Giovanni Maria Artusi
                              c. 1540-1613

INVERSE SITTING
OF THE MODERN WOMAN, 1927

When the image
becomes the idolatress,
the vista animate,
each aureole, curve, cleft
and smile a seeker of art
so intimate as to melt
a seascape to solid blue,
she assails in knife and palette
a quiet retribution.

If you leave her to the device,
hide her colors
behind a drape of gray light
so that she relies
solely on chiaroscuro,
she yet finds an edge to fire,
etches the empathic
filigree onto soul.

The tease is in her lambent,
fluid brush, exuding sepia
with every stroke.
To males of her commission
(each elemental sinner)
perspective pulls lapel to pocket-stitch;
she flies them out among gas giants, haunts
them as a Botticelli angel, bitch.
And woe to women
posed to her critical style;
she will find details

of palsy in a wanful smile
complete with adder eye.

Let her muse be one of these—
pressed into caricature, or released
an ascendant starling, or a man
stupid in his sentence.

(More like quiet *revolution.*)

She points out Cassatt's daffodils,
smokes the skulls of Miss O'Keefe;
she is artist and model
of love and lust, lurid in command
on either side of any canvas,
always just beyond
aesthetic reach and yet,
the commonly
uncommon lens betrays
an always hidden certainty,
benign to coaxing of patina's rust,
bodily resistant to trends

and eerily free.

THE TWO SAD SISTERS

So two sad sisters up the cherry lane
sold many modest baskets of globes, garnet
in their season; the lithe limbs, the cherries,
splayed out surely toward their succulence
and not too dear, were excellent in pie.

The sisters had goats; a red-haired he-goat
whose mate had died, several comely daughters,
and one with child, the father's child, as such
are he-goats and such epithets are made,
but milk and cheese would tithe the sullen winter.

In bristling frost, the March of an expecting,
a beautiful young goat gave way to birth
but by a fate of turning, breeched in rib
the kid could only writhe; the while, women
hands up to their elbows deep, swore and swore.

Then standing overhead like gray angels
the two sisters let the daughter die;
having cut the broken child from itself
the two lay as life's wracked figurines
in a squandered manger, wiping eyes.

Backed within his stall, the he-goat brayed
as if it were, and was another day,
nothing to him, cast among the stubbled
orchards and the house, its door-crack dim
with sun of a delayed retribution.

Yet that and every summer, down the lane
on every several openings of wall
into a curtained window, pastries cooled
on ledges, some with edges dripping
onto muslins, folded bright with stain.

A CROPPING IN WINTER

The corn blooms invisible in December,
plucked of handfuls, dropped
in deep baskets of tired wicker
lined with snow, and brought straightaway
into the silo of the cold sun.
From here, and likewise lost of pronouns
dim ancestral girls, purgated souls
pinned to aprons, accept
the baskets of the men, grind and mill
the amplitude of grain daylong into night,
when as if to contradict an intercourse, the banjo
of the solstice moon is strummed.

Bread that is made
is for the bible of new spring; it is eaten by dreamers
who dream they live yet celebrate
no living thing for long.
What they grow into autumn is temporal,
flushed with meaning as a severed eye
beholding God.

So comes the eventual
and ever, gained into white quilts
and choruses of icy lace not understood,
but sung.

MILKING

The timothy in clusters dines on plates of light,
filling green with incandescent blood
that gowns their slope in arcane majesty,
loaned from the hallucinations of Eden.

The brindled Holstein, alpine in its fortune
marries the grass to its inner churn, illumines
the role of an Austrian boy, who leads
her with a switch back to the milking.

It's good milk; silken fiery streams that sheet
and fill these spiritual silver buckets,
nudged with turn of time and alchemy
to wheel a glowing cheese, stacked and tabled.

We carve a convex sun of it at breakfast,
on crackers milled of bright significance;
within our crucibles it feeds the day,
the grass, the cow, the milkmaid, and the boy.

We celebrate the way its rays imbue
all forms and masks, the divine showing
warm and white, prismed to spectral solace,
substance of this world, and its delivering.

MY POEMS ARE LITTLE CRIPPLES

Tootling along in a black space,
here and there a hum and squeak,
a quelled bellow, nervous laughter;

they preen in a mirror under matchlight—
jealous of one another they jostle,
love an audience of shut-ins;

they marshal themselves, motley
in a phalanx full of weaknesses,
are blown apart with the first volley;

they pick up their arms again,
their legs, prop their holey torsos
and speak with a silly hope,

go home sheepily to the deaf ears
as if already dead and the diners
talked around them and above them

wallowing in the stiff, prosy song
of the day, always the same—
more war for fodder, price of cheese,

addicts poised among sunflowers.

Close the poem! There's tired newness
to it, that will fade with the hours.

BY ALL ACCOUNTS

It was a funny day.

As the block of buildings crashed
like cardhouses around a deaf beggar
and horses of fire-engines rebelled
in the streets,
Barrymore sipped *Domaine Baraillon*
from a clean glass
at the one open bar in Union Square.

Chippies and pimps, fearing
the end of world, stripped
and fornicated like Dante figurines
on the steps of the courthouse,
while the great Caruso sat on his trunk
in gray light; shivering disconcert
and afraid of having left that voice
in the crumble of a fifth floor bedroom
at the Palace Hotel, he sang
"Il fior che avevi a me tu dato"
to a barking spaniel

and a man in a blue suit.

MISTER GARBAGE

In the panoramic scape
of this, life in landfill of minor gestures,
useless things heaped in awful
majesty and never again regarded,
live we.

I have decided to search
and everyone stops to laugh, one then many,
then several, then none as they move
in their directions.

This pile wraps smiles
in fishpaper, stuck to an accounting
since paid. That one holds a polaroid
faded by a sun also dying—
a boy and his father.
This was the rind sucked dry
and flung to silent landing, these
the grounds of divorcing.

It is infinite, action behind a
trillion breaths.

Where is that thimble in this
Anapurna of swill, the vessel of meaning
filled with the seconds when
we understood.

Keep looking, keep looking.
                    Don't walk away.
Okay.

Be good.

SNAPSHOT FOUND IN A DICTIONARY

The dunlin,
a brown and white sandpiper, lights
on leaves of the Dutchmen's breeches,
the two spurs of its flowers
looking like angel wings
astride the bird, who turns his long bill
to the shutter, quick-shutter
of a Brownie box camera, September, 1955.

ABOVE THE FLOOD, AS WRITTEN

I.

FASTEN SEAT BELT   USE SEAT BOTTOM
WHILE SEATED   CUSHION FOR
                         FLOTATION

ABROCHE SU CINTURON USE EL ASIENTO
                         PARA FLOTAR

We can sit in pairs.
It is a froth a mile below,
thick as a marble mantelpiece
of wet significance you could vanish through,
but all below it and into the civilized ground
the H's and O's marry into a deluge
of earth, a small shard of God's and Noah's masterpiece
of trial and oblivion
that spins itself about a largely unchanged world,
changing it slightly.

A bus floats away;
beautiful women terrify the trees
with their slipping fingers—
soup for a leviathan's children, soup today.
The bridge to Nineveh, in Texas,
crumbles like cake to a smiley swell, the Trinity River;
Mexicans sing in circle.

Next week, dry here.
Crickets return, then locusts, dust.
Above the clouds, a merry sunshine.

II.

On glass-flecked beach in Mindanao
it comes, on the raping wind
halloing the huts, scattering star-fruit
in the bible of different tongues.

Later, later North, the water turns
to swan-down, cold and shimmering
as welcome death to tired souls,
and Europe is a muffled sound
under bellies of serpentine drifts.

Two dead, twenty thousand dead, six, twenty-three.
All immersed in some kind of unbelieving, some funny
kind of permanent, perfect glee.

This is where the forecast and shadowing
meet. Always somewhere, always circling,
painstakingly mercurial yet precise
in its random indifference,
its perpetuity.

NEW ANTHEM OF THE SUN

After the tears
the impostor, now gone for hours
and reliable as a bad suitor,
has no claim here.

I am the sun.
And I am striking
for a new dignity.
I beat the signals out
electric in long waves, a lasso
of worlds.

The song banks off Martian moons,
sets them to billiards.
If there are accountants there,
they weigh the profit and loss.

Thick men of Jupiter
roll in their beds. Hot ones
of Mercury bounce their wives
like basketballs,
bang their heads.

The Uranians walk
in a fog to castanets
and shakers,
hum a kind of soca.

Saturn senses it is not the time
to be just beautiful;

Neptune abstains, of course.
To hell with Neptune.

Venus, aligned with my attitude
in the night sky under
canopy and screen
winks its understanding.

Copernicus was right.
I am right.
We agree to disagree,
that cliché of bygones sailing
in the ether,
unreflecting in our trance,
satellites of radiance

failing.

GALE FARM

When you are gone
my hurt comes back
as if in season, a replayed reel
that amplifies to howl,
a horse whinny, wild,
hogs in the slop, milling
without elbow room and wondering
in the black and white dust.

I run with it, gate to tree
calling out
and kick the slant-door
of the root cellar
like a girl.

No one to help me.

The worst of it twists
like special-effects, muslin
on a lazy-Susan that passes
for sinuous pipe of tornado,
that pretends to rip the door
from the little house and do it through
and through, and me inside
(and do me, too) in my
lonely disorient without
the semblance of healing, without you
on my trip of missed paradise,
no emerald, poppy-red or blue,
wiped off another Kansas map

at half-past three
in the afternoon.

SOMEWHERE IN THE CORNER OF REGRET

I would like to think
a world could be devised
that would undo
the doing that hurts and defiles.

Measured by a calculus of second chances,
a life where reversal balances
the forward frenzy,
the dash
to a pool of no water.

Take this whiskey
and this glass.

Having fumbled it
to the fanfare of gravity,
and just beyond the pity of my clamber
it shatters on the floor.

I am left undrunk, unnumb.
It too.
All we were counting on
seeping into a floorboard,
cutting the bare heel
of next September.

A world, rather, that could
expunge regret and sadness,
that was not always devolving
into chaos and the misfortune of an audience,

shards that recrystallized as a talisman,
drink that shimmers brownly golden
of reverie, a mouth to return it to,
bottle to re-cork,
a letter to evaporate hints of rain,
a chance to understand, to remind,
to revel, to float in the interminable
sea of warm content, to define
love with gesture and confidence,
to anticipate, to hope,
to breathe and know that one is breathing
in the sextant of eyes,
to tell time "stay awhile," or at least,
for God's sake, countenance
retrieving.

LEAVES AND WATER, STONE

Aurelius likens a stream to it,
this passage of the sacred, these saucy blunders
natural as November, its cold spin and its decay,
each exfoliate leaf turning in the cylinders of water,
the eddies forking to the greater river, sea.

You are that one, at that time,
and this one say, is me, both grave and golden
in our crackled veins
that each sucked sunlight till too late, till rains
came and the pinching wind, the falling
bowling gliss and so unglamorous
light-landing that came to this,
a clutching stone, a letting go
to other stones and letting go,
dammed in clusters what was once so sylvan,
so well chalked within a sketchbook, lately thrown
unto the compost, into loam, to all that comes
and all that goes so small and vastly onward,
always of a mind, if not
or never quite together
or alone.

OF SENTIENCE, OR ACCESSORY

I wear you like gilted edge
on the fine tissue of a day;
it soothes my darkling allergy
to light, indigo without you.

I wreathe harmonics of your voice
above the car-horns, the news
and neighbors, all the chatter that
recesses into tone-deaf wells.

The scent of a love-making you
suggests from stacked oranges
and wafts about the stale street
of breeze, and hint of coming hail.

I taste the coffee off your lip
with this, a third, savored cup
inside a sidewalk window, framed
for the artist who declined his paint.

And till the ever-if I touch you
in this wise, the way of lovers
catalogued or long mistaken
in my self-intentioned blight—

I do adore, as then and now
among the sense and shiver's
second sight, that raiment's
cling within, without, my night.

DEFINITION OF BLANK AT THE TELLER'S WINDOW

Surrender him
the bag of sugar,
a rhubarb stalk,
the sour that adheres
like silver to the plate
of an erratic mind, sweet
that empowers him to dream
and count up
forty years on the wind
of lilacs,
his mother's voice
calling him in.

NATURE TEACHES BEASTS TO KNOW

The stones among unkept arbors
are dull with rain,
      walks oddly cracked
to defy the indiscriminate talk
of superstition. I've never come here.
This, the memorial garden
of my very close friends.

These were bosom confidants,
the accomplices of minor intrigues
and major events requiring filled photos
      and toasts of drunken men;
these were women who would have
slept with me, the varietal chums who occupied
hours in the circumference
      of a glass.
They have left me. But I am also ugly,
having shoveled the other into the common grounds
of our effigies,
the dandelions' grass, the slurred address
of pretty birds.

Why, tell me,
did we assign such value
to a bond currencied in wartime lire,
in bright collectors' yen? Oh, the godchildren
who wander into the forest
never to be seen!

There should be a menagerie here,
feasting on imagery. We group
        out of instinct, the Grant's gazelles.

But we separate out of desire
to be new in laudedness,
from new forms that can appreciate
a singularity of purpose,
such design as gods remand
to only-ones, to carvèd tributes
among the several hills
that range to west and windward
        of this sinister place,
the bit, embittered memories of pieces
of names, a semblance of history
squandered for good reason,
        or bad refrain.

DALÍ'S OLD MAN TO THE LEFT OF THE SEA

I am the man encephalic
propping my head, blown obtuse
on the Y of a branch, an augur stick
set astride a plain chair
on sand ground fine from old skulls,
and there the morphic echo,
bell from the town campanile,
transparent ballerina,
hoopskirt of an old woman,
of Belial incarnate, turning the wheel
that saps a string of albumen
from the sutures
of my embarrassment.

I am impossible to dress
and hard to love.

PRAYER AGAINST OUR BLACKNESS

The black factory stamps shadows of us
just off the outline of our bodies, away from the ground,
and the wall.

Each is a mild evil, stays mild
except in its quieting abundance
marshaled into a cloud, black cloud
with yeasty fingers
that sweeps the cottages of our good love
into the open sea.

We always challenge the challenge to our shadows.
It is the act of a false saint,
the maintenance of impossible pieties,
unequivocated gall.
Even the ones to whom we profess
channeling the plasma of our souls—
do not question here.

The quantumness, this multiplicity
of division of inches,
these hundreds of miles of separation
over the flat lines of calendar
to find we have changed
into new things, new hats and trousers,
frocks that glitter, taste
athwart old taste, the almond sweet,
now bitter.

How to polish this dull refraction off?

Steel fibers, novenas, the restoration
of trust that comes in the not-
quite-dying fever? Perhaps if we lend
accolade to weakness, light it up,
parade it as a fetish of some pre-Lenten
carnaval so the hoot and whistle of not
forgetting sin may yet deliver it
into the lap of a warm madonna
and make her smile, and child of the image
become our child, and sea give back,
and houses leavened and breaded
for the rising seat of ourselves
in the posit of normalcy become an article of faith,
if not erudition.

TOWN OF LUGGALO

While I am in this trance
of sweet fate
and at hem of its dream, Julie,
we reside in the town of Luggalo.
Just you, I, and the apportionments
of ourselves in mystery of love
that begets the father and daughter
from a greater self, a plural sought
in other avenues, a place
where we can meet, remain in
now or then
and call it just our home.

Luggalo!

When I am gone you are the mayor
and keeper of its blocks, the envelope
of twelve souvenirs, a golden key
of such satisfaction you handed me,
as in-hand in your yellow jumper we
had strolled past statues of our best times
strewn with garlands
on the pennywhistle street.

We are the purveyors
of special estate, portraits hung
in a long hall frequented by visitors
from the hamleted countries abroad
who wonder what each painted day
was like— theirs as ours

when we were for each other
not card nor carol sung
on the receiver after ale, but
commune of a mute devotion,
spoken through condensing clocks
and watchful signs on borders
braced and healed, real in the mindless heart
of memory, directed to this point of map,
town of wonder, said after
what you could say of our name at the age of two,
Luggalo, that place in which I've slept
and will ever wake to, years hence,
even in the widening of your eyes.

DECONSTRUCTION

This is me, after hours
of unsatisfactory discourse,
of philosophy and laundry lists,
attempting to explain it all
in a poem.

This is me standing in front of the house.
I am looking at that corner
of roof-trim that needs fixing—
such an old house, and poor carpenter.

This is a photograph of both us out there,
taken by Julie who wanted to use up her film.
She will find it years from now,
and affix it to a nondescript album
(the kind that are stacked
and adorned with printed flowers).

This is me cut out of stiff tan paper,
overlaid with a red square and two
brown rectangles, black ovals for shoes;
I'm pressed into blue background
with a stapled green band at the bottom,
and the brown house is a square, the
black roof triangle, white curlicue
for smoke, red chimney. There is paste
seeping through the edges. That sweet paste.

This is me an open oval
on loose-leaf.

Eyes, no mouth.

This is a smear of carrots
on the wall. It is also me.
This is a cry, an attempt
to communicate.

This is me.
Where are you?

This
is me.

DESOLATE ANGELS

I believe the desolate angels wait
at edge of our calamity, poised, preening
to wax their wing upon our waning light
and soar at last, to the last of everything.

Old guardians, kicked beyond this scene
draw lots for the next few unencumbered souls
that fill the offspring newly sprung from water
to a warm pink vase, with a card of offering.

Gabriel, horned and Azrael, his broken lute
a-strumming form the yanyin of embrace,
the death of life and lost in life's place
another living name, a new forgiving.

MAYAKOVSKY

"I have seen Christ escape from an icon,
and the slush tearfully kiss
the wind-swept fringe of his tunic."

from "A Few Words About Myself," tr. G. Reavey

On the third try
of spun chambers, each months apart
and as if scheduled for a haircut,
Vladimir Mayakovsky kissed the sky
through the blown open
sorrow of his dim sequestered heart
and Russian spring seized
with tears on his doorstep.

Don't cry, his open mouth
seemed to say.

He had aspired to be
that cloud in trousers, a scented
turquoise mist beyond the lethargies,
the devoutly alternating
devotion and defilement of a current
of women, the meaning
beyond what he could say.

It is hard to be a Bolshevik
and a saint. Harder still
to be a man worthy of caress,
a purveyor of dreamt clay
fashioned into reality.

One searches through his posters
and polemics as one digs oysters
on a Caspian bank; and then the two
handsful of poems. Much work for morsels.
But what of not tasting,
of the empty days and normalcy
of breathing that betrays the calendar
unto eternity? This he portrayed
in the prisms of a soviet
altered with the bile of misgivings,
and a heart burnished
with the silly hope of transfiguration
yet beating above fettered graves.

MORNING

(by Vladimir Mayakovsky;
translated from the Russian,
by A. Rocheleau and V. Richter)

Sullen rains squint his eyes.
Behind
such bars of iron thought,
of the electric wires
and feather-beds alighted on,
the legs of the rising stars
lean.

But the death of streetlights—
tsars within their crowns of gas
made more painful
for the eyes,
the fighting bouquet of streetwise sluts,
the fitful prickling laughs
at jokes, yellow
poison roses
that grow in zigzag.

Behind the hubbub
and tumult, pleasant to
new sight—
she-slaves of the cross
suffering indifferent calm retire
to the coffins of the funhouses,
while East throws in
its one
burning vase.

MONSTROUS FUNERAL

(by Vladimir Maykovsky,
translated from the Russian
by A. Rocheleau and V. Richter)

Sullen to black, people appeared
solemn and heavy, arranged themselves
as if paymasters or recruiters
of a dark order of sulky monks.

Lament of crows lined windows,
the sky's chalk, colored in storm;
all was so matched and fitted
to the terrible expecting.

And then yawned, groaned unwilled
the dry ochre of the dusty air
where climbed and rolled
the quiet caisson of a funeral.

Disturbed, the mass as one eye
threw its glances to the coffin,
which burst and bellowed out
"they are burying the laughter!"

A hundred-breasted furry stole
roared; billioned by multiple echoes,
it followed the procession
and at once, knives of cries

sunk in, forcing to understand nothing.
This was the mother of the laughter?
To whom, yes whom can she go back?
Look, wearing his boldness, this one?

It is big, the nose is big;
the standard Armenian joke sobs.
We still have not forgotten how
he twisted his mouth; behind him

ragged and without favor, screeching,
a sarcasm adjusted its canter.
Where, if he's dead, can she bury her head?
Already, the bleats blocked skyward.

But still, from where the little cries?
Why, there were regiments of smiles
breaking on a burial mound
their so-fragile little fingers.

And so, through their formation
that whetted together a cried-out
Symbolist, came a Terror that skipped
to a prominent place of mourning,

his sodden face a salty porridge
squished into wrinkles of a sullen forehead
and if someone is laughing, it seems,
as if, somebody just tore out his lip.

SPOILS

The caravel of emeralds and gold
three days out of Panama, turns a pin
of Trinidad, pulling its longitude
up thirteen salted weeks of a blue sleeve.

It hopes, hopes, plies the wind with prayer
of old Catholic arrogance and new greed,
smiling into the sun of its comeuppance,
storm off autumn rocks of Tenerife.

The shoals dance with madlights, yellow, green.
Fish in their finality comb the bones
with kiss of working women's lips and teeth
until relics of men assort themselves.

The pillowed sob that wails in Cadiz
does not assume a history of the scene;
timeless, Incans, small-pocked and minusculed
spin the opal clouds, 1533.

FAITH

I believe in you
because I have no time for the government of stars,
no scissors for time's twill
and no direction for the scissors,
little heed for direction
nor place for heeding
or comfortable place
for anything but a comfortable creed
that ceases, never, to be believing.

THE AUTOPSY OF PAUL

He is wheeled in
as still as soft statuary
more reposed than disposed of.

His chest is opened
to rolling hills of irises
where his heart once was
before it was given to another.
The brain is a good solid brain—
an apartment house of infinite characters
playing various games—
knucklebones, backgammon, draughts,
sin upon sin, a quantum mechanic
boxed with shame.

But long ago
he severed his life
from the possessive ambition of apostrophes,
left the capital off his i
and became at once organic and spiritual,
the subtlety of grass,
a bottled flame.

I read his letters
as if they were meant for me,
postmarked of a nearby city
and closed with personal salutation.

Not only can you weigh the soul,
you can weigh the soulless of their heavy lead,
and count their exit wounds.

In my best prayers
I take his place beneath
the scalpel there, as he took.

Him or me, a road to Damascus points one way,
magnetic, even unto death.

And hallowed be its name.

FALL DOWNSTAIRS WITH ME

in your liquid dress of blanched organdy,
your empire waist a circus in my hands;
unsettling smiles to pall expecting guests
we shove the chandelier and bumble light
in unstrung love to twelve cornets and a melody.

Fall darling! With, against me to their gape
and gasp long frozen to the fashion face
and hung like sweatered consciousness on hands
of measured time, the kind that regulates
a normalcy as clear and clean as grime.

And we shall laugh like pretty fools in reels
of Chaplin and Lloyd, willing specimens
of the comic danger of feeling, to kick
and somersault our decorous selves
upon the landing's Persian rug, unreeling,

dusting off and dervishing ourselves
to hail the gypsy fiddler's tarantelle
and dance into the waiters' bright applause—
I will be your tumbler always, this way,
sum of this effecting that we cause.

A MEMBER OF THE CONSPIRACY

My last *Pall Mall.*

Sex is written on my face
if not my mind.

I walk through a park
of defected carrier pigeons
whose messages curl yellow about their toes
but flash a thousandth of a second
every thirtieth frame
behind the irises of lost eyes.

I turn over queens in the sweaty
semblance of all that has come before,
and the nothing that may be.

You are in my sights,
the hairs of my tis-of-thee.

I am Oswald in the lunchroom
waiting for instructions;
Umbrella Man unfurled,
the third tramp, the brute in Mexico City
fading on a polaroid.

It has always seemed an advertisement,
these get-togethers;
so much is said to walls, to chandeliers,
to divans, just beyond gazes,
words with entendres, the missed
and mean.

The third Mason on the left.
Near the fire-effigy.

That's me.

THE DEATH IN THE ROOM

Is not always a palpable thing,
yet there it is—

I shall call it a him, crouched
on a stool in the corner, always present,
and obsequious in his negating way
as if to say, pay no attention.
He wears, for me, just now,
black pants and a black sweatshirt with a hood,
      and he shades his eyes
      against the contrast
      of the colored TV. He is slight,
I mean his build is slight
like, what's his name, the young actor,
      always young, Sal Mineo.
He is a panther of conflicting emotion.

I see as redbirds flock and blow
in Italian breeze about the screen
      and around the coffin
of a dead pope, he takes notice.
The scene that comes in threes.

Down the hall,
he is playing jacks with a comatose
child. And he follows at some distance
happy couples down walks
      of the April snow
who couldn't, couldn't possibly imagine—
he dabs the darling eyes
of the survivors, second

and the seventeenth
to know.

Occasionally
he settles to dinner
in the extra chair, eats nothing, drinks
only water.
He is the one common relative.
     More identical
in his difference
than the African prototype of man,
or the glowingest apostle
of the light. Centurion at the cross,
imported swordsman who takes the head
of Anne Boleyn, barrower
of plague-dead mothers and their kin.
     The death in the room

serves a tallied clock
of the veiled god; he is not bad, not unpleasant,
not necessarily, by his smile, grim.
     He is
what is that was, and what
will be in each dark corner
of each lit square, of each
soft footing of our imaginings
to get to him. Please, we say, please
     must it be, or *could* it be, or no,
we most often forget about him.

He grants us in the majority of our moments
     that silent wish,
the blind longevity

of the single, long, second of our lives
      never to intrude, secondary player
without a line, and waiting

    to begin.

THE RAYS

I had just returned to California
to gain the trail of the dyed-brown
China White then polluting both coasts
for a book a love affair would cancel,
and just in time for when the townsmen
took their shiny hulls to chop
of sharks and haul the mating mantas in,
feast of June among the opals.

Bruce and I did not hunt rays;
we drove to a sullen southside dock
and thought to order our skiff and tackle
only to get drunk at a nearby dive—
and *if* we had gone, full of inebriate
and brave song, we'd have keeled,
drowned as babies, baby men
without the requisite lack of memory,
that ruddy windfleck of real fishers.

Nonetheless we feasted on others' dead rays
whose wings lived still before the coals,
living things not yet disencoded
of their species to inanimate chemicals
in the chemical of our laughter,
the mix of beer and Bodega Bay
that drinks to us in malady, that
hoists the prelude night, and morning.

UMBRELLA

suggested by J. P.

Walks, she, beneath a black umbrella,
pelts of rain articulating scorn
that slides off the slick polyester,
wet-circling a fugitive still dry,
though each drop seems somehow
to find the skin, the veins,
the spongy heart, its matting
damp with shame.

Umbrellas are funny things,
almost insane.

KHRUSHCHEV, THE CANNABIS KING

Letter to the editor.

From my thesis
for the Russian Department
of Columbia University,
spring of 1971:

the Premier took to an Indian variety
no doubt furnished by the husband
of Stalin's daughter, the swarthy one.

My sources, here and in Moscow
are inviolate; the man smoked incessantly.
We know of the demands,
in the middle of deliberations on Tito,
for Borscht and crackers.

The shoe as Giapetto's hammer.

We see him at Risk,
the pieces everywhere, the dash
of missiles erect or flaccid,
like so many Cuban cigars.
Why so upset, he asks?

Way back, we trace pictures of him
riding the Flying Elephants at Disneyland,
trace them for children spared the atom bomb
to color in.

And even after the worst of harangues, a smile,
succor of the lollypop schoolboy.

Deposed, he tends his garden, his garden!
Bourgeois, bourgeois, all bourgeois—
and his rolling laughter.

FLYING MACHINE SUITE

(16 poems based on the drawings and notebooks
of Leonardo da Vinci)

FLYING MACHINE

This machine should be tried over a lake,
and you should carry a long wineskin as a girdle
so that in case you fall you will not be drowned.

— *Leonardo, B 74 V*

It resides
        in a tree of mathematics
an instrument
        nature
        plays
in flawless
reverie
        of singsong dawn.

Man attempts to extract
        in its sleep
        the still wing
        of the hummingbird,
the gull of arc and suspension
        on gossamer wind-
                        strings,

the slash of kite
that rips the sky
to a blue
     bleeding.

The life which rides
within
conforms better
     to task
     than that of man separated from them;
but it does not stop
his will any more
        than the shrike
     will lay mercy upon
the mouse,
and not impale him.

Hence, this contraption.

Spring of horn
fastened
     upon wood of willow
     encased in reed
for impetus.

Double canes
soaped,
     wire holds the spring
and it is not straight.
Spring of wing.

Net. Cane.
Fustian. Taffeta. Thread. Paper.

The greatest jet
          five centuries on
     fires
     into the element off the simplest
of the twelve designs,
and hardly the most efficient.

It is bad imitation,
     and the forlorn standard
(turned to wormwood and dust)
         becomes
     a full-scale cartoon model
         in the Museum of Science.

Steal it tonight.
Launch it
     from the roof
overlooking the lake.
     Wineskin as a girdle.

Intuition, he thought
is ecstasy,
     waiting to awake.

DUMB PAGEANT

Leonardo, Ludwig, cap. 180

I paint the souls
through articulation of the limbs
and I watch
for instruction
the natural movements
of the dumb.

When the mouth is stopped
the body graces itself to the world
in small motions
quick and deft,
humanities tuned to a singing fork, sung.

They play
in their silence as I play off the palette
in lines cast
to the natural center,
each move anticipated
as a storm or lover

by minds that talk a streak of light,
and yet say nothing
in their sum.

IL ORSO (THE BEAR)

Leonardo, Tr. 70 a

We are like
the black bear, beautiful
as a child, honey-nosed tumbler
simpering in spring.
But we grow, we grow
and sever ourselves to the grove
of thickets, the drought and early frost,
the bulk, burden of scrabbled berries
and a foolhardy charge (king of the forest)
into two violences, necessity
and power.

A stretto of breath
belies our station; campfires
trace the shadow.

As him we sleep one-eyed
in a trough of sprigs and acorns
near the wolf-gnawed hip
of a deer's sorrow and dream that black,
that bruin's dream
of night's incognizant tomorrow.

SCIENCE OF THE WIFE-AND-BABY KILLER
AT HIS SENTENCE

Leonardo, C.A., 123 r. a

The condemned man before God
pulls from his satchel three epithets
written backward and
read only by a mirror.

When asked of his crimes—
dirty dishes, dalliances of pretty men,
punch and pillow,
the sleeping beauty
and the angel boy,
the widowing fisherman and his bags of cement
he answers to the light, asquint:

Weight, force, a blow and impetus are the children of
movement
because they are born from it.

When asked why so long
a list of petty mayhems led to such black symphony
and why, in the end, he was caught so easily, he says:

Weight and force always desire their death
and each is maintained by violence.

When asked why he, in the face
of eternal damning, shows no remorse
and is not kneeling
he can only admit:

Impetus is frequently the cause
why movement prolongs the desire
of the thing moved.

Interesting arguments.
Nonetheless.

He is transferred to the appropriate ring
of hell. Encased in ice,
the devil and he debate the natural
and unnatural laws,
and consider the effect of time
on the movable
and the immovable thing.

SPRAYS OF OAK LEAVES AND ACORNS

Leonardo, Drawing, 1506-08

In their perfect form
the fruit softens to the eye,
each boyish phallic top
a third encased in its coronal cup
and hung, clustered neath
the morning dress of leaves, undulant,
green, even unto the red chalk
of this rendition, grown grateful
to a sap and gravity of seasonal mission
and to settle soon, several to the ground,
with, beyond the full hands
of already wintering squirrels,
deepening the deft forest
beyond the platitude of humankind
with a strength and grace that all except
a kissing rain or wind, belies
the human sound.

MUSICAL DEPARTURE
FROM A NOTE OF ANATOMY

Leonardo, Quaderno IV 9 v

Twenty-eight muscles in the roots of the tongue.

After the kiss,
a small slide in satin.

Twenty-eight bows
for a viol.

COPSE OF BIRCHES

Leonardo, Drawing, 1498-1502

I come from and to
this copse of birches more real
than I, more tactile, deep
and dense than the wood I walked to
in the morning of an old life,
        than the indistinct trunks
of my certainties, this copse, these trees
and what may lie beyond them
ask me to imagine more
than the artist intended or the world provides,
and isn't that irony good, chopped fodder
for a holocaust, a natural fuel
for pagan blaze, for small crosses,
for wine under shade.

ASK THE WIFE OF BIAGINO CRIVELLI

Leonardo, Quaderni III. 7 r

Not alone in that
sense of necessity,
however the demand.

Ask how the capon rears and hatches
the eggs of a hen
when she is in the mating season.

Wife hatches the chickens
by making use of the ovens in the fireplace.

(Those eggs which are of round form
will be cockerels
and the long-shaped ones
pullets.)

The chickens are given into the charge
of a capon which has been plucked
on the under part of its body, and then stung
with a nettle and placed in a hamper.
When the chickens nestle underneath it
it feels itself soothed by the sensation of warmth
and takes pleasure in it

and after this
it leads them about and fights for them,
jumping up into the air
to meet the kite in fierce conflict.

I knew, Bella,
that it was not only me.
I sing of the charity of pigeons,
and the sacrifice.

AN ASS AND A COW

Leonardo, Study, 1478

It was a century of ten thousand nativities,
and each artist prepared a catalog.
Here, he starts with a cow and ass,
and the ass is half-disappeared
in the dream of having carried Mary to legend—
      both beasts attentive as actors,
as children examined of their Latin,
the horizon of their gaze
off the page.

Baby Jesu, immaterial just then.
(He shall be incorporated later.)

For fun we can call the ass Giocopo
and the cow, Liberti. What they are looking at—
the shine of a Magi crown
      or hilted dagger, a sheaf of oats or timothy,
an oncoming landscape, or God,
we are unsure.

Today, and for point of argument
you can be, if not a wise man, Giocopo,
and I can be Liberti.

Let us assemble our manger slowly.
But assemble it.

ON MINDS AND THE NOONWARD RACE

Leonardo, Codice Atlantico 204 v. a

Radiance, heat, image.

The mind passes in an instant
from east to west
and all the great incorporeal things
        resemble these closely—
the shrike in its sylvan dive
impaling the mouse devoutly,
the unfolding of bells and heaven
        across the campagna,
opinions of popes, the iris of eye
of the dissolute man, his yawn
of no particular hope, a life so planned
        on palisades of wet

Sorrento sand, its sea that sunders
tumbling into each demand, impenetrable
to penetrating scope,
        played
off a godhead's circumspect
        serenity and stand, darting
among shadows to the high sun, gone
that which was at once, at most
and once again
so close at hand.

TWO MINUTES OF A LOST CONVERSATION
WITH THE DUKE OF MILAN

Leonardo, drawings, 1487 and 1491

Excellency,

I harness horses middle to the scythes
in front, scythes in back, and as the wheels
trailing hinds will turn, so steely blades
will wheel and whir across the terrible air.

One of these will decimate good order
while our gay-plumed rider combs his hair.

And Excellency,

I can fashion sorts of sloping milk-bowls
ironclad with oak to buffet blows
and gears to speed these dreaded naughts along
in sunder of the pointed palisades;

octets of men will smite through holes with brilliant
cannonade the unresisting throngs.

But yes, Excellency, the *Festa,* the songs!

According to your will, apart from questions
of conquest and defense, a marvelous
mechanic bull that snorts a purple brimstone,
turns about in perfect circles to amaze
even the most sullen conspirator,

and twenty-three original fool costumes,
in styles your guests will press to face and savor,
tacked of organdies and silks purloined
from chests of Marco Polo, still the brightest
bolts of red and orange ever known.

OF THE RELATIVITY OF BIG AND SMALL

Leonardo, BM 19 r

It is not so big a world
as cannot be known and somewhat conquered;
it trembles in its spin,
its blue wildness, but nonetheless.

The earth is moved by the weight
of a tiny bird resting upon it.

The finch is therefore master of a globe
and sings of it in verse
each fine morning,
even as the stem of the poplar
shivers of its enormity, slightly,
and ground smiles
its grave awakening.

ABOUT THE GROTESQUE HEADS

Leonardo, sketches. c. 1490

Sometimes I gall
at the flimsy compliments on these commissions.
It is not hard to paint, really.
Rather, it is hard to find subjects
one wishes to explore beyond
the blunt chalk of an afternoon.
In any regard I am compensated, and somewhere in the well
one always finds an angel, drenched, or a madonna.
And so as it is possible to wrest
beauty in increments from a plain face,
it is easy to magnify the ugly feature in proportion
to my dislike.

Eight heads.
These are the last eight people I thought not much of.
Actually, the center one is me,
just to be just. A bad day.
Should one prefer the monkey to the pig,
the anteater to the hound?
The beholder sees,
though blindly, blackened
by flatterers along the way.

HEAD OF A MAN IN A HELMET

Leonardo, study for costume, c. 1491

There is the unfortunate nature of accuracy.

What he means by the helmet
cocked above the head, that it carries a face,
    and that face appears to be the same
as the face of its wearer, and becomes the same
thing evident as you and I, in all our candor,
pull mask from headdress to reveal
    faces, countenanced with similar,
different lies to which we had just feigned
abandonment. Love and piety come to dance
by invitation. And in this static duplicity
we free each other to the semblance,
    sporting the visage on helmet or coronet
and beneath, to steps of renaissance,
the *ballo,* comes a prayer, three lutes,
acceptance without guarantee.

THE VEIN IS ONE WHOLE

Leonardo, Fogli A 4 r

Clutching the earth
like a ball of sand
the vein is vein of one hand pulsing whole
and vast as a corridor from Fiorenze
to Trieste, aqueducts and pinpricks,
boulevards and vias, alleyways
blushing to the smallest of address, teemed
with aspiring and life.

The vein of a man
and man of his vein, clipped
at the mother's gate
into swaddle on a cold night,
grows with each suck to a forest of poplars
on his own promenade of blind luck,
to meet into flesh a woman
cast and carried on a vein, one vein herself
in majesty conjoined
and splayed to a future, to branch
on branch, moving the sap
of anointing, the race of red
into its own gay stretch
of populating vein, inviscerate in its generation,
in a hundred, thousand generations of whole,
of one blood, one vein, one line
of innumerable vessels that are one vessel,
one drip, a dripping stain reporting
to a sacred heart, one all and all-uncircumventing
passion of the same.

"The vein is one whole, which is divided into as many main branches as there are principal places which it has to nourish, and these branches are subdivided into an infinite number."

CARD HOUSE STRONG LIKE TYRE

Leonardo, Codice Atlantico 244 v. a

Two weaknesses leaning together
create a strength;
therefore the half of the world
leaning against the other
becomes firm.

For a quarter century
(fleck in the eye of God
but of some length to small sights)
we have leaned,

buttress right and left
communed to fall upon themselves
but yet supported in a miracle
to house the frescoes
of creation.

It is not so weak, lest
it consider itself strong.

The earth quakes,
the eaves drop their mortar,
yet it stands. And it will fall
only from its prides, not its tears,
it will leaven dust on a day
when judgment falls
to the horns of archangels;
the institution and sacrament
wafered into reality and sacrifice

goes on amongst the tourists
and appraisers, a monument
poised to ruin, yet shivering
ever to erect itself
in the light of a benediction.

§

FOUR DEADBOLTS LEFT OF GEHENNA

In my alternative universe

we go to the SaveMart,
meander past silk flowers and rotisseries
to the blue aisle and the pegboards
that cinch the world
to tolerances of a thousandth of an inch,
dropping the steel Yale deadbolts
into our basket.

The cost is $43.96
for all four.

We pass them on to men
of little means named Julio,
Fernand, George and Ralph
and they
affix these with their portable drills
and screwdrivers
to separate doors
in separate cities.
It takes seventeen minutes
since they are talented—
all four.

These are employed
to make doors not open.

Because of this
the planes do not fall.

The twin inhabited
pillars of salt, massive
as a heart
do not dissolve.
The eyes look, the ears hear,
the days bought back
go by the wheel like water
in accordance of another seer.

No need for extra checkpoints,
painting of irises
with accusatory light,
not much trouble
from the swarthy types,
advised of entrances
made chaste on wayward flights.
No untoward wars among the goatpaths,
tyrants left to their lieutenants
and their syphilis, their milling throngs
to time when birds of septic paradise
fly out the pages of real Qu'ran.

In my universe
regret, the alkali, neutralizes outrage
and common sense
blooms among the magnolias.
My universe
(and I admit as much)
all depends, and just depends
on simple locks
accorded simple men with keys,
unwinding the
impossible clocks.

A GRAFT OF APPLES

For centuries to tell—
a blithe horticulture, raked of graves.
Seed of the Smith-Jones apple will produce an apple tree.
But it will not produce
a Smith-Jones apple tree.

Ghost-fruit of our ancestors
cluster and speck unnatural crimson
in other orchards, seaward, foreign.
We are as native as the knife can cut,
the tar, seal.

The growers cared too much—
crotch formation for the understock,
the young and vigorous best for topworking.
Beware of rot.
(A whip-graft sometimes takes, sometimes not.)
Sometimes the union is unholy, of false protection,
a pasty coating applied with a brush.
Some say: you removed the wraps too soon,
just as we started to grow— girdled the tree— rabbits follow.
Others rail
release was not in time.

A basket of reasons—
scion and stock repulsive, no apple with plum!
It was the wrong season— we were not vigorous,
dry, lowed by chill and frost.

(Most grow best with prayer, in Northern clime.)

But as with fire-blight's indecision,
sever six inches below the visible symptoms.
Assure that seemliness to persevere,
brother and sister of later confection
latticed in hallelujah's
misdirection— the pale admirers of character
throng a marketplace street
to feel and pick the halest, sweetest orbs
of this, American vivisection.

CRAWFISH AMONG THE LANDED OF JACKSON

The mound on the kitchen cutting board
invites ritual; they call me to it with the grace
of tradition, lovely hosts.

There is a human, dark, eglantine
raised from the cracks of neat southern streets
heartless as hedge-clippers, quietly insane.

Best to bend the head and twist,
like this, like a straw, siphon, savor
the juice of its small being.

Beneath the pile, *The Clarion-Ledger* examines
crumbling infrastructure, Medgar Evers' name
appended to signs at the airport.

He shakes his head about that, the roads
and bridges, I assume. There is talk of
a murder trial, white killing black.

Used to be there was no trouble here;
they wanted work, knew what to do,
they liked us and we liked them, she said.

There's no respect, that's what gets you.
It's time to go. And thank you. Through
the porch door, the white swing moves.

Crickets stand, attending without surrender.
In dusk the pretty doors all seem unpainted.
Moses, Pharaoh, such an old story.

The paper said the Woodrow Wilson Bridge,
above the Pearl River which affords me now,
is, itself, in no danger of collapse;

this, I think, the crawfish know.

BLUES

after Gwendolyn Brooks

Young boys, young boys.
More blue murder.

Too many days
(with your best clothes on)—
the miserable pretty pray.

    Oh Lord.

Black, the tan
poor-white and the Chinese man
remain a one-song choir
for an audience of night—
across the daylight, sorry.

    Too many.

Lord says pick yourself up.
Go on down the lane.

Wrap this up in twelve
tight bars. Turn again

and play.

AND WITH FIRE

Age ignites a returning
to green gardens and panoramas,
to villas of biography.
Andantes cross like deft swans
the pool of our reflection, the sated smile,
recompense.

But I would propose a discourtesy
to the images that hound and mortify
and still, if dwelled on like a mystic,
bring tears.

I shall repair to them, disguised
in dress and empathy, with tucked away
dry yarrow sticks useless save to flame and ember,
and vial of alcohol pungent
in its clarity of remembering,
to set fire to the anteroom drapes,
the basement boxes full of masks.

All there— the time we betrayed each other,
mansion of the nouveau riche
going up like tinder, bit players flying through
windows.
Factories of useless subordination,
embarrassing tenements
shacked of laughing, the laughter
turned to piccolo cries
of *save-me,* all right, the ladder here,
now find you live elsewhere, eel!

Acts of drink and recrimination
in the theater of grave children, sorry
in their holiday frocks and trousers,
hiding under beds— pulled free
of their few lines and brought to the
autograph alley, as the place
smokes and radiates the cause and effect
of falling stage lights, a flashpoint,
the cattle-like evacuation
into nothingness.

They search for me in the squares,
but the sketches are all wrong.
It continues throughout bad summers
and sledded winters, across incorrect years.
I have been Saladin, my dear.

Now when we look back, at least for me
and as long as I can trick the unwinking moon,
the times play reminiscence
and are quilted into dreams of the best colors,
fabrics, the major chords, sweet breaths,
indomitable resolutions. I will share as much of this
as I can, and say nothing of the fires,
vague headlines only which now,
I seem almost to have forgotten.

We should *all* have such wonderful lives.
And matches, matches.

MISS JONES

In the last frames
of a famous blue movie
intransigent nudes punished as suicides
try and try, failing to finish.
For eternity they will attract each other
just enough to join in the futility
of their manipulation,
and wail the ingenious
ecstasy that is empty pain.

Right now, across the rainy evening
blotted of moon and gaslit
to a windy squall, I could
take the phone book, voluminous
as the numbers of Nineveh
before the retribution,
and call a hundred women
who would writhe and wrest
a conclusion from my voice, unguent,
urgent, until their eyes
flamed and their hearts leapt
in the wet of their convalescence,
their newness.

I would have only to summon it.

And they, their voices coiled
in the antiphon of pleading
would have me rise, godlike
and shower the dense stars

with all the clarion that precedes a fall,
the animal delight that leaves
religion to its gutter,
with nothing that passes
in this world for something
and disappointed, drop
a desperate pair of ones
to the valley of the shadow
fearing no elaborate evil
or its opportunity.

A HORSE THIEF, A HANGING, AND A CRYING GIRL

It is not the same at 48.

I have become, in glass
and off-hand photograph, an unkept
waxy figure of the notorious me,
destined off its pedestal at change of owners
for some more current rapscallion
or cad, or top-draw murderer
in the unlit corner of an unnecessary museum,
in a western town
not important enough to name.

It is time for swinging.
My boots click novas to a moon,
my buckle willed
to a Spanish livery-boy.

Save the tears, darlin'.
Collect them, feed the violets
in your window. We get what we deserve;
the appaloosa was lovely but
all mounts are temporary, a wash
filled in a snowstorm. What we value
and kill for as a hand of hearts
is a psalm from an insincere
mourner, a whistle, a shovel,
a rolled cigarette.

If you love me, forsake me.

Shake the silver from the last,
lean leather that I owned
outright, kiss the air of subtle going,
take this tether in your hands
and to the evening of our destiny
let it fall, and in its falling

wake me to a tinhorn light,
glowing.

WALLACE STEVENS

Tapped a Sheaffer green
marble-finish fountain pen, the butt-end
against a leather shoulder
of the blotter on his
mahogany battleship of desk—
cool in grey gabardine,
warm from the long sip of his Autocrat
coffee.

His choice was:
pursuant to surety bond
of a city block, imburse
the Chinese launderer
whose 57th Street palace-of-pressing
burned in a semi-suspicious
morning conflagration (in which an upstairs
relative died a human torch), or
as his investigators
and several ambitious underlings urged,
wall it off, stretch it,
go to court if necessary
and fight the babbling Chinaman
with the weight of Protestantism
and a battery of New England granite—
everything this building still upholds.

> The Chinaman spins on his Oriental celadon—
> even as he burns within.

Wallace Stevens' signature paid the claim,
modest for the time, and he returned
to a turned-over legal pad,
making French curves with
his Sheaffer, green
marblesque pen full of blue-black India,
watching the first Yangtze
and its tributaries map the adjacent window
with October rain.

ENOUGH OF THE BLUE GUITAR

My blue period came and went
with the shortage of sienna;
tears are unique only to reptiles.
Humans dance and paint blurry-eyed with them
and wail in seventh chords,
open-tune to the misery of being alive
as if they'd rather be dead.

But a stone hears no music,
no bent notes or glasscock glissandos
through ears of a stone head.

Wake up!

The old man who strums upon his heart
has survived his children,
buried his wife and the innocence
that came with the first pint of semen,
thrown away calendars
with parts of him noted in the squares.
He has left, he thinks,
these six strings, variation
and theme.

He is a cliché; so are
poems with blue guitars,
Blind Lemon Jeffersons,
Spanish paintings so cobalted into misery
you pay to see the superlative
spiraling down.

I am walking in the October sun.
Done with the azure brush, the solo run.
This is my last, up-tempo blues.

My last one.

SHOSTAKOVICH COMPOSES IN LENINGRAD, 1944

The notes stand as beggars in a bread queue
on a soggy street, St. Petersburg in May.
They file to their slight filling,
mouths open and sing their solitude
up into threnodies, bombard
the staves with their attentive drive,
each one bald or bonneted, relentless
empty silhouettes, or blackly furious
following their flags.

They slash into the owned body of the Russian people,
rebels, infants of icon, and slaves united in the orthodoxy
of the pocketed Marya, of mother and country,
doing godless and individual things among masses
of sound.

Will the demagogue like it? Is he around?

The page is flipped as bows glissando
into a pool on a melted steppe,
and schoolgirls are hidden
from marauders.

It ends quietly enough,
the vestiges of piano haunting the literate
mind
that is illiterate in the face
of carnage,
that is flecked with wizened blood
and the loss of fortissimo,

the clouds
over the felled horse,
the decayed rider,
his tumbled book
of psalms.

EDIFICE (IN THE RAIN)

Continuing old poems
I have returned to this place,
again confounded by its all-right-angles,
the smooth cold of reflection.
You make up its whole,
and against its ebon sides, enclosed against
the storm, I can play a triple-header,
my ball to bounce so
cleanly, my invented infield stabbing
mosquitoes with a frog's tongue.
I play so many innings waiting for you,
the ball against the fence, the fence gone,
the house sold to strangers.

You have many faces here, drunk from
the wash of years, the television square that
so describes you. Old Pete, who cut his teeth
on a branding iron. Dan Matthews of
the Highway Patrol.

Out of the clear blue of the western sky comes...
Sky King and his niece Penny, whom I think
I married.

I never saw you cry, just occurred to me.
And my children have never seen me cry. Just
occurred to me too, and not yet to them.

But the face— so many heroes would be cliché.
Just as many Jack Elams, Anthony Zerbes, Henry Silvas,

villains who died a hundred times each,
felled by Ben Cartwright,
or the stern, widowed Rifleman (who wanted so much
to cry and cry). Each was flawed, I thought, left
in a bowery by their mother, torn photo
tucked in a gunbelt.

They are all you to me because metaphor is easy,
poetry is easy, and reaching you is hard.
I am building my own place,
hardly a taj, just down the street, square by square.
I hope for others it will be a welcoming place,
with a Poet's Corner of no Dryden or Gay,
with the same contradictions, a place to think,
to marry oneself to yesterday,
divorce it, pray.

The rain has stopped. And goodbye is superfluous.
Pretend with me.
See you when you get home, okay?
See you when you get home.

SAPPHIRE BULLETS OF PURE LOVE

title suggested by John McLaughlin

They say he died smiling
shot through with sapphire
bullets of pure love, rattled from
a magazine of secrets,
that his heart exploded
and became a radiant afterthought,
that the pooling beneath him
was the color of tourmalines
and that opal, flecked with turquoise
were his tears.

THERE ARE SPRITES OF THE PITIES

There are sprites of the pities, as there are
sprites of love; they soft-alight the shoulders
of the lost, while others of the lovers
only, dress and talk appropriate their part.

Pity-ones are purply with black trim,
lovie-kind a brilliant pink, with gauze
in the accouterment; they whistle wide
their call, while brothers brood a hymn.

There is a navy of them; elect of old,
their roles against the urge to re-inhabit
so-embodied souls engender comfort
or a cheer against the warm, or cold;

I've whistled with a brightened one along
thinking all the world was limbed upon
a nightingale's song then found, at last
to be so utter and completely wrong

as tears would fashion from the real ether
graves of satisfacting pride, and measure
fit discomfiting for those who lose
their all within a moment of ill weather.

Commiserate, ambassador and me;
we fold our invitations of reunion,
setting all our boats to greenward drift
and one sweet square of calendar to see

the swift or subtle shift again, when youth
recalls its dancing onto bitter shore,
and every sprite-and-man can yet reside
within a single happiness, and truth.

NARRATIVE FOR A NUDE POSTCARD

"Men seldom make passes at girls who wear glasses."
— D. Parker

In the photo, circa 1924
she sidewise kneels on the divan,
orb of her bottom cushioning hidden heel,
the other exposed, right instep flat
against plush, just revealing
the tip of toes.

Her torque of thirty degrees,
the arc of hip,
the accent navel, nipple, prayerful knees,
arms spread in tilted crucifix
to leftward light, inverts the V
of the casual, empty left hand
with one that holds open
at length from bottom of spine
the only extant edition of Millay's *Renascence,*
opiate eye
fixed to a verse on page 18—
Strange how few,
After all's said and done, the things that are
of moment.

Strange how in 1999,
I drew to this book (this one)
in an Albuquerque bookstore,
green cloth frayed at edge
but legible as lovenotes
left on ferries and I,

having received this curious
quaint postcard from you,
now realize in another life
I had taken the picture,
posed her among sprigs and books
and pillows as some prelude
to an understanding, and that when
we were through with the
figura dolce, I walked
a man enraptured into her meaningful embrace,
unfolded the V of her thighs,
her heels at my shoulders
and face to my face, sheathed
this trilling heat and her willing why
into thrall of an afternoon,
touched at the soft core of her
emollient self with a self-dousing fire
and *we were those lines,*
that photo, devour of time,
that light, those shades of grey
that were really vermillion,
cerule, the pink of Arctic salmon,
vair and eglantine
the eternal, ephemeral cast
of articulate flesh, the
flash of discomfiting rhyme.

I WOULD RATHER MAKE LOVE TO MY WIFE

Than write.
I would rather not write another line.
I'd rather, all in all, see the garbage collected weekly
than read your new things, and that is selfish.
But I would rather the garbagemen
were artists at what they did,
fling with élan, and be painted by Hopper.
I would buy that picture
and then go home, and yes, make love,
love down the hall from the picture,
forgetting it.
And I would rather
she think my love as fathomless
as cello's descent
in a Beethoven quartet she would never listen to
because there is a time and a place,
but I will settle.

All these issues!
It's just, you understand—
you write so well—
I would rather make love to my wife.
The rest is a poem about art
and artists, written by
someone else.

SUGAR RAY ROBINSON

Sweet as
sweetbeet sugar,
everything cleaned and pressed.

174-19-6. 103 KOs.

Fast and pretty, pitiless.
The Cadillac, pink, is parked.

Sure, I stayed too long.
But they say I was
blessed.

At the end I was
maybe too old to realize
        a coward
needs something to fear
to be at his best.

Nubile shadows
once the dowry of my energy
        and ambition
seem to rest as the dark fills in.
Their laughter
reinvigorates my folly
of belief
that sincerity precedes sin.

I stand in the rain, all wet—
keep a clutch of good

                    crisp climaxes,
          undated signs of sorrow and regret,
stuffed into overstuffed boxes
of French cigarettes.
I was white, man,
on my Harlem thoroughfare

it's easy to forget—
swing right, stay light
slick hair
slicked back, whack

back
          to black, blue-black
like a bootblack's ass
naked, pocketless
poster of the past.

Feet in molasses, one long breath,
bells wake me
in my sleep, sleep me
          into death,
spray-paint the night
with all that Sugar

decorate hell
with a wicked left.

RECKONING

I am watching the strewn wrecks
of twenty years' abandon
multiply in panorama
among the gulls, the children we are
no longer playing safely.

In this harmonic of the fourth decade
we lose our minds
to the apparency of what was missed
while we were busy gaining,
crying in beds of our passion
and the births of our legacy, of the half-
dozen thousand nights
where at least one thing
that wasn't spinning lay beside us.

Now it bores, it stains
with accusation, it regrets,
it becomes furniture bound
for shrouds and cobby lace.

Such is the fashionable amnesia.

We dive for flattery as if it were bread,
the pockets of our emotions
picked as we stoop, strive
for the re-and-reinvigoration
of things that sing and vibrate,
we clap our hands,
we tarantella badly.

And tonight perhaps, this night
we kill our lives for a newness
known by fugitives.
Then, the hours on, we'll lie awake
(on left side stead of right),
not with that piper-so-enticing
but some later migrant
of the cucumbers, to recall
a single curtain of stars
permanent for undeserving vows
and dreamlike, catching wind
above such sea of years to free
inside its bond of persevering

all that were the reasons
to be proud.

FAREWELL, GOOD RABBIT

Once I sat in Vegas
with a blue martini while the conjuror
separated people from their heads
and their bottom halves walked about the stage;
he drove a Corvette through the air.

I enjoy the awe
of my newest stupidity and really,
I miss the ball in the fingers,
the coin behind the ear;
I am a dutiful audience nonetheless,
and similarly pleased.

I often sit among celebrities in the parlors of their minds
watching the automobiles float.

I pay strangers my trust.
My own expertise with rabbits,
freely given, is purloined for a thousand acts
in small venues.

Use the bigger hat I say,
and the white one prefers carrots.
The folks will love you
in the adorableness expended
of a good rabbit, and
the curl of purple smoke.

But please, I am not offended.
Be careful; the big time can be cruel,
and don't do the torture cell!

The glass will mirror you, and what you see
will unnerve you, and you'll forget
where the latches are
in that clarity of upside-down,
and pure water will fill you to the toes
in genuflection.

STATION

Occasionally, we strand our Jesus
at the station;
in the saturate amber
of morning,
break our fast with assassins
and plan to do away
with *evil* in the world.

Not for us but for our legacy
heave the cold hail
at those who will their treachery,
our lovers and suppliants
left to a wonder, an empty outline,
a happenstance unexplained,
till the eyes' gates in sweet
eminence fail

and only He remains.

SESTINA FOR THE SIXTIETH PSALM

And my legions fall, prostrate or scattered
in the distant mist, lines turned to breaches
nulled in reach from the far face of holiness
and sickened to a man, the right, the left hand
waving to surrender before our pledged city?
Wanting, wallowed at progress of their armies,
the cold, clank regimenting of their armies
disciplined in death and refusing to be scattered
in the ply of patience that takes a city—
darkly marshaled foot-falls find our breaches,
shed resolve, cuff the even hand,
aspire to defy the bond of holiness
and by such crimes belie that holiness,
ring in the hollow of unwilling armies
raised to prop or splint the shaking hand
yet render self as fodder to be scattered
like a fist of rye in windy breaches—
seeds that fall on stone in an empty city.
Wine-astonished vision! blur the city
to the hallow of your word, your holiness
to turn two allies tight to four in breaches
and to lines affront these foreign-facing armies
unto salt of Edom's valley; scattered
as a flame with iron-casting hand
(to burn the dead denials with that hand!)—
your wake, the smoking stubble of their city,
right reversing, rigor black and scattered
at the rally of the hours of our holiness,
their gray and green disintegrated armies
offer mortared walls that mark their breaches
to testament, to the apex of their breaches,

offering sequestered peace with open hand
and glint of word translating arms and armies
into hilted swords, salvation of a city
and a city yet recalled, within your holiness—
its own stone heart, its landbound pride, scattered
to the banners flown, to shepherd-scattered
armies in your hand and heal in balm of holiness
the breaches of belief of man, and city.

OF ORCHARDS, INTIMACY

You think we halve jubal fruit
to get at the beads, that we flame into gutters
to satisfy an insatiable, insentient need;

true, a few admire the triplicate mirror,
count women, caught between tissues of pride
and greed but these are uncounted,
no person more memorable
than a dried seed.

I think the men that oared for Troy
were idealists; died for the concept
of intimacy, the moment, in word
or look or touch when we slip into
another's countenance and feel God, any God
in the one shiver of true acquiring,
in the true orchard of living trees.

THE DAMSON SONG

There is a poem that exists
in the half-light of its morning,
that strolls a broad
flat space hearing its heels
click soft on pavement,
that awaits a population
of objects that are beautiful,
odd to each other
but purposeful in their strange
levity, their fortunate being.

Here we are now, within the outside,
arriving from the right periphery
of the poet's eye;
it is not warm, this place, yet
no jacket is required; I would
wrap my blue one round you if it were,
turning slightly
to that new sun, source illuminate
at our shoulders
giving us slow time.

To this small orb, what happens is:
what didn't come before, but
to the others, did, curls its damson-pink
and severed skin until
the flow of its élan
sweets down to wrists of
our own sepal-hands, and drips

itself to separate
ground, standing us so ever still,
subject new, of so-old songs.

THE RAGA OF CHOICES

with consideration of Sant Kirpal Singh

And so the man was sentenced to
a hundred lashes
      or
eating of a hundred onions.
He takes the onions, eats ten
      as the eyes water, water
and he says, no, how about the lashes!
He is certain this taste will be better
but they are pain of a different
etch and after ten it's no, the onions!
With ten more orbs the
stomach convulses— bring me the lash!
      And so it goes on.

A man is faced with a
beautiful woman
      at full flower and devours her,
savor and scent. Each day
for hours he immerses himself in her—
ten days go by and he is offered
the alternative of a slice
      of the best cream pie.
No he says, but on the tenth month
of the tenth day, he says yes.
It is the best cream pie and each day,
another piece. But no woman.
This goes on for ten days then,
the woman burns in his memory.

I deny this pie, good as it is,
give me the woman.

The woman is gone.
And for his fickle nature
the man is sentenced, as is custom,
to one hundred lashes.

Or a hundred onions.

RESPONSE OF THE DONKEY-MAN

I am like his bobo, Alcorizo the critic;
I write well sometimes, but am gullible.
When Buñuel points me to the tree below the crag,
I see an eaglet in the nest
                    and fire.
The price tag on its fat, stuffed leg smells of my tormentor.
And how he laughs.
Then the restaurant.
Such a woman! Her gaze across tables
knots me with the lust of a schoolboy. Forgive me Buñuel!
I must speak with her! Forgive me! She and I must go—
                    don't be angry, Buñuel!
Yes, like Alcorizo,
I elope with every dream
split wide on hotel bedrooms sliced
with moonlight, my tongue a scythe
from lover's tit to belly
and just at the navel I read the lipstick:
                    "from your friend, Buñuel."
The whore snickers. But unlike Alcorizo,
shameless tongues like mine
resume their southern slide
into the film of my silly self,
surreal.

TRUSTING THE MOROCCAN, 1974

" ... and besides, how could anyone be so
idiotic as to open himself to the dangers
involved in telling the unadorned truth to people?
You even have two pockets in your kif pouch—
one for the kif you smoke yourself and one for
the less good you give your friends."

— Paul Bowles, American expatriate

At a low table
teased with flame of a green candle
and the smoke of sandalwood
we eat fresh *majoun*
(a spread of boiled kif,
wheat paste and currants)
on old soda crackers
and listen to the storyteller
as I fumble for pencils on the rug.

In a mountain language
unwritten and far from Arabic
he is translated to say
it is not a good morning—

> *I have syphilis of the mouth*
> *tuberculosis of the liver*
> *cancer of the heart*
>
> *and on the way here*
> *three Spaniards confronted me*
> *and kicked my teeth out*

as he smiles toothily
and sips
the strong tea.
Tangier is a prism of brown
light split into reds and tans
and the account that follows

I fail to remember.

REVERIE OF THE WHOLE EARTH CATALOG

I. And We Shall Inherit

A root cellar crafted of barrel and trench
to keep the collards fresh all winter.

Where to place blows for a lap weld.

The key to firing steel which betrays a rainbow,
light yellow, straw yellow, purple blue
back to gray, and then dull red. With red
comes the allowance of it bending and twisting
without a break— it goes to sunrise red,
maraschino, even brighter red, almost orange
then white. It starts to *glow*
white, ascending to its liquid self, yellow again
but incandescent. More heat brings sparks
and the metal is burning as if it were
gopherwood before the storm,
too hot to work, save to hammer.

Card and inkle-weaving, Osage braiding
bag and backstrap looms.

How to true a footing.

Stockpile tins of Multipurpose Food
from a bomb shelter in Wisconsin.

Package of bees with one
bred Italian queen.

A soft ring of inflatable pillows
designed to commune souls
in play or seminars. Inexpensive alternative
to institutional furniture.

A manure gas plant complete with latrines—
process of anaerobes turns everything
to carbon and methane, lighting the house,
humming the refrigerator and the modified
John Deere!

Herter's Yukon folding sleds.
Eddie Bauer Frogman Mitts.

A way of locating the lode
by panning. Flags erected mark the spot
on which colors are found in the pan.

The hearing helper helps you hear your hounds.

This: you must corner a square-logged house
so the joints will drain.

A tier-shelf bed for dung and mushrooms,
sugar-baby melons on trellises.

A roof, truncated iscosahedron
to resist the snow.

The way to spade adobe into wooden forms—
dry the bricks, stack them loosely
to cure in the sun.

A mix of turnbuckles.

The best bread, from wheat ground just before baking.
A carborundum
grinding stone lasts forever.
(It will be recovered by silver men
after the next star falls,
and they'll know we ate well.) The best wheat?
Deaf Smith County, Texas.

*II. Just as the Negress Sees Herself for the First Time
in a Good Mirror*

So they gather
in the Palace of Fine Arts
to divide the unspoils
in a round of democracy.

Amid volleyball
and styrofoam swordfights,
sticks of sandalwood
curl yellow-black from
their smoky ends
a call to order.

"20,000 dollars and what to do with it."
They mark up the big board.

World game.

Original big people's research computer.

San Francisco free
school.

Divide equally among many projects.
Population control/education.

Essay/speech contest on...

Film / Hopi land
protection.

Free all political prisoners.

More wine.

THRUSH, UNINDICTING

The thrush does not debate the light
that wakens it;
its glassy highs not forced, the swell cajoled
or cadence managed by circumstance.
It sings, merely.

On avenue of our regrets
and the failed waves of
dead struck anvils in the mind, the self so serious
and centered as to cancel a season—
around that such of us, there and up
about the wire, a thrush relays
his sarabande.

Sadness, we deign, comes painted
to the lampposts and taxi doors,
to the sidewalk and elm,
to heavy bark
to branch but not the reddened breast upon it,
shivering with sound.

Sing! it says—
you were made for me
to trill through such indulgent lenses
common, calm, thrilled beauty.
Come, or I, awaiting on
to strike of eight tomorrow
neath that eastern shadow, blackly green
in its anonymous intent will healing drift,

a spendthrift spent for you to say again
what lovely song,

what sweet lament.

SEA SONG, SUNG ON A BALTIC FERRY

The Estonia, September 28, 1994

The interesting thing
as they bobbed alike behind windows
or were pulled in grim inventory
from the cold sea
was the rarity of single spouses
who survived.

"The strong remained with the weak"
and for these, do not mourn.
There had been decisions, and great fortune.

Better than the vow,
the clean rings gleaming,
the first climax in the screaming night,
the times of creation, the aspects
of success and memory
was this singular god-gift
just next to salvation—
that see, love is real, *really* real
that now we demonstrate
and sing it into the salt
of our fluid being and walk heaven's prow
coupled into eternity,
our names face-up and floating
on the manifests and papers,
we stay an element, a green wave, a tide,
a morning of pink sun,
a confirmation.

NOT THE EVE OF SAINT AGNES

At that time
when the day dabs black into its brightnesses,
the tweed of noises
unravels into disparate threads
that tie up nothing
and lose, each to silence, and you decide
whether to love me like a failed angel
some hours hence, and the children
find the places in the cubes
of their own memory
that will forget, in end, most of all of us,
I hope you will say yes.

And we genuflect.
Or I genuflect and you bestow
what have you on the limber cork
of our floating bed, that has floated
several centuries of seas it seems,
or seems in one flecked opal instant
new as a Florida honeymoon,
the currants sweet, the palms green
replete with those who saw us off,
relatives and guests now lost, whispered
into gray or dead, yet found
within its welcome circle
faces of these self-same boys, or girl
who earn their sleep in a fine house of flowers,
ringed with night-lights
and the unused trumpet of morning,
its sound a kingdom come among

the company we keep,
among the brilliant blacknesses,
the dawning.

HAIL CAESAR

His was a life of stupidity and resolve,
the like of a man who would kick himself
in his own balls
and revel in the splendor
of the attempt.

He is not alone.

His legions manifest
their formations
across broad boulevards
heading south to the Forum,
hopscotching in armor to the tribute
of women, themselves felled by their own ambitions
and itchy feeling,
corsets and camisoles in flight.

Let us pray, slightly, for successors.

Writing old history poses the difficulty
of no paper, or ink, no original light,
no readers or considerers,
only stiff binders opening like the legs
of forgotten girls and unkept mothers
pageless to past and unprofitable,
birthing possible motives,
dim passages, destinations
afire on sight.

We have returned. For what.

Rubicons are narrow streams
easy to manipulate and cross,
not unlike emptying oneself of the previous night,
playing with warm gravity
against a stone,
hardly momentous.

But Hail! The real story. The O's
of *O what might.*

MEMOIRS OF THE CHEVRON REFINERY, RICHMOND, CALIFORNIA, 1978

I. Isomax (Part One)

Barry and Dave tell us we can do it.
Bruce and I will try.

In an Oakland library, I study a book on plumbing.

Just say: "We were with Dave Vick on the Utah job."

I don't know what the foreman
of Coast Counties Construction asked Bruce.
But the man eyes me like new bait
and when he asks, I blurt, indignant,
"well, I'm no 'A' fitter
if that's what you want."

(I was no 'B' fitter either. I could maybe change a tire.)

Hired, I find myself the next midnight,
on a ladder without harness,
forty-pound toolbag across my back,
holding on with one hand
sixty feet off the ground,
tightening bolts on the side of a furnace
with my inch-and-a half open wrench
the size of my arm,
brick-stacks flaming jet fuel
to the right and left and me

actually doing, somehow,
the most dangerous job
in America for thirteen-
fifty an hour.

II. Isomax (Part Two)

The smell of garbage-pail eggs
always, everywhere, here.

Safe enough they say,
unless you open a line
into your face
and a whiff will
expand your brain into your skull,
bleed out your eyes
and turn you to a turnip.

Today I work a maze of small pipes
to get to a joint, to loose the opposites,
pull the Flexitallic gasket for a new one,
tighten up, the way I came.

Going back
I bang my hard hat,
explode my glasses,
lean on a hot steamline
for a moment's bacon,
endure
a slapstick treasure.

III. Five Cat

Picture the incessant sniff of a ripped-open can of motor oil,
sticking your nose in it.

And having some African bug.

I spend an hour in a hot port-o-let,
releasing from every letter O,
and suddenly understand Dante
in Italian. *I am in hell.*

Virgil-my-savior accompanies
Barry and Dave, their shift over,
and I lie with the tools in back
of a Dodge Ram pickup.

IV. Isomax (Part Three)

This is rich.

Bruce and I scale the side
of a heat exchanger; I leave
him a story below, go
with Shorty to the top.

In minutes we smell the sweet irises
of another planet, and look
to each other, knowing we shouldn't.

At the edge I see Bruce has fallen,
not awake, to a plank that kept him alive.
I don't recall the ladder, only reaching him.
On his feet, we all look round
and try to breathe.

On the ground, surprise.
A spaceman in a Scott-Air suit
is blowing some nitrogen compound
into the intakes. Error
on a clipboard:

Ha. We weren't supposed to be there.

V. The Phenol Plant

There are showers everywhere
just in case you—
open a line that says "down"
and isn't, like this one.
The back of one guy
remaining faceless to me forever
runs for water.
Puzzled, I look at the leather
covering my fingers,
wet, dark, and mushing up.

Pulling off my glove,
I see the fingertips of an eighty-
year-old man, one
without prints, for a while.

VI. HF Alky

Walking past
The Ammonia Plant which bugs the eyes,
pinches the nose,
we come to and skirt the edge
of the forbidden.

At HF Alky you work
with a full suit, tied at the cuffs.

Hydrofluoric acid.

Shorty says:
"If you get a drop of this
on your bare arm
they don't call for an ambulance.
They call the police—
'cause you'll be dead in ten minutes."

VII. Ortho

The Ortho Plant
provides forty percent
of the hazardous waste in Richmond.

Staple of gardeners
that garlic smell,
savory, sickening,

the scent of a gigantic
No-Pest-Strip,
the smell that comes out
of trucks in the nighttimes
of Orlando, keeping
the mosquito to her swamp,
only *this* is like I'm
right behind that truck,
on a Vespa scooter,
a king-size chigger soaking it up.

VIII. The Empty Vessel

One wouldn't think this
would be
a great place for a cigarette,
to get lost awhile, climbing
through the portal
of a carbonized steel
barrel fat as a beer vat,
tall as a bell tower into black.
Poisonous, flammable?
Shorty doesn't think so.
And that will do for us.

We watch ourselves
dissolve in the fireflies
of orange light. Normal thing
in a peculiar place.

IX. The Last Spot Bar, Close to the Main Gate

The juke
plays Johnny Paycheck,
take this job... and it
wasn't even our quarter.

We line up the brown Coors bottles.
We are going home.
In two more weeks, they lay me off.
Bruce a week later.

My good friend would become
a software analyst.
Shorty, whom we knew nothing of,
partner of the irises, provider
of hiding places, who can say?

Gette, I come back to you,
to New England with a diamond
in a quirky setting, courtesy
of Standard Oil of California.
Urban Cowboy. Pipefitter—

same job Travolta had in that movie,
though I think you are prettier
than his girlfriend, and he,

much better at playing me.

FOR MAGDALENE FROM MEN WHO THINK THEY ARE JESUS

I forgave you from the small cross
I had erected out of pities,
pitiable god or son of one
spinning on the tree of his sentence.

But I had not peeled away
the crown of sureness I grew
that kept me scourging like a Pilate,
possessor of prepossessing truth.

I cuckolded myself on pride,
bitter wine sponged into mouth,
ears blocked to last-minute confession,
to Romans rattling their bones.

I forgive you not catching and killing me
before I did you in with hope,
before I could thrust a foot at your hair,
the brush of tears and gratitude.

It's I, now, who prays to your likeness,
writes you into books that disappear,
immolate in a reminiscence
that generates visions, pairing into view.

It is not wrong to pray to a woman;
but wrong not realizing who, to whom
and what, and where your existence extends
to sow devotion, expiate, and root.

A WARNER BROTHERS OF THE MIND

In the shadow-body
where instead of the efforts
and counter-efforts of a race,
species forming its arms, legs,
evolved torsos dependent on light and air,
and lower things to barely
mine their measure out of sand
comes a real life, sculpted on
the billion stories of decision and panic,
love and failure to love, in films of instance
and interminable period, emulsions deep
of hue and smell and every fifty senses
to become the real body of us,
the real lives.

It is corpus cinema, and it, after everything,
survives.

Flashes, fragments,
plots, arcs of action and character,
flawed often and seldom corrected.
Filed with meticulous care
in rows of vaults that require
vaults just for the catalog,
and a motorcycle with a cart
to reach each one along the
wine-graped vias.

Take mine.

MYSTERY TRAIN

Each clockwise loop
was a hundred miles and seven days
by foot, each passage of the metal
tunnel painted as stone
a new mountain of an old range
the coolies carved through.

At eight, the electricity beneath my fingers
was the awful responsibility
of a commander or small god. And my soldiers
were safe in the open car behind the engine
resting for then
and dreaming of their plastic women.

Each passage I imagined the scenery changed,
the conversation of men erupting
in hard laughter, laughter of hard existing
among the acquiescence of fate and duty.
It was like life, I thought.
And took that train.

I think back on it; how the current
of the humming transformer could flip
with the lever to the left, how in a miracle
of polarity having to do with the insanity of globes
and opposite affinity, the rig could reverse itself.
It could not go fast, the engine
pushed instead of pulled, but it would go.
I would do this sometimes,
but found the clocks would seem to shiver

and go back, and my mother would call
again what she had just called.

It was me perhaps, fancy. And I had then no reason
to go back. But where is that Lionel? Given away
as I went to baseball and budding
backyard girls, gone to the oblivion
of trash or attic. I want it back,
to place it counter-clockwise on the sizzled
tracks, to place the tunnel but the men, missing,
me alone in the coal-carriage back, to watch
from the unpaned window.

Regret is the impotence of not re-living,
reality, a false sum of perfectly
good addition. Subtracting it all in the scaled
speed of what would have been a hundred miles
an hour, a careening of curves, a wild
dash to birth, or just a slow, steady dismantling
of structures and alliance, I would take either
as I would take good jam or butter
on toast prepared for me.

Upon this circulation
I have a mother who did not dispense herself
among the flowers, a father who drinks again
but breathes, and there, young man on a stage
who reads his piece on the astronauts
to fine applause, to the *wunderkind-boy* under
blinking treelights, face illumined
in a ball, holding a so-heavy box,
sound a chained metallic sound
calling him within, forward, aboard the callow hopes

beyond somnolence and heaven
while time slides itself a dream-current
between yesterday and tomorrow,
and where all the stations are peopled
with everyone you know,
and they smile.

Other Poems

(New Poems; Minor Pieces; Occasional Poems
in the form of Odes, Epithalamions, and Elegies
[including a Song]; various sorts of
Greeting Cards; Lyrics for the Libretto of an Opera,
and a Few Noble Failures)

although not intended to create a separate volume,
the final segment of this collection is also dedicated:

for Maurice Methot

I DREAMED OF ELEPHANTS

A colony of brilliant performers
for whom whips were unnecessary.

They danced,
they cartwheeled and somersaulted
and lived to give pleasure
to the children who adored them.

There were large, so large, ones
and small ones too, a troupe,
a battalion that could have taken
Hannibal home, so hallowed earth
would never
be sown to salt.

These were, and are, the elephants
of peace and joy that children understand,
and parade of them
before our newest selves

means everything.

READ THIS POEM

As if it were a wrapped potato
baked on a white-hot grill,
yours to complement
a steak and salad, functional; it goes down
with the butter of conversation
and you know that somehow
it accompanied something better and
was probably good for you.

Or read it
as fudgy brownie with the best frosting,
good as illicit climax and
just as guiltless in its coming
if not departure, reprocessed
as a broken dream.

Better yet, finally,
dare to consider it a dangerous thing, run!

It will follow,
yes down that avenue, that alley,
corner you,
stay with you
and even then,

you'll like it.

THE BRIEF OUTSTANDING

Commence the long breath, the ribbon of air
with a cold blue slap and a bright eye,
stumbling into forests of ottomans and chairs,
cracking hardballs into Dutch elms, birches
kissing the gingham queen—

sweeping the hours lost in a vacuum bag
searching debris for emeralds and a just cause,
finding in face of your frightened daughter
the heaving pause, clutch of small celebrity,
a halo of gauze, the brief outstanding

that we live for, don't we, on that ribbon of air
passing through the wood flute, on autumn banks
of a river that retires, stacking the images
till a last, sweet snore retreats unto elegy,
but not before.

THE LANGUAGE OF THE ROLL

Keats to Woodhouse, December, 1818

Woodhouse, Richard, look.

As I said, the poet seeks the interior
as he smiles at the surface.

He disappears as he becomes.

The ivory, smooth to polish,
pregnant and solid,
the magnet of the elephant's pride,
indulging the exotic, the India of its origin,
attracts to the ferrule, the shim'ring sheath
of its translation at the moment of
impact, tense to the sweet reaction
of the clack, self-speaks the language of the roll
steady and voluble in its rotation,
in its new preparation, the knock and bounding,
making a geometry no less complex to follow,
computing Io's union
with the spotted orb.

This is us, this is what I mean!
Who would deny the billiard and its balls
our life, survivable for them,
for their context, their politic, not ours,
their religion of the never
inanimate life, even as they wait,
within our story to comment or relate,
I am of billiards in their bright majesty—

you are, we, they of us, they are, in the angles
of their love and their posterity,

what we are.

VETERAN'S DAY POPPY

The timeliest hero shares minutes too few
with what will become of the man he has saved;
there is no reward, just the next thing to do.

Abreast with a medal or metaled clear through
the chest holds a motive engraven or graved,
the timeliest hero shares minutes too few.

Of bronze and of pigeons, the pensioners knew
a laughter of fate that disjoins the depraved;
there is no reward, just the next thing to do.

Remember the living, the dead that they slew,
the murder implied in the pennants that waved,
the timeliest hero shares minutes too few.

They lived for their friends and if living, renew
the ones of the mud and the missions they braved,
there is no reward, just the next thing to do.

Battalions aground, the crosses of dew
in the morning of meaning and misery are laved;
the timeliest hero shares minutes too few,
there is no reward, just the next thing to do.

OCCUPANT

The emory works itself
into plane and curve
of vessels coveted in the course of life,
the blues dulled, the reds, carmine red
devitrified to just less than a sheen,
something less than its living.

We become soft sculptures
of what we used to be,
hardened some by what has been,
but warmer still
than stone.

We still feed, still breathe,
one apart but one
who knows the others
on this block, a group,
are single, same.

Almost everywhere
there are families in frames.

Some pray to God, characters
in their own fine operas.
Some refrain.

Some work the jobs they can,
some disregard old calendars.

Some try to remember, with force
as if squeezing their mind.
Some remember to forget.

But we are not dead, not dead yet.
Poems should end with hope.

Hope should end with deliverance
on the spot,
or at least a note saying:

how come not.

THE QUICK EVANGEL

Belay the quick evangel in the light
that knots and frays misgiving's cleat,
pinions us to dimmest gods and fright
as we, your children anyway, retreat.
The posthumous delivery of heat
melts not a rock that rightness turns to keep,
confessing cores of memory replete
with innocence, betrayal, and evil sleep.
We are what we become as lambs to sheep,
as manger-moles to men who flood the land
with promises as high as mires are deep,
who lift ourselves as strength can stand
until can never stand against its power
and fall, evangel, endless in your hour.

A PROSE ABOUT POETS

In my story, sixty thousand Pleiadians
from the fourth planet of Zeti Three, their spirits
loosed here, mix with the vociferous doves
and paladins of a hidden confederacy.

They speak in *poetry,* the native utterance
of the whitelit star, stuck on its bluest stone
and etched with the full, impossible brownness
of misunderstanding and routine treachery.

Devalued as coal, they strive for ears and patrons,
and hear only each other's breathing; profligates,
a few, curious of silly bells and horns
sex the wanton wanly for a fractured hour.

Confused by history, they seek a conference
round figurative camps of fire, of wet wood,
and plan the torchy revolution of the mind,
a plan for the wrong side of gravity and light.

And they devolve among their hum of hivy jobs,
almost sweet, the janitors and secretaries
and a kind of teacher-elite, who stretch themselves
on the poets of centuries, unable to reach.

The politics are thick, writhing in a cosm
of Hittites, Canaanites and clanly others
battling for pecks in incognizant air,
a bloated fantasy of pikes and foamy bricks.

The right side of a drip-drop scansion, forms a draft
of columns orderly as phthisic monuments,
parthenons of cadence, arched pantheons
of dead letters, prim violets, billets-doux.

The left, reduces like shadow to a shatter of tears,
narrations of monotony disguised as reason
for the sake of the wearer, shoddy design,
a fodder of epithets dried to a cheap concrete.

And the self congratulates the self, as always,
undressed in the parlors of reading and bars
of fine indulgence, one vibrant note amplified
in collusion, the conspiracy of applause.

Thank you, thank you, thanks for now, forever, all.
In cavernous night sky, a twinkle, then it dies.
Poems worth a glint of shiny dimes, perhaps
are saved within a beerglass, emptied as it falls.

PENTIMENTO

Between anticipation and remembrance
the sliver of an uncorrupted experience
whistly whines as a grassleaf harp, on lips
of the child you were, or child yet to come,
the here or where of this our ransacked present
stilled of stillness in its ever forward run,
searching seconds of the green, to russet-
red to merely brown, the seed to seedling
stretching boughs that shiver back to ground
seems never grown, though there, and never seen.

Anticipation sexes life with wets
and pulsings, hear the sighs! the aftermath!
a climax so, so narrow it's a myth
worth telling after Sunday's psalms and beer—
the weight of memories, month to minute
in the library of a soliciting benefactor,
called up from daunting stacks a fragment
of an intercourse, a discourse, or a cheer,
loading volumes for the dromedaries
decked for desert journeys, wells of fear—

Come, come to me Ma, from porch of Junes,
of nights smelling pine and pink, white lilacs,
come too Elizabeth, in figure of your fifteenth year,
to me, my tan, mean soldiers on the floor,
missionaires of visionary noons, and more
your laugh, my toddle-girl my Julie fair,
your mouth a coo of evening's Orphic seer,
remember on your wedding day, the old man

fixing one crooked orchid in your bouquet,
anticipate, remember, go, go, stay!

IDYLL

Of Caffeine and Birds

We sip in the nave,
the wrought-iron veranda
of a cobbled coffee-shop
        mooning up our day;
above, in the bottom crook
of the second S
and invisibly obvious—
            nested finches, married so
            and similarly landed
            to a happy circumstance,
                behave.

JESUS OF THE VELDT

The aardwolf pulls and tears
at his carrion in haste,
taking the sins of the world
to his shaggy belly.

His shadow eliminates
every hurt and waste,
dissolving to a dusk of landlord
predators, freely.

MRS. BURT PLAYS RUSSIAN DANCES

Oh won't you stay, my pretty plaidskirt maid!
Washed to warm in this, our heyday's whee—
a troika or a darting Karabushka,
tunes that cling to violins and me;
I am your fine, third-graded Cossack boy—
I've waited turns amid the plumes and preen,
stopped my steppe-worn tramping feet for healing,
with your style and circumspect, redeem!

A whirling girl you seem alive with future—
follow me or I will follow you,
grow into my yearn, a wife, a teacher,
waltz me into catacombs of truth
and be not slivered memory, for years fail
frail men, only strong of shell
and shorn of substance, partner me in rain,
in hail, lift the sun into its swell—
dance me into dreams of fire and feeling,
dance me to and far beyond, the bell.

WHEN

I have vowed to change.
      And this, as human does, I do.

I will not covet my neighbor's
wife as some Persian fluff
to my Siamese
when Yeti slide by the window,
when Amelia tramps in
unfogging her goggles
and La Gioconda moves
      that reticule from her thigh,
      and sighs;

I will not stack my possessions
as an effigy of me, or hold them
as totems to the empty breeze
when the Large Greys come clean
and throw a house party,
      since they are actually miserable
      and love company;

I will not commit the sin of pride
and defer with modest smile
eyeing the periphery
when Germans admit they shot blanks
at Audie Murphy, and the Pisan Tower
      leans back, killing
      the souvenir market;

I will make my peace
with God
and we'll walk as father and son
in fields of forgiveness

when the Gulfweed Sea
in all its isosceles
spits forth a regatta
that heads immediately
for Bermuda.

I will write the book of dreams,
cross the sound in a bark of my own building,
take homeless from the alleys
and hungry from their lines of hunger,
the warlike to a soft and sudden seat
and they will war no longer
when Easter Island announces a reunion,
the platypus grows feet,
clowns engage in crying jags
and Cayce re-ignites
his psychic lamp on Arctic Street.

And I will countenance you
for all your worth to the world and me,
appreciate the nuance of your news
as I do your navel, your truth
as something more than
lithe and labial
when the Chosen One roars back
from ether (trumpets flare!)
and on my forehead
foreign stamps:

IT'S TIME, BEWARE!

(yes, then I might)

confess myself, admit was I
in the confusion switched the cups,
palmed the rubies, shunned a good hand
    like Peter in an old garden,
        Azrael in his retreat
and like all of us, there's more,
more to tell and more I'd tell you
darling then—
within the sweetest when we call
    whenever,
when forever blows itself
a candle out
    never to repeat
        or ever end.

REUNION (DURFEE PRELUDE)

— for Ken A.

So you and I,
a nickel spins on a tabletop—
that falls yours or falls mine;
we take it up and spin again
a gyroscope of time.

So you and I transcend
the swath of pages, there and there
on the table's top, in the wide
volume of our dual lives
and new type set in retrospect,
royal purple ink cascading
through sections yearly lived
to be yet carefully inscribed
on a tabletop, thick oak and varnished hard
against the pits and mars of bored
or intolerant young men on verge of expulsion
from an old school's gray womb
into torrents of recognized success, or sirensong
of an unsafe, unsure
singular muse.

There, in the monument of red spires,
carillon and pigeons,
the observatory neither of us used, where,
somewhere on a passage up or down the grassy hill
commenced a line of maps, hours, wills, a table set
so you and I, meet me and you, commence the coin
that spins, still spinning, long
and true.

THE BAKER'S GIFT

She marries, at 33.

I've walked a paper floor, suspended above heaven
holding white shoes in my hand, fearing a heel
would poke and tear this tender love unleavened—
"Cana vintner, Baker-man! Does he know how I feel?"
When I was thirteen, the well of my quiet disease
distilled overnight to vapors of singular devotion;
I've held, since then, to the unsure fear of release
a child's face knows, just at the carousel's motion.
Lace amid pearls, I wave to my parents at the gate,
gathering satin and tears at the self-same age
of the baker who calls, "see, it's not too late"
from that radiant hill, from the last, turned page
where endless bread divides, given one to the other,
shoes on, your hand in mine, my husband, my brother.

THANK YOU, DUNCAN HINES

The mix is done.
A cake, the oven, orange heaters.

They wait.

Couple of courtship begun
in the radio parlors of Roosevelt speeches
content themselves now with the usual company,
smell of vanilla, and of peaches—

ancient, smiling children they are pleased
so pleased they scraped so long
and well that bowl,
and lick

to very last
its spoon, and beaters.

GREETING CARD

How life distills into memory—

one drop
per thousand gallons
but each drop

a perfect paint
elegant perfume
the drunk intoxicant
of a mind regaled

by heart-strung tunes.

THERE IS NOT

There is not for a man enough sense
in the present or futures of tense
to resist that ensnare
on the sirensong stair
where a woman awaits, and relents.

MILK OF MAGNESIA OF HUMAN KINDNESS (DOGGEREL OF CLICHÉS)

for my students

You have soothed the savage beast within,
and I have walked a razor's edge to reach you,
yet now, just now, it finally dawned on me
the lessons that a laxative can teach you.

EPIGRAM OF THE FOURTH GRADE

I liked to read.

In *Time Magazine,* 1965
they questioned, yet again, the existence
of a Creator, making him
as Nietzsche did, a Created
who could be killed.

It became a slogan.

In a *Weekly Reader,* that May of my tenth year
from my seat at the fourth desk,
second row from the bright window,
I read about the search for war criminals
in South America. Eichmann
believed what Nietzsche said,
and sought to prove it.

Things were interesting.
They twined and turned round, I knew,
even then.
And it came to me, the jingle,
as I liked to write, too:

>   "Doubtful says that God is dead
>   and that's why men are meaner;
>   Hopeful says that God's alive,
>   living in Argentina."

No, God was not a criminal, nor his son,
killed as one.

Mrs. Mullaly liked it.

I had made my first poem;
the jingle was an *epigram* of sorts,
I would later learn.

But outside of a commission
for Class Day, 1967,
and verses to gain a nice girlfriend
when I was seventeen,
I was not a poet then, or that whole time.
Not until Eliot,
a few months later.

Back when I was ten, I wanted
Donna Clarke, the most beautiful girl
in the school (I thought)
to *also* be my girlfriend
(for whatever that meant),
and right after I had written that jingle I wrote,
right after
— and thank you, Mrs. Mullaly—
I thought not of Nietzsche,
or even God,
but of gold hair, a smile,
and the larger poem
that is the absolute life
of a child.

AGAINST THE RUINS

The architecture of us never comes to catalogue
in shelves of British Library-decked decorum,
twelved into itineraries, walking tours of Kent,
but rather, they present as left-living small creations,
real smiles or their memory, estates of dolor's sense.

O! but in the minds of us, we stacked the pearly marble,
hoisted high and chiseled, emoried smooth in its perfecting,
arched the nave suspending Gothic predicates of graves,
stained the glass rococo in the light of our misgivings,
circumstance and argument, flailing at our dreams.

Such edifice of foam and reverie, you and me, assuming
we'd remain the virgin's ever-asset of assumption;
borne of monumental issues formed from here or there,
we were so sure we would, we could sustain the grand
of our designs, the periods and eras of our weigh—

but they go, don't they, disrepair themselves of wind
and sun, expanding ice and rain, surrender sin, and pain—
and all we realize, too late, the effort to enleaven
what's important to a permanence of state, restates
that life will always gainsay us, demolish us within.

Perhaps a little sign instead, that children play around
will mark us, or will poem in a volume in a drawer;
lie me, us, a promise everything that goes comes round,
as wrens alight upon some carvèd stones not teetered yet,
as whenever touch the mind of God, our buildings fall.

NOEL HAYNES

in green surges like the valley
our mouths are filled with water.
in such rain even angels
fail to see the ocean
scattered with halos.

                              N.H.

To touch the standing
cellophane of a cigarette pack
so lightly
as to leave no dent
        so I
approach this work of yours
                this
quadratic of image—
        x as an Ashbery conceit, *c* a sigh,
metaphor to the second power
        [a sportive punctuation (.)]
the badminton with Bly,
softshoe shuffle
in spaces Merwin marks
(showing up in rumple of
        an out-of-date tie)
        a loosed and dangling
participle
                in corner pock of Ezra
Pound's inveterate
        inflamed Italian eye— my friend
as one bomb salesman
        to another—

color walls in chalk, gall
        and gossamer, do that
dada
thing you do

to *who* the every what
and where of
fine
fluorescent whys
     and be for me
the lightness of a contrail
seer of smoke and letters,
past and future perfect numbers,
settled to an imperfecting

       pi.

THE SECOND RUNNERS-UP

A poem for the also
of the story,
the Annes and Josephs
to their Marys,
Elizabeths to Johns, other Johns
to Peters, swift embodiments from God
to Son, to Spirit, *that,* the lovely
       primary, second
runner-up endowed to masses
in its majesty,
amorphous yet diademed
in spread of sash and diamonds
to the so-arrayed lilies,
to mothers of fathers and scions
and daughters holding lilies
in the aisles of our days,
       to the goat-paths
of Africas leading
to the church of sunbaked clay,
the prayer of food
after fasting,
the new rain and blades
and the fruits of their blades,
hosannas parading
to hand-drums, to O's and to consonance
       and here and there
the apparitions come to children, chosen
in their small, ept, magnificence
to be, themselves, second runners-up
we line the roads to praise,

and may we all be
seconds, really thirds,
depending how you count—
running up

the stairs, the ever stairs
of heaven.

THE ART OF WAR

When all trees fall
instead of one
do they make noise
if, when it's done
it's deafened as it stunned
the village
and villagers
in dell before it?

And what of the usual
raff, the pillagers
(elected of hell),
the Visigoth, Eulan, Arab
and American,
one in rushes by a Mekong
flat, replete with lorries
and rat-a-tat, the little, late plumes
or, predictable
as Dakota dawns

the counting cold, then heat
of the very
long?

No answers. The
questions are wrong.

One figures, figures
then forgets philosophy
for the simple sings

of good war-songs, the sex of hate
as all the meatmen, we, in silkslings, pulled
and always hither milled
by one good clapping hand,

arbiter and profligate,
the us and it, so
ever stupid still
lies still

and strong.

A MARKET FOR SLAVES

STRATEGY 1

The vague
chiaroscuro on the cheek—
the blemish of light
that leaves a forehead
disconcertingly,
even the delicate hand
that brands itself askance
        with SEX, SEX etched
into photographic plates
to reach the eye
in mask
but play the brain
(or so the not-so subtle psych-types
say) forthrightly
pull us to a cigarette,
beer, a kind of underwear,
a homogeneous day-and-nightly life
so purposefully prescribed
and underscored
everywhere.

STRATEGY 2

The movie frames
grab milliseconds like moths
metamorphosing idea
into emotion, but held always

on the tensile surface,
while below, *it's there*
la la la la
and *there,* la la— the intermittent
image of a godhead
flashes in wild bestiality
　　　　CRY CRY　　　DIE DIE
and we almost feel that ominous
diving into self,
a preplanned
drowning off other determining,
the funeral of feeling we buy
buy, attendant, consuming
consealed, consealing.

STRATEGY 3

The group in the picture
having such a good time
is no group—
rather each sets apart in his own universe
eight separate sets of eyes
cast each to different point
of that imaginary cube
which confines us to the pentethol
of confusion, a fine old sleight
that isolates all possibility
of fraternity in the freeze
of hypnotic loneliness
light years from the warmth
of unison.

SUMMARY

In the quarries of our native alienation,
we acquiesce to anything—
without a need, a knowledge, or nativity
of temptation.

PEOPLE WHO LIVE

There are people who live apparently,
who draw and divide.

People who live on the shell of an egg
with no egg inside.

AT LAST A POEM FULL OF BIRDS

St. Kitts!— no talk of slavery, sugar, and black sand:
you can write of those and I'll be first to read it.
But I must set past passings right, right here,
inventory the majesty of friends in these hours.
Just birds for me now, these! the sounds of color,
songs of perch and fishing and nature's monogamy.
Avocets, plovers, rails, crakes, gallinules,
egrets' snow-blind drape of noon's green scenes—
sandpipers, godwits, shearwaters and oystercatchers,
petrels picking silver shiners from the skim,
terns and cuckoos, pelicans, gulls and ibises,
boobies and gannets swording the opal sea—
pintails, teals, ospreys, coots and guineafowl,
frigatebirds that gyre in the blankets of sky.
Zenaida doves, the fulvous whistling ducks,
swifts that angle over stilts and still caribs,
swallows and martins, vireos and warblers,
banaquits, caracaras, siskins and crossbills
crossing in twos the scooter-studded street—
grackles, redstarts, shanks, lapwings and swans,
whimbrels, kites, falcons, and New World quails—
the snap and catch of their light, shadows in paint,
live the moment of the raising of their number,
of their twilling and of their punctuating jewelry
on the day, as their scales, modal-piped and pinking
into tropic nights remain!— and I've sailed away.

HAVING MISSED THE BUS TO THE AMERICAN HAIKU CONVENTION

I.

the slip of derailleurs—
my fix on her white bikini bottom

somewhere kigo
maybe mountain, snail, wind—
searches for this line

a hundred egrets
fat pairs and chicks on thorn tree—
snow on tropic boughs

Ezra Pound throws dice
that come up five seven five—
loses to shinto

II.

among paper lamps
courtesan spreads pink petals—
Basho reads to drunks

black characters spill
syllables to dance in eye—
wet them to hearing

juice of ripe orange
glistens onto rice paper—
now it sticks to you

EIGHTEEN (AGAIN)

for Karen

You are eighteen; and a happy birthday.
(No matter, twenty-seven years between.)
Apples abound, their round, russet remorse
still free to be sweet, still red, still green.
And you can be but one turned year to me
even as children pass in their race of lives,
as seasons spin their sunny-dials to a shimmer,
so many harvests, apportioned by needful knives.
Eighteen was a time of snow, a fog of wonder,
the walking streets forgetting pain for hope,
and as pain yet sears, hope hails, still, from corners
of us, hands held in admiration, from each end's rope.
We pull ourselves back, far friends once more,
share pictures of happinesses, sorrow too,
regale the paths we took, survived, and see
what we, both eighteen again, well knew.

MOTHER AND CHILD

written with my daughter years ago

The blossom in the bud turns to the light,
more beautiful for some perhaps, for waiting—
the gift of slow reveal, unseals sight
and turns itself about a window's grating.
Summer comes to bless, dismiss the winter
of its emptiness and swell a spring;
watered, sunned the shoots must disinter
to wonderment of this, this little thing.
Mother, new to custom, rocks her gently,
child of love's found promises and dreams,
rose and gold, with eyes that watch intently,
life abloom that knows more than it seems—
born, it grows to vine, to someday seed
a circle sown, a cultivated need.

DEUS EX

The gods we make
take to their age like figs
beyond season— even as we aspire
to them, they come down to meet us
bruised, beaten.

What was Zeus
bellows bylaws,
bloated and unwell, sowing
the not-so-secret seeds and paying
off maids for the next flawed Achilles,
behind the neoned
Olympian Hotel.

Hera is a glacier—
given to drink and crosswords,
her plastic surgery hides no disgrace
that wouldn't wear the smile
off any Fury, or Fate.

Ares, impotent
as a sea-snake erects himself
only as a shaft of light, flailing
in invisible exhortation, fight! to minions
of the timeless trail and trench, clusts of sordid
Arabs, Greeks, a few reluctant
French.

Athena, manlike
needs a husband, has no sense

of humor— she was never a child and has always
been a headache to her father; if only
she were an ounce less wise,
an ounce more wild, she might
be worth the bother.

Hades, on his second wife
shows up only for funerals, takes
no vacation, whiles
time in a den decked for decadence
hiding one or another sick
abomination.

Apollo as the favored son,
spoon-silvered and heir to everything,
sunspot on the sun, feigns the straight-arrow
as calculus of life's position,
inherits the mortgage of a world undone,
a dividend of perdition.

And Aphrodite, unplanned child
of the foam, amply breasted, too fine of form
to contemplate a mind, too perfect
to be alone, transmits sex
for adulation, adulterates love,
peels it from the bone.

They exist in our hemispheres,
halls, our palaces, toilets
and thrones, their throes
degenerate any perception
of worth in emptying, wailed tones
and mesmerized, we follow these
despots, deacons, doctors, drones,

emulate the spider, the hatching mouse
and wait for matching myths
of some reality

to make us whole again
to finally bring us home.

LONELY

(an assigned poem of underlined words—
Evan Rocheleau writes for his mother,
with edits by his father)

When you told me, I knew what it was like
to <u>receive</u> a message that a <u>friend</u> had died.

You have been gone a <u>hundred</u> days.

On an <u>acre</u> of tears I <u>built</u> a <u>museum</u> of memories.
The museum is closed; a <u>guard</u> stands
under one <u>fluorescent</u> light. I am the guard.

But whenever you return
it is like something I <u>heard</u> on the <u>radio</u>
about someone lost coming home.

<u>Unbelievable</u> they said.
It is how I feel.

And the museum opens its doors.
Out I <u>tumble</u> into your arms.

APPLEJOY 33305

(written with my son, Evan)

The man who tied the rope
saw the first firefighter to jump off the ferry
heading for the towers.

He couldn't forget the name.

Neither could the officer
who helped him take
the elderly man from the stairs
of the South Tower.
   He saw him run back up again.

The name was pasted on to
his heavy
   black jacket.
It was Applejoy 33305.

Five minutes later that tower came down.

In the North Tower
a crying woman was pulled
from underneath a desk, and handed
to another firefighter going
   down the stairs.
She remembered who found her,
and the sight of his name.
So did the Indian man who welcomed his ax
breaking through the elevator shaft.

So did the young banker
he told to leave, that he
would take care of the blind
      burned man
      on the fifty-first floor.
He sat on the stairs with that injured man
      as the last tower came down.

His name was Applejoy. His number was 33305.

How could it be?
Several people swear
      that Applejoy had never left
      the South Tower.

Yet others knew him to be
in the North Tower.
He was there for sure
when it also came down.
How could it be?

It could not
           be
despite the witnesses
at the ferry and the towers, including those
who owe him their lives.

The reason is simple.

The New York City Fire Department
      has never

            in its history
            had a firefighter

named

Applejoy
Number 33305.

POINT OF READING KEATS ALOUD

The point of reading Keats aloud
    alone in a large room at 3 a.m.
is to drape the edge of conscious thought
    with sound,
and in an ether equidistant
    to the separate gravities
and logics laughing
gayly in between the zero and the one,
    to open drapes to real self,
and selflessness so lost in lesser latitudes,
    then found.

FOR LECTURE AND EXPENSES

(From *Discourses on Art, Science,*
and the Meaning of Things)

When the famous doctor
(what's his name?)
grew acres of tissue from
a single, little
chicken cell, a shiver-
ing mass more real than
the cliffs of Dover or
any mountains of orange gel
for whom old racehorses
gave their lives in obscurity,

and that, this wild succor
of bit-parts, still alive
after fifty years in some big
laboratory endowed in per-
petuity by Arab sheiks
and a few old British
scions, might allow us to
contemplate why
seven
separate sea-
lion heart-cells, placed in prox-
imity on a borrowed Petri-dish
would start out seven
diffuse meringues
but merge
in thirteen seconds to a perfect rhumba

of ersatz sea-lion
circulation,
does this mean that if you took thirteen
great pianists and set them side
by side playing Schumann's
Toccata that
soon, by the thirteenth
(or fourteenth) measure they would,
rubato here and caesura there,
in a full or even waxing moon
be converted to the most perfect
rendition, the one in Schumann's head
before he leapt (moonily) into the Rhine—
or one *even better?*

Is Art a fabric
of ambrosia or, like Science
the amalgam of so
much English chicken meat,
so much orange jello, or, as are
so many things in Ripley's,
is it better to wonder,

and just not know?

Thank you (anyway) for your attention.
I have to go.

NINE JUSTICES

Brother Iscariot,
hungry, thirsty
sits at a long table, alone
as scraps of bread
that's just bread, or last ounce
of wine, just wine
drops from his mouth
like a missed opportunity.

Nero runs round
in a sheet of flame
a fat old phoenix
without wings or destination
shouting Sulpicius
Galba's name.

Salieri hangs
from a harpsichord string
and his toes just miss
the piano, keys dancing
in repeated sing of Mozart's
Sonata, 17 in D.

Danton's head
talks to itself about good government
and prospects for attorneys
in the New Republic,
while Louis,
grand-fils du Roi du Soleil
full of cheek and similarly separated

yawns his pantomime
scream.

Break a leg, John Booth—
he relives the shame
of his pratfall from the rafters,
ruining his exit
(and all he was after)
with a choking, inaudible
"Sic Semper Tyrannis!"
and fact that Mr. Lincoln
thought him a good actor.

Hitler is tied
to a table and brief-case
while satyrs
dressed in skins
of little Jew babies
hum the Seder songs
coloring on his landscapes
with sticks of ash.

Señor Escobar
lies prone in a snowstorm,
the dust of dead mothers
atop a thousand hypodermics
pressing, pressing.

De la Beckwith
stands glued to a replica
of his own driveway
as black youths hold
his arms out like a Baptist
Christ, chrismed with the

long kiss
of Medgar Evers.

And Atta, Mohammed
awakes in the 83rd floor of his heaven,
watches the man, face in the plane
from the narrow window,
clear as Koran, sees it is
the God of Abraham—
no, his own God
no, the same God!!
and falls, as if to fall, forever down
through that shaft of salt,
disciple dismissed
by his own hand.

BORODINO

Whenever, looking at my watch, I see the hand
has reached the figure x, I hear the bells beginning
to ring in the church close by. But from the fact
that the watch hand points to ten whenever the bells
begin to ring, I have not the right to infer that the
position of the hands of my watch is the cause of the
vibration of the bells.

> — Leo Tolstoy, *War and Peace*

Little corporal.

You, mounted on a wax stallion,
grand paralysis of epaulettes

you are no calculator;
place adder with the wolverine
and cross yourself out of the circle,
commences,

and in an hour
lose yourself below the hill
in a fog of saltpeter, smoke
and trumpets, the gravity of flags,
reports that are old
before they reach your tent
but seem so real, accompanied
by frightful or ambitious
compliment

so you say
bon, avance

but stay behind as first lieutenants
turn the lorry wheels,
dead to the once-*belle*
camp-girls' lament.

And when in afternoon,
the fragments of too many lying lead-men
cause retreat and slog reform
to the pace of a dying dog,
and when dogs have already
begun to pull at reddened uniforms
of new fathers (made in Ghent), your soldiers
order you to end, *assez, finis,* and you say
your *oui, victoire,*
the victory.

Yet robbed or wrecked of heart
your army, cleaved of a third
follows Kutuzov's, cleaved
of a third, past the flames of Voronezh
to winter in an abandoned capital—

    to lie with a dead woman
    strains the covetous lover

and showing you the future
in her entrails
and in the soon cinders
of this Oriental prize, you find the truth
you never speak, on
the sledge of your long way back,
at Elba, Waterloo, or on that windy
sea-stone in the vacuum

of your final throe and hack—
soon reflected in the snow
that pinkly blinds upon the rise

and frosted to a cold, stone look,
or lack, in pairs
of your remaining

corporals' eyes.

THE THIRD SECRET

As she walked on strands of air
above the hedgerows
      she made me understand.
(It was all without words
so mine in the translation
succeed, hardly.)

At the podium, now
I stress, inarticulate
for a worker of sound and epithet,
her final endowment—

> *It is possible*
> *to free*
> *a child and the snap-*
> *dragon held in its*
> *mother's shadow.*
>
> *It can be arranged*
> *that a sun paints pink*
> *the ancient hills astride*
> *two speckled sides,*
> *and treaties of a reuniting kiss*
> *wet as ripe currants*
> *between man and woman,*
> *multiply.*
>
> *Decide among clean*
> *common rains*
> *such countries' cities' streets can drink*

into pairs of sober eyes
and truce these new, benevolent hearts
to stop a clinging madness;
the least, pay pence to chance
and not undo
the flickering hour
before it starts—

One thing sure.
(And welling in the throat.)

War is not kind.
It simplifies by
complicating lines
of little lives and makes
its luck an everpresent lie,
a certainty divided
by a multitude of errors
fractioned to
the plenary of its penitents,
and in the last assessing
dust, betrays the one
enlarged
undeafened cry.

Reconcile! Reconcile!

And forgive me
in my lapse
the occasional urge
to ask why.

MAYBE, A VIAL OF HELP

Which is the glue of us—
make no mistake. It is more powerful
than crushed atoms, more beautiful
than suns, and it survives into the last breath
of each and everyone, however low, bereft
of hope and filled
with a victim's contagion.

The oyster sucks the salt along the shore.
And the shore is made of oysters. Always an equation.

The last act of a suicide
is to help the world be rid of him, and
the act of creation is the first act of help,
seizing the mother's body at the crash of relation
with an aura of its new life,
and she exists now to help the other.

If you ask
that particular suicide, he will stop
at the rail and change your tire first.
And the baby will help
and help and help
until you deny it into a dark angel.
And then it will help you understand
your mistake.

The leaves of hardwood trees
collect the weather in their canopy
for the ground of humid frogs

both yellow and crimson,
scattering seeds.

Can I help you?
I'll seduce a waitress tonight.

We are paraders of help.
Nightingales and avengers
and small vague supermen
clambering into tall buildings that are ready
to come down, or cowards that help
by identifying themselves—
they all stand round.

No one there to help? The floor
keeps you from falling
to the center of the earth.
The earth gives you a place to stay.
We help it out, celebrate Earth Day.

Consider the specific gravity
of help. It clings, conspires,
brings the bouquet
to the wedding party,
buries and prays for you

but to whom, and for what...

help me with this... hey you... hey.

A FRIDAY

We would nod, now,
like November pigeons.
Much is the same for each,
if we gathered around coffee.

The visit of the principal,
the early release into seats
of surprised buses, quiet ride home
that comes when innocence
is confused with guilt.

Then the beautiful smeared
mascara, smeared legs, the hair
minus the hat, the
waiting on the asphalt,
the gray conveyance, flag
on the long box at center
of a history book, a black horse,
drumming.

We carry these icons
around in cellophanes of a small wallet
in minds of our eighth, ninth, tenth years
set under California palms, Iowa rain,
or the cold hearths
south of Boston.

The old mothers, Persephones
robbed of him, met us at doors
with eyes as wet coins of carrots

blended into faces; if you listened
hard, strung house to house,
remained that echo of first wailing;
in others, young women
had cried silently, like maenads
denied their supper.

Kids we, afterthoughts of accessories
but for that day, that weekend
we carried the cards of adulthood
because someone had to be hard and sure,
go about business.

I recall as the images painted themselves
in charcoal late Friday afternoon,
I went and ate peanut butter cookies,
indicting myself
because they seemed like the best
I had ever tasted.

I pushed outside into the cold,
an air cold like ice-water down the throat
and walked to the Reeds, where I swung
the swing in our thick coats
with four year-old Cheryl.
I told her a great man died that day.
I don't know why. I didn't even know why
he was great. Cheryl kept swinging.

Fact is, we all took that piece of ourselves
reserved for national tragedy
and buried it in similar backyards,
and dig it up on occasion, as when
the parade thrums, or a dog barks

into the night, or the calendar comes round
and again, there it is.

My children will have the towers
falling down. They don't understand the other.
My grandchild
will have something else and so,
won't understand either.

The same, disparate things.
Persephone, maenads, supper.

IDEAS FOR THE HUMAN SONNET

we slave at these friendships,
only to lose and forget we lost them—
    (was it my fault?)

we are hounded by dogs of the fact
we can't forgive ourselves—
    (but you don't understand)

we bow to authority, though it's clear
that the blind lead the naked—
    (still the best bet)

the happiest moment of a life
always has to do with love—
    (there it was, there)

the hero gains the shining, unimportant
moment of self—
    (and barters it for others)

an artist sits in a field of lavender
and sees that his mimicry is hopeless—
    (he could open a shop)

God made such worthy plenitude of parts
that no woman is not beautiful—
    (unless they try, inside)

faith is more real than reality
in that it is harder to destroy—
    (funny how the flames seem cold)

what comes first, that feeling of love,
or the decision to feel it?—
    (and does it matter?)

and as pain can be the sweetest of sweet
depending on enormities of its outcome—
    (rave on, you now, rave on!)

I AM JIM MORRISON'S PERSONAL ASSISTANT

Another dream movie.

This one starts with a *trailer.*
I am trying to keep a house full of
drunks together during a storm.

It is New Orleans, or seems to be
because I am surrounded by old French drunks
and one of them, of course, is my father.

He is being propped up by another drunk
and my sister Connie (who is playing her share
of cameos these days).
As the trio stumbles down
a hall to the right, I am really trying to
keep this old tenement, or dream
together. I try to close the door
onto the windy street, but there is no door, really,
so I pull the wall over; it slides easily
to make one.

Yes, a big, big storm coming.
"Get in you drunks!"
Coming Attractions ends there.

I find myself in the living room
of my old house at 1738 Meridian Street,
Fall River, Mass. I no longer own
the house, but was let in. Only a few,

the beautiful people vomited from a bad night
in the Sixties and allowed to age, are around.

I know who lives here now. I want to
meet him. A publicist quizzes
me like Himmler, then lights a long-stemmed
bowl of hash, offering me a drag to prove
I am not the police, and he is disappointed.
I remember that smell.

We discuss the poems put
to music, and he tries to cross me on
"Light My Fire," which of course
our man didn't write. I tell him
I like "The Crystal Ship," and of course,
"The End," but I also like the music-hall
staccatos of the organ on "Love Me Two Times"
and the way that line "Love me two times,
I'm goin' away!"— is sold hard as if it were
Blind John Milton,
providing Milton could sing. He, the PR man
just looks puzzled,
which is my objective.

An old redhead groupie, but not the wife
who must have suicided with smack
as reported, lounges on the cushion-chair
where I used to watch *Tuesday Night at the Movies,*
the console color Motorola
between my mother and father and no drunk-fight
because it was Tuesday, not a Friday.

This redhead wants me to go.

Impolitic, I tell her to sod off.
(After all, it *was* my house.)

Then he, Lizard King comes in, escorted.

Not any older,
open shirt, hair like Shelley writing "Adonais,"
lounging on Ma's chair to the left, the one
with the green ottoman.

I want to be profound
but can offer only fan-like epithets,
a sycophant echo, to which he responds
"yeah, so what, blah, blah, blah."
At this I say "you're right,
I'm telling you bullshit like everybody did."

A makeup man gets him ready.
Jim Morrison is now in silver face paint
like the Tin Man, covered with beads
and wears a *Paris Bombers*
brim-cap. "Get the bats!" he calls.
We discuss heavy philosophy without using words.
He decides he likes me, and I like him.
He is going to play softball— he has
a softball team. "We don't play, really.
We all just stand on the diamond and pose."

"I can appreciate that," I say.
I offer him a rosary of purple glass
that belonged to my mother,
and he adds it about his neck. He asks,
"Hey man, would you like to be my personal assistant?"
"Yes," I say. He scribbles a note with a number.

And I leave; I can't wait to tell everyone,
to tell you.

I knew you would ask
me for that number. I have it.
It's here somewhere. Put the *First Album* on
will you, or Side One of *Strange Days*
and the TV, whatever that movie is,
turn it down.

ON THE MYSTERIOUS DEATHS OF TREE-SITTERS

We don't need you.

We have been here, our coniferous
selves resplendent
since afterbirth
of the earth's first tumult, fertilized
by ash, cross-pollinated by wind, civilized
into rows of our own configuration, kings
of the landscape, we *are* the
landscape, we.

Drive your cars through us; we live.
Chew us up with automation, we outlive
the machines, hell, we have outlived
fire since before you were semen in
a salamander.

We do not require welfare,
platforms, protests—
and the resentment builds. If we wanted
to, we'd throw apples at
schoolgirls. If we wanted to,
we'd hold our breath
and you'd poison of dioxide
faster than your Studebakers
and cigarettes could ever kill you.

Investigate all you want.

They slipped in the night, plummeted
like one-winged doves into the mulch

and will be remembered at their
funerals with folksong.

How did it happen?
Leave us alone.

The ridge is everything
it was meant to be, and without
a single eye glazing it over
with wonder or wasted
watercolor.

We outlast everything.
Our lifespan is infinite
as far as we can see,
and in your jealousies, your
desires to plow or protect us, you waste
the little time you have to bleep upon
some rural speck, or complicated
urbanity.

Don't you understand? We grow
from pulverized rock, from sand.

We're sorry for your loss,
but we don't
                    need you.

It's you who needs the shelter
of a hand, to grab you
when you slip or are pushed
into that funny gravity
          we so ignore.

Buy your postcards
3 miles down
at the Humboldt stand.

*Greetings from
the Redwood Country.*

    And come no more.

OUR COMPLEX RELATIONSHIP

The perpendicular, acute
the hypotenuse
the root

the ninth skew-line
parallel to
a universal
truth.

Love is mathematics.

I am the plane, willing, sane
on which
you grind
your Pythagorean boot.

POETRY LESSONS

These are the snapshots
when it comes up in middle age,
what you hated about those days,
over drinks among married professionals
if it comes up at all, as a rule.

Iambic pentameter,
the regular drip upon the crown
of a head looking elsewhere.

Feet, that fetish
sucking each dactylled, trocheed, toe
till Christina Rossetti
or my next-to-last-duchess
comes to the fore and dies
under some metered moon.

Schoolgirls swallowing rote of sonnets and haiku,
and Longfellow—
that ignominious tool.

Swallowing whole "The Lady of Shalott,"
an intellectual act approaching pederasty.

Nothing too funny, nothing just right
in the lovemaking of words, nothing about tears
in a Cuban jail, or
growing up hard in hailstorms of silence,
about caged birds and the fear of flight,

on finding a voice,
leaving a trail.

But there it is, Chapter 22,
skipped to a lou in THE ART OF POETRY,
the required and spent matches on a wet fuse,
like stopping at Stuckey's
with a bad bathroom you can't use
somewhere past Synecdoche,
Synesis, or the vaguely quaint
and often quit-claimed
metaphor of muse.

They say
we are living, dying;
we have better things to do.

UNWRITTEN NOTE

after William Carlos Williams

It occurs to me
I need you to fix the dishwasher
    and save my life.

You have a knack—

rescuer of soul
smoldering poison at its polyester edges,
for a man's dark
face in a storied window
    barricaded
far above the neon, trying to hold on.

Yes, you know
how to open that latch when it sticks
    and I need
    you now, later,
in all my laters from years of yesterdays
and for all the wounds
that take, better their tincture
    by your touch,
that instinctual, insurmountable
woman thing.

I don't know what I did to it—
stuffed too full of the dirty,
made dirty by inconsequential
hungers, by years
    of casual abuse.

There is justice in this
predicament, this quartering of hours
        in a day's aloneness
damning me with details of what
I let slide, a depreciation of
the hearth's old inventory,
and every heart's slight.

Let's not wait for death.
        Fix the dishwasher.

Plums in the fridge for you.
My thanks.

DECORATION

I don't own
that pair of celadon
fish-beast vases
with seaweed mountings
(Chinese porcelain
and French-gilt bronze)
circa 1725—
they are in the National
Gallery.

But if I did
I'd place irises in them,
frame their baby-blanket hue
between the scope
of your bare shoulders
at a small table
overlooking
the Bay of Biscay,
and once consumed
(of your eyes)
forgo the blue on blue,
the incalculable value, vista
of things like these
      for want of you
and deft simplicity,
of all you say in silence
smiling at this untrained gaze
on something, someone
plainly reminiscent
of another art
and truth.

FOR ORI

Ori, my boy, this is what I love about you.
Always master of effect,
despite any slight that might have affected you.
Here we are! Have an apple.
On such Empyrean day, set for voyage
our near-sights hoping neath a present dew
of time and place, silver images
and endearments mounting
like so many scrawled inscriptions
on the program of your life across our way—
connect this afternoon.

We make bad mourners. We just won't do.
Instead we fumble in the grass for the one thing
on which admirers can agree—
that someone young as you, cast to the emerald air
shall likely don the raiments of an uncontested heaven,
hear the blast of associate stars, or at very
least acquire and for our ears arouse
the one ascendant ever
of an offering in fugue, to place where you espy the scene
without encumbers, with whys of truth,
in company of newness and a new health
to sift and rise, rise you! flying from the prayers
of our affection, and look, apple ours,
at apples out
completely newborn eyes.

FOR ORI: THE CHRISTMAS LETTER

nine months after

Ori, hello again.

Here's how it is.

Your father folds you into his days
off the airy portent of the answered question:

What now?

We fly.

Your mother, saved
in the broad arms you yet extend
from the covers of your bed
sleeps a beatitude of peace.

Your friends
including a few who discovered themselves
too late,
wear you in reminiscent smiles,
sniff the incense that discomfits
beginners' loss.

And your first, pristine amour—
what a love she was!
keeps your talismans in her special drawer,
the sealed compartment of her heart.

Me, I make no bones,
I paint you vividly in brightest pastels
in the tentative sway of baby hips, to wend
new caravan from there to here,
new name, the Prince of Possibility;
your brother, elsewhere older than you now,
is proud of you.

Yes, you are stranded into these minds
to a soul of our estimates,
a broad fabric wefted of the metaphor
that reality is to dreaming—

thank you for the gifts, they
come often.

Under tree of my design, tinsel-light
embracing, all the presents you refuse to open,
always, until morning, remember?
We expect no less.

Inside these wraps, without giving them away,
enjoy the various missingnesses
that keep our bond in you.

So we turn, good fellow, we turn—

and joy to the world!

GOOD POEMS BY NAZIS

Aside: *I would rather read a good lyric*
by a Nazi than doggerel by a saint.

And in my dream
I steal a note from Manson
to his forgotten wife, 1955,
and make a found poem.
>   (Yes. *Steal* it. Charlie gives me no trouble—
>   I say I'm no LaBianca, no plump starlet,
>   hairdresser, you will taste gun metal
>   my friend, I'll dress you for Thanksgiving—)

The lines lie out this way:
Rosalie, Rosalie
the stars tip through the brown light
>   *of my sung soul, the tatters*
stitched into our wedding clothes.
Never learn not to love.

I become a collector.

Gacy's pastel clowns
are like Chagalls to me, spilled out
during a toothache
>   in the Russian winter
>   that passes for Chicago.
I hang three in my living room,
serve ginger ale
and dip with little dipping cones
to the invitees.
>   The film that lights
the far wall is Kenneth Anger,

the devil's secretary, thirteen minutes
of Vivaldi score, a midget in a wig and a tall frock
who minces, capers among the fountains
of Tivoli. We watch, guessing the director
    might have sacrificed
      to Crowley's name, the entrails of some whore
whose one misfortune
was to stay too long, or come at all.

    Which leads me to the modest works
of Rudolph Hoess, commandant of Auschwitz,
    solidly middle class poet,
father of four, whose children
play in the gravel yard among dahlias
while he organizes sonnets in the
style of Schiller, an imitator perhaps,
    but organized, an olfactory poetry
infused with scent, and marginalized
by the chance importances of history.

Amateurs, professionals, it blurs
in its confusing.

At a banquet that closes
the manifestation, Poe is drunk,
Wilde is not buggering but buggered by a waiter,
Picasso is asking a female journalist, as
    he does young women,
if she would like to practice a Latin word,
and all is right with the waking
world. Art is art,
and writers write not who they are,
but who they are not.

ATLAS, REVISED

Herzegovina.
Brigadoon, without music.

Borders leach, paper fells the eraser—
the run mascara of skewed lines
tilting, turning, in gall, in godless greed;

mapmaker, throw new dirt into old holes.

CHOCOLATE PONTIFF

Like bunnies at Easter
I crave a Belgian chocolate
pope, hollow with the air
of perfect selection,
a curl of smoke.

I would suck the head, use
the arms as diffident
chocolate cigarillos in a French movie,
crack the legs into shards
of hope.

The tongue does not blaspheme;
it melts the secret
opened on a Saturday,
that Ağca, broke, couldn't help himself
to sweets or salvation.

Before this I'd confect a prayer,
a Hail Mary, a deliciousness
after the taste of the host,
wonderful,
where the bread multiplies in me
and I can ask
for dessert.

KEROUAC, DISEMBODIED, HEARS SIDE ONE OF "THE FUR ALBUM" THROUGH A CAR WINDOW, ABOVE THE PACIFIC COAST HIGHWAY AT BIG SUR

He has spent time here, around here, since 1969.

A certain tumult
red, red, red, red
like eyes in my mother's mirror
like my crying eyes,
blood on the teeth my of my trap,
my anger.

They call, gargling monstrosities
sucking, sucking souls, forcing
me to compromise.

Allen, your thing for Neal
was different from mine. I love
you before our Buddhic light,
though you still sometimes wallow
in your mother's filthy madness,
and your own filth— me, mine was different,
different filth, but I still love you, man,
even in your doom—
these monstrosities have your reservation,
and your room.

Beneath the tumult
ring-rosying round my soul,
traipsing lovely in the etherum
greens and purples synesthize—

It's easier to smell the universe without
a corpse to haul around
and heart to keep frozen so's
won't degrade in the expediency
of one life, overdone, plastered to page one
of the *Lowell Sun.*

Calling, calling
my daughter calls
above the old drone of TV and coils
of burning Chesterfields—
Wolfe, that big bad
loup, loup, si le loup y était
il nous mangerait...
Was I good, could I have been as good,
can you love me and press proud
my Tangier picture to your heart
ton père, perdu, perdu?

Generations change, revealing games
of altering postures,
alternating names, but the same
wives who longed for the icons of *Life
Magazine,* closets of perma-pressed
Nazi clothes, exist of interviews on the Beats
— pages forty to forty-three—
legacy of excrement
smeared across gray memory.

Celebrity
celebrity
milltown boy
makes the scene, to be, to be

so happy
ha-ha-happy
everyone is envious of me,
I'm so happy
I could scream.

Allen names his ashram after me.

I hear the inverted choir:
Marilyn. Lady, Mardou and the opera divas
who loved the wrong men,
clutching their breasts and wondering
what it was that did them in,
incapable of love, wailing to remember,
caught in an accounting of "how" and "when."

Was it me, I'm wind, it wasn't me.

One star falls far beyond the surf.

Someday I'll come back to the living.
In a blond body contoured in California,
and will try to be serene.

For now,
the music stops, and I dream.

* *"The Fur Album" is a song cycle*
by composer Maurice Methot.

JUNKIES
(OPEN POETRY READING, 7 PM)

So here again—
without a stall, or stadium.

I recognize faces,
cubist angles, countenances from Dante
or the back corner
of Birdland,
smacked up in the cold light.

We have a point.

What silvers the vein,
aesthetic hum of an anesthetic presence
desires an audience,
an ear, a commiseration.

We understand the strap in the teeth,
the lines along a dull tattoo,
the dizzy, shameless
deliberate self.

Once I told an acquaintance
who thought to dabble
that commitment falls like cement off a ruin,
buries you but, done right
(shiny, white)
is each time a final, fertile slice
of sex and deliverance.

Which brings us here—
to a mass if not a cure,
the string within a shibboleth
pulled at, something cheap,
eviscerating,
paramount and pure.

UNDER CONSTRUCTION

Every time there is a new religion
they refurbish hell.

Of stucco, naugahyde and fire,
every imagination
drafts its misery in a contest
of climate and color,
ingenious in its appointments.

Cain, first inhabitant of the Semite god
had it good compared to the drover
who refused Muhammad his water.
But all things come
unto salvagers eventually.

New blueprint artists,
new carpenters.

(There are ironies: the suite of Caiaphas had a receptionist
but the calendar had no squares.)

Traverse just here
and the carpet is pulled up,
so trampled is it with betrayers large and small.
Marble tiles mined by Thracians
and polished by minor prophets
are inlaid across the expanded
foyer of judgment.

There, the desert motif,
locust wings and thorns.
Judas, loosed, walks round and round.
A portrait of Adam and Eve
is dimmed by a burnt backlight,
and Zoroaster's candles drip
down rusted shafts.

Seventy virgins are waylaid
into wallpaper in the bungalows of purgatory.
The six arteries of Islam
are corrupted with dogs.

Three popes are there
in purple and cinnamon, still infallible.

Enough of this—
take down these pilings. Those red drapes.
We know we can do better.
It can all be fixed.

Heaven, meanwhile, is different than this,
I promise it is. The halls are permanent
there, made of choice impossible foams
and air, where the chaste and kind
may visit well within the essence of
their own small lives,
inevitably human though they are

and rare.

AURORE AND ALBERT

Two sides of a French-Canadian dime—
child discarded in a dark corner of Quebec
who found his mother, cried and moved on;
little girl left to the sickness of a new century,
almost the youngest, in her mother's coat
at the confluence of two rivers, great and small
that fed the mills, disgorging their threadgoods
to the sea and the world.

At fifteen gone in a tanker's hold,
he came back and left, back, and left,
boy by imitation becoming a man
chose her from the sisters, bought her Snickers
the quiet one, willful, strong and funny,
funny enough to wait for him with all the prospects
of a heartsick seawife or at best, the bride
of a cottonwear weaver.

On the last cruise, past San Luis Obispo,
San Pedro, San Diego, two shifts before the canal,
El Niño works its windward spit
and *Swifteagle* lurches toward the Baja coast
caught like mullet in a peon's fishnet,
cracking the captain's china, and the hull—
half-grounded on rocks as sharp as life's
cold knives, and sinking.

"So I'm s'posed to die now, right?"
He pulls beneath lifeline suspended above
a chasm of sea between ship and island—
if he lets go then, these pages erase

with a wash of generations yet unplanned—
"her..." he struggles on, "she... " he falls
with her vision to an apron of wet sand, grasping
a Virgin Mary.

His mates replay the story till they die
in the watery war of forty-three
or safe in their beds at eight-one,
but two weeks of oranges and reddening sun
resolves in a rescue that makes the papers;
he signs his discharge, doubts removed,
he will weave cloth feeling the warm earth
from inside his shoes.

Dime for a ticket, Gable and Bennett
with the last rattle of plank, he runs
semi-sideways, running down Pleasant Street
to a stoop of black bunting, to the awful hush—
"Is it her, for her?" his legs removed
as if suspended, as if falling, held up to find
that the last tragedy of her first life lies
with a father, sleeping.

Saltspray of tears reflect on faces
pulled by the gravity of fifty years—
millwork, flattening of asphalt, children,
the pigeon club, golfing and clothes from Cherry's,
Vietnam and Grenada, Berkeley and Florida,
laughter on the porch, the burning of our cathedral,
the times the Christmas tree came down
in dashed dreams, reflecting.

French Canadians love and cry in private—
that line of her's, "What a life!," it rises

from the chat and clatter of our newest progeny,
photographs to add to the endless album
of family, of our own passions and misgivings,
of our own lives forged from two random hearts
and all the moments of rough poetry they lived,
without reciting.

GEORGE, A BALLAD

"Giddy-up go, Daddy"

You drove the drifting snow along,
you drove in days of heat,
you separated right from wrong
with pedals at your feet.

A trucker's life's a simple one,
you go from A to B,
you try to make it back again,
again, to family.

"Goodbye Annette, goodbye my Gette,
and goodbye Annmarie,
I tried my best to be the man
you'd look up to, and see."

Your baritone could fill a room
with confidence and quips,
yet melt to squeak of sentiment
as tears slid by your lips.

Calendars can fly away
their pages with a breeze,
but memory calls the living back
and brings us to our knees.

"Goodbye Annette, goodbye my Gette,
and goodbye Annmarie,
I tried my best to be the man
you'd look up to, and see."

Working man, your day is done,
deliveries are through;
rest yourself within His arms
as we deliver you.

"Goodbye Annette, goodbye my Gette,
and goodbye Annmarie,
I tried my best to be the man
you'd look up to, and see."

BARTO IN MOUNT DORA (I)

Barto comes home,
his Lake County roots
dripping with spring rain,
replaced to warm soil

where boys still slalom
through the orange trees
on skis of feet, tossing mandarins
past their prime and retreating

to shade of a recovered sun
dabbing its light through the scrub oaks,
painting the dusty football
that bounces in jagged rhythm

off a narrow street, and pierces
like Prokofiev fortes he summoned
behind the window, yearning
just then to be among them

again, among them more often
than a blue, blue moon,
Chopin's moon, that shone on him
even at eleven.

*   *   *   *   *   *   *

Barto comes home
having reverberated
the Albert Hall and the salons
of Europe, a handsome face

on shiny discs, the medals
of posterity, home from the wars,
the rivalries, comparisons,
Kissin and Pogorelich, the glove

of the aging Horowitz heating
the fist of a young Rosenthal—
how all such pocketed metaphors
blithely erase for the family of friends

who came in their Sundays to melt
with that Smith boy into seamless wonder
by the first minute of the K. 311—
six hundred ears of an early harvest,

one with the parents who sat behind me,
stranger among cousins and uncles
but returning like Barto, like Mozart to Vienna
to the heart of hearts, to the inevitable home key.

> * *this is the first version of the poem; it was
> written long before the concert pianist and poet
> Barto Smith (known internationally as Tzimon Barto)
> and I met and became close friends; the later version
> bears little resemblance to this particular piece*

FOR RITA, ON HER BROTHER'S PASSING, FROM EVAN ON THE EVE OF HIS PREMATURE BIRTH

Grief let fall into our pocket,
hold on to a joy in exchange—
the gift of friendships's matching locket
for yours with the broken chain;

a man who walks a tunnel of light
we think in our blind eyes darkness,
touches the tip of a tiny hand, right
as he passes to God's great promise;

a godmother lost of companion and brother
(but kept in her heart as an ember)
deserves not less from a family who love her
than a godson who fights to remember.

FASTENING

We become each other's
inseam, zipper, glue

you become me
me you.

ODE

Someone said the best lovers
are poets-in-the-sack.

So I'm John Keats. No, not
the one of urns and nightingales
and irretrievable eves, but the boy-man
who rhymed intolerably feminine rhymes
and followed the script of every
well-versed fraud since the advent
of Christendom, who stumbled,
stammered and poured
the tubercular pathos of his inner chords
like butter over a lyre, who overdid it,
who strove for something mad,
ending up with that curious
look, the one that says lo,
if you only, only had—

then, looking into some
semblance
of his own *Chapman's Homer*, found
truce with the word and fashioned
into the quiet glory
of your simple need
what he'd never understand
and not quite believe,
prismed in the dower
of a smile.

MELANCHOLIA

for the psychiatric dead

Too many trails.
Too many have expired.

You have taken the world
winter-borne into drugs, vibration
and death,
denial drummed quietly
in the name of your private monsters,
the mirror-men.

Willingly from Wundt
to Pavlov, Skinner to Osmond, your parlay
gained favor in the
funereal parlors of state— Bismarck, Lenin,
Heydrich, Dulles, and the pharmaceutical giants
of yesterday and today.

You ground artists
into sepia powder, writers
into words stranded on disconnected tongues,
poets into self-loathing
seeking their private gas and gunshots;
actors become driving, diving drunks,
dancers spin down dead
like depleted gyroscopes,
our geniuses buried
preemptive, in steamer trunks.

They have not forgotten what you pretended,
and what you did. Neither have I.
Your race to create
an uncreated race will stop
on your doorstep. Ids, idiots,
idiopaths will take the truth and wrench
soon enough
the jugulars out of your lies,
laying you all in the foyers
of false mansions

knowing why.

FRAGMENTS OF RENGA
FLOATING ON LAKE, NAGASAKI

                                                            release

                                         the past

                                              coins

                                    among

                              koi

                        on archèd

                bridge at

                    lantern's

                          glow

                  on mulberrys'

                silken

          joy—

deca-

        quadrillionth

           anniversary

              of now

RICK'S ENVELOPE

There is an envelope in my side pocket
where all our memories are kept;
it has thickened with years, a currency
grown of interest, its investment sure.

There we are, the laughter watering
our eyes to our wives' disapproval,
or our shouts at the arrogant umpire
who calls your daughter out, then mine.

There you are, in the most-affluent house
by the brilliant lake, our beautifuls
beside us while your girls, our girl,
our boy, too, play off-Broadway.

Time has passed, and as you prove,
we're passing off, and passing to,
the fragments of us laughing at us—
here's to me, my friend, and you.

AMARANTHS
(STILL LIFE FOR A SECOND WEDDING)

Still wet, these hues before a frame contract
their silent gift of likeness, to be hung above
a stuccoed hearth or cross the wall entacked
in soft, still brightness of a perfect love;
the past, its faults, in withers drop and fade
neath skyward twine of newgreen blades enthralled
in sunlight shadow, dabbed of bluish shade
and bled with berry-dots of heaven's call,
so that all in all, on whispered breeze begot,
the toddle's eye of one day's gleeful glance
to a picture's dusted leaves, will leave unforgot
the searching, feelful grasp of gloveless hands
that made these amaranths, sprung in purple glass,
the brush of simple somethings meant to last.

BUT GONE, REMAIN

for Richard Masi

They do not stay that go, but gone, remain
and in that paradox of shades we sort
our knowing black, from white, from gray.

While all are saved, some are saved and used
upon their blessed days, as matches struck
to evening skies, as lights that guide our way.

YARDBIRD SUITE

(Homage to Charlie Parker)

Mama's boy from Kansas City.

Wanted to, but
never met Stravinsky.
(Second
most original musician
of the 20th century.)

Appetite for everything—
chicken, one thing,
yard-birds.

Yard bird.

Yard
or Bird.

With his own Manhattan
Project,1945,
he pulled the changes from "Cherokee"
splitting Barnett's atom in a chain
of 64th notes, radiant
in its reaction.

And yet

still a Negro.
Negro to be polite.

The cousin-fly himself, of thirteen million
chiggers on a summer night.
But *genius* to his black confrères,
and to all the night-life diggers,
most of whom
were white.

Before the streets could simmer
and ignite,
they turned the white-to-clear in
the via of veins
as he bent the spoon
of jazz ignominy, king,
and cooked.

Bebop. Bop be.
Diz and Miles.
April in Paris.
The spring with strings,
pretty like the angels.

There are different ways of fight, or flight.
Tan children, white wife.

WESTERN UNION
MY DAUGHTER IS DEAD I KNOW IT (STOP)
MY DARLING FOR GOD'S SAKE HOLD ON TO YOURSELF (STOP)
PEOPLE HAVE BEEN VERY NICE TO ME HERE (STOP)
MY NAME IS BIRD (STOP)
LET ME BE THE FIRST ONE TO APPROACH YOU
(STOP)

Stop.

Back in town,
death clown.

Alone, speck in a circle round
he listened to the honks of big Buicks
and strains of saxophones coming
from Birdland across
the street, barred to play
at the icon-crèche
named for him.

Instead, he soaked his feet.

On the way to Boston,
dragging his chain, he stopped;
on the couch of a baroness,
he lay watching Dorsey's jugglers on TV,
downing glass after glass
of ice water,
water for fire,
the steaming insides of his laughter,

the laugh-and-laugh, opera laugh
and died,
at fifty, no, sixty,
no, thirty-four
and a half.

SAGITTARIUS IN BRAILLE

syllables are spots
a zodiac poet finds—
bright winks in cold sky

arrows for the blind—
perforate the paper now
strike the face of time

APPIAN WEDDING DAY

To marry
in the Roman way
— when there is no love—
it takes eight small gods,
parlor gods we'll say—
in order to consummate.

In the courtyard
of a minor magistrate
amid laden trees
of olive and persimmon
the first one joins our rite:
he has a cough
as deities of pedestrian
account are subject to chill,
but in short, his affair is over.

The second leads the bride
by lorry to the villa
holding the reins of
a different horse.

The third escorts her to the atrium
telling her to wait,
looks about, and leaves her.

She is ready to flee
when, late, the fourth
arrives to keep her there.

The fifth unties her girdle
and lays her in sheets.

Sixth, subdues her.
Seventh, spreads her.

The eighth, accomplice to
every such invasion
directs the penetration.

Where does love come, voyeur?
Is it Venus herself
who bonds the spirits,
binds the flesh, one
flesh fired in its
temporal need or revulsion,
that seals
the postdiluvian heart?

This is the difference.
Love, love not.
This is why, in Venus's name
we seek, even if as eternal fools
what we do not find.

The demi-gods, the eight
owned of forgetful
lives have their names, too—
forgotten, trunked,
mortified.

Because and as such lives,
theirs, ours,
in new as old Latin

blur the facts;
they are heard,
overheard, always, in the myth
of their significance

these rituals,
these acts.

THE LILLARD BELLS

dedicated to D. D. Palmer, the doctors
of chiropractic, and Harvey Lillard,
the first patient, who regained his hearing

If you have wondered, or forgot
or taken for granted what's clearly not
in a weary world, deaf within ear-shot,
of one who makes way separate from the lot
on unsoiled paths paid no less dearly
by years of toil, no less sincerely.

He is the child who saw the sky
and wondered why we did not fall into it
and did not believe when told as writ:
"Deny!" we see with God's own eyes
our minds and perfect bodies glide
with innate resonance, and eternal wit.

He hears the bells of a prairie morning
careen through decades of father's sons,
the babies saved and the crooked walking,
the cries of a million, the cry of one,
the tiny hammer strikes its silver awning—
when Harvey Lillard rises, it's begun.

SAVANNA'S SONG

At her time, and in this place of water
cradled in pools of Christ's tears, come to this
as did her mother, father, finally a daughter,
union's youth and bold experience, kissed
with balm of tolerance and a high, sweet laughter
born beyond this earth too full of indecision,
but one in witness, blessed here and ever after
with God's eyes firm upon her, full of vision,
Savanna smiles in the light of Sunday morning—
in stained, reflected rays, the world is dawning.

POEM, AFTER THE GREEK

To write these
you have to believe
you are really Leonidas
holding the pass at Thermopylae
with a bronze gall—

or at very least

a homeless man in east L. A.
capturing his diaper box
for a night in fall.

It's not about words.
It's about little victories.

That's all.

NUDES DRAWN ON A NAPKIN

— after Matisse

The lines shiver.
Sensations condense into picture, see.
See how you love me.

PILSNER'S WAKE

"... fanno lamenti in su li alberi strani."

*"... they caw
their lamentations in the eerie trees."*

— Dante (tr. Pinsky)

(Matthias Pilsner, speculator, Stuttgart, 62.)

No postmarks
on a Hallmark card
from hell.

Congratulations.

On this occasion,
after the screwings,
subtle ones
strewing crones and babies in your wake,
one that topped the one before, and before that
better than the trapping of your first wife
in the sticky cloak of the beneficent spider,
than the deal that ran
the old company dry as July biscuits,
all the little monstrous ironies struck
beneath the baritone of the communion-giver
(Body of Christ, Body of Christ)—

how marvelous a resume.

But
on this occasion, that tops all others

in presences of friends and sons and brothers,
we open the bequeathment with a broad smile—

you leave
a red ledger
a pall, the imitable
style.

For the carver:

"His the voice of sweetness,
   of marzipan designs;
   he claimed to walk the narrow,
   but he read between the lines."

Herr Pilsner, comedian,
wilkommen!

LA BAISSANCE DE LA FEMME, VAMPIRE
(SEDUCING THE WOMAN, VAMPIRE)

He must be discreet;
careful in his postural dissertation,
of placing hands and feet.

The man is servile;
small before the woman, glistening;
orange spot beckons at her belly,
or perhaps the hands pray
from a countenance tilted, look askance

or in the humankind, her kind
of *l'histoire fantastique*
she calls with brood of lip,
low moan, the spasm, glance—

bite the head off— still he sets
to writhe and dance

because he knows
the every cost and meaning
of the symbiotic, solemn trance
and in that moment
eternal as an afternoon with God,
quick as point of a lance
he wants to be devoured,
sucked clean, sucked dry,
not of seed or blood,
but humour in the eye,

the marrow of romance.

POETS AND INSOMNIA

Enter night.

Coven
vampiric or otherwise unseen
in mirrors
of our visible selves—
lawyer, nurse, shovelman,
pupil
of the worst teachers
or the best priests
extend, occasionally
to the commonplace world
an ironic light,

lambsblood lesson scrawled
on the faces
of angels and beasts

as we gather near,
but not at the cross

in hope
to see
the second sight
and rock
our restless act

to real

sleep.

HAMELIN STREET CONFIDENTIAL

He lives in my wall a cha-cha,
comes out from the plumber's
chiseling back of the door
and its dirty calendar
confident in his tux of darkness,
slumming himself with taxi speed
to the square at 45th and
Refrigerator—

catches jazzy hum,
sixteen separate crumbs
and a black olive, tapping one
foot to Lester Young's
"I Cover the Waterfront."

She arrives, late
and they break away
to Soho's safehouse back of second-hand
couch, squeaking the biology
of field-mouse.

I will find the pest and kill it
this I vow,
but I have not killed greater enemies
and I'm tick-tock painfully
aware of that now,
thinking of you—

a sip of this
and I'm winking into
my own half-sleep anew,

as nightlife wanes itself
in subtle sinks, on stair, in vestibule—
these sounds peculiar (not really, *too*)
to low-rent apartments

with the rent due.

RIMBAUD

The Flytrap

He was beautiful.
Boy-man
blessed of blue-eyed portals
to a separate heaven

seasoned with hell.

Brilliant as a small sun
boiling of its own fusion,
lighting self upon itself,
sucking radiant
to reside in a garden,
a forest, steeped in its blue-
green shaft, its hood aflame,
attractive.

You wanted to love him,
(you did love him!)
murder him.

Verlaine, that shiny fly.

Every time the older man
went back to God, from him
he came.

The soft pod enclosed,
the teeth of chlorophyll

softly jailing, the bed so softly
sailing off
with his soul.

Next. The years would try anything.

The poems had no origin.
No destination.
The images were tourmaline,
agate, sharp blue diamond.

You say he died too young.
He was never really young, or old.
You say the devil had him.
The devil never had him.
The devil was a cuckold.

Rimbaud
skipped the opal sea to Tangier,
enticing the sailors,
haunted the Casbah for hashish,
nursed a cancer in far Aden.

In hot air
the flytrap dried, shriveled, died.
Just the air, just heat, just fire,
just a sun, misplaced
in time and place
and never

really there

appeared to be laid
neath a grim French stone
yet appears in our dream
beloved, bewared.

SLEEPER IN THE VALLEY

Rimbaud: a translation

There's a green hollow where the river sings,
stringing its silver rags among the grasses;
where the sun, from proud mountain shines:
the little valley bubbles back its beams.

Young, bare-headed soldier, mouth agape,
his neck bathed in cool blue cresses, sleeps,
sprawled in grass under sky and clouds,
pale in his green bed where the light rains.

Feet in soft sword-lilies, smiling as smiling
sick child, he naps; Nature, cradle round him
with your warmth: he is getting cold.

The scents do not shiver his nostrils;
he sleeps in the sun, hand on his chest,
quiet; there are two red holes in his side.

LE DORMEUR DU VAL

C'est un trou de verdure où chante une rivière
Accrochant follement aux herbes des haillons
D'argent; où le soleil, de la montagne fière,
Luit: c'est un petit val qui mousse de rayons.

Un soldat jeune, bouche ouverte, tête nue,
Et la nuque baignant dans le frais cresson bleu,
Dort; il est étendu dans l'herbe sous la nue,
Pâle dans son lit vert où la lumière pleut.

Les pieds dans les glaïeuls, il dort. Souriant comme
Sourirait un enfant malade, il fait un somme:
Nature, berce-le chaudement: il a froid.

Les parfums ne font pas frissonner sa narine;
Il dort dans le soleil, la main sur sa poitrine
Tranquille. Il a deux trous rouges au côté droit.

VOWELS

Rimbaud: a translation

A black, E white, I red, U green, O blue:
vowels, I'll reveal one day your latent births;
A, hairy black corset of dazzling flies,
buzzing, bumbling about cruel stench,

shadowy gulfs; E, dolor of vapors and tents,
proud glacial spears, white kings, lace shivers;
I, crimson, spat blood, laugh of beauteous lips
in anger or the drunkenness of penance;

U, cycles, divine vibrations of viridian seas,
peace of pastures sown with beasts, and wrinkles
of alchemy imprinted on studious foreheads;

O, supreme clarion of full and piercing sound,
silences traversed of worlds and angels
— O omega, purple ray of his eyes!—

VOYELLES

A noir, E blanc, I rouge, U vert, O bleu: voyelles,
Je dirai quelque jour vos naissances latentes:
A, noir corset velu des mouches éclatantes
Qui bombinent autour des puanteurs cruelles,

Golfes d'ombre; E, candeur des vapeurs et des tentes,
Lances des glaciers fiers, rois blancs, frissons d'ombelles;
I, pourpres, sang craché, rire des lèvres belles
Dans la colère ou les ivresses pénitentes;

U, cycles, vibrements divins des mers virides,
Paix des pâtis semés d'animaux, paix des rides
Que l'alchimie imprime aux grands fronts studieux ;

O, suprême Clairon plein des strideurs étranges,
Silences traversés des Mondes et des Anges:
— O l'Oméga, rayon violet de Ses Yeux!—

THE STAR WEPT ROSE

Rimbaud: a translation

The star wept rose to the heart of your ears,
infinity rolled white from your neck and loins;
the sea red-pearled your ruddy breast,
and man bled black on your sovereign side.

L'ÉTOILE A PLEURÉ ROSE

L'étoile a pleuré rose au coeur de tes oreilles,
L'infini roulé blanc de ta nuque à tes reins
La mer a perlé rousse à tes mammes vermeilles
Et l'Homme saigné noir à ton flanc souverain.

TEAR

Rimbaud: a translation

Far from the birds, the herds, village girls,
I was drinking, kneeling in some heath
surrounded by clusts of hazel wood
in afternoon mists of tepid green.

What could I have drunk of that young Oise—
voiceless elms, flowerless grass, covered sky.
What did I draw from the colocasian gourd?
What gold of pale liquor made me sweat?

As it was, I should have made a poor inn-sign.
Then the storms transformed the sky toward night.
There were dark lands, lakes, poles,
columns under the blue night, the stations.

Water from woods lost itself in virgin sand,
the wind, the sky, threw icings to the ponds,
and I, as fisher of gold or gold in shells,
say I lacked the worry of that drink!

LARME

Loin des oiseaux, des troupeaux, des villageoises,
Je buvais, accroupi dans quelque bruyère
Entourée de tendres bois de noisetiers,
Par un brouillard d'après-midi tiède et vert.

Que pouvais-je boire dans cette jeune Oise,
Ormeaux sans voix, gazon sans fleurs, ciel couvert.
Que tirais-je à la gourde de colocase?
Quelque liqueur d'or, fade et qui fait suer.

Tel, j'eusse été mauvaise enseigne d'auberge.
Puis l'orage changea le ciel, jusq'au soir.
Ce furent des pays noirs, des lacs, des perches,
Des colonnades sous la nuit bleue, des gares.

L'eau des bois se perdait sur des sables vierges
Le vent, du ciel, jetait des glaçons aux mares...
Or! tel qu'un pêcheur d'or ou de coquillages,
Dire que je n'ai pas eu souci de boire!

YOUNG COUPLING

Rimbaud: a translation

The room is opened to a turquoise sky;
no space: big boxes and bread-bins!
Outside the wall is thick with wort
where shiver the gums of goblins.

Such as genies plot so well,
this expense and vain disorder!
It's the African fairy which provides
the blackberry, and hairnets in corners.

Several enter, discontented godmothers,
in trains of light among the sideboards,
then stay there! The couple is absent,
not seriously, and nothing is done.

The groom has a wind about him that
blurs his absence here, all the time.
Even the water-sprites, mischievious
come to wander the spheres of the alcove.

At night, lover oh!, the honeymoon!
will spoon their smiles and spill
a thousand copper strips of sky—
then, what will matter to the crafty rat.

— If it doesn't arrive like a pale wisp,
like a gunshot, after vespers.
— O saints and white spectra of Bethlehem
charm, bless, the blue of their window!

JEUNE MÉNAGE

La chambre est ouverte au ciel bleu-turquin;
Pas de place: des coffrets et des huches!
Dehors le mur est plein d'aristoloches
Où vibrent les gencives des lutins.

Que ce sont bien intrigues de génies
Cette dépense et ces désordres vains!
C'est la fée africaine qui fournit
La mûre, et les résilles dans les coins.

Plusieurs entrent, marraines mécontentes,
En pans de lumière dans les buffets,
Puis y restent! Le ménage s'absente
Peu sérieusement, et rien ne se fait.

Le marié a le vent qui le floue
Pendant son absence, ici, tout le temps.
Même des esprits des eaux, malfaisants
Entrent vaguer aux sphères de l'alcôve.

La nuit, l'amie oh! la lune de miel
Cueillera leur sourire et remplira
De mille bandeaux de cuivre le ciel.
Puis ils auront affaire au malin rat.

— S'il n'arrive pas un feu follet blême,
— Comme un coup de fusil, après des vêpres.
O spectres saints et blancs de Bethléem,
Charmez plutôt le bleu de leur fenêtre!

SHAME

Rimbaud: a translation

If the blade will not
cut into this brain,
this pale mass, greenish, fat,
of vapor ever-new—

(ah! he should cut off his
nose, lips, ears,
render his belly! abandon
his legs! O marvel!).

But no, really, I believe
for the head, the blade,
gravel to his side,
fires to the gut

that have not struck, child,
pest, so stupid a creature
he must stop a moment,
trick and betray

like a cat of the Rockies
stinking up his sphere—
yet at his death, my God!
rises a prayer!

HONTE

Tant que la lame n'aura
Pas coupé cette cervelle,
Ce paquet blanc, vert et gras,
À vapeur jamais nouvelle,

(Ah! Lui, devrait couper son
Nez, sa lèvre, ses oreilles,
Son ventre! et faire abandon
De ses jambes! ô merveille!)

Mais non, vrai, je crois que tant
Que pour sa tête la lame,
Que les cailloux pour son flanc,
Que pour ses boyaux la flamme

N'auront pas agi, l'enfant
Gêneur, la si sotte bête,
Ne doit cesser un instant
De ruser et d'être traître

Comme un chat des Monts-Rocheux;
D'empuantir toutes sphères!
Qu'à sa mort pourtant, ô mon Dieu!
S'élève quelque prière!

LA MAISON DE MOI
(THE HOUSE OF ME)

Cette demeure de moi, vient aux briques,
un portique, éclats se ramasser, malheurs lourds,
l'escalier posée les tapis de l'ésperance
couches des bêtises et l'intrigue, lucarnes compliquées
sont braqué au ciel, au secours du faucon triste
(la charogne vue ou bientôt d'être), les fenêtres
clair de la naissance, calamité
et fermé pour telles tempêtes ce qui peuvent voir,
touché, senti comme mousseline ou toile
sur un arbre du hamac, separé du monde
par pierres glaciaires extérieurs, runes nordiques,
épitaphes indiennes, carillon sous le vent
menant à porte ouvrie, une vie parfois
une chambre des pieds essuyés, avec portraits.

Dans une aile, une crèche vidée des importances,
les larmes de pneumonie, l'éloquence meutrie
de l'arrivée tardée, entravée sur une mere,
la tendresse de la soeur qui peint l'enfant
une fille tzigane pour le premier Hallowe'en
et un chambre avec barres pour sommeil roulant
pour arrêter le monstre au dessous—
les paquets, paquets des soldats combatent les guerres
sur un plancher de silence, frappé avec pointes
ajouté aux questions tamponné d'alcool,
les dagues de la glace en la folie fondue
suée au chahut atroce des nuits de vendredi,
les uns plus vieux fuiant à leurs phares,
la lustre balançant comme un gibet.

Je grandi dans elle, les ajouts étaient surprenants;
le conservatoire rempli avec les modes et gammes
Lydiennes, le rock et les ragas, le blues, Basie,
au sous-sol je voudrais absorber Thomas Wolfe
et monter mon séjour sur la route des fous,
je m'ai enroulé la route pour revenir
comme le courrier non ouvert, au lit sans des roses,
la matrice veillis des maux, les marguerites sculptées.
le numéro de boîte aux lettres sur la route la moins,
vous attend pour escorter sur ma course de la chance
dans ce domaine, la maîtresse de lui et de moi,
la pommade dans un bain merveilleux du salut,
la beauté rayonnante qui expose sa grâce tranquille,
la peine d'un visage tuméfié, en quittant.

Les années d'enfants sculpter dans marbre le plus doux—
le relief est partout, les reflets sur les balustrades,
la chanson dans le jardin des asters, symétrie de l'ardoise,
les tours de pour toujours dans notre rêverie,
les années de réaménager, moulé à partir de l'image
a un manoir actuel, en vie ce bâtiment respirant,
cette génération assuré de ses corrections,
la chute de plaques de plâtre qui libère tous enterrés
vivants à aimer, dormir parmi les cuivres et les fleurs,
dans la chambre de nos aubes, des décennies délivrant,
les jours patriciennes et délibérées, libéré comme des soupirs
dans les écrans d'une véranda d'été, la cadence
de permanance tout sauf assurée— puis, le percepteur.

L'addresse pour tenir compte des couloirs tristes
où émane du Ministère de Chances Perdues.
Les enfants, plus âgés marchent en file dans l'allée;
vous vous rendez et je ferme le sanctuaire

de notre dévotion, la plus belle de toutes les chambres
dans mon coeur et parfait comme un tombeau
scellée avec de la cire et de glycine, et je propose
la métaphore à un endroit sur une autre rue,
où les vendeurs colportent près de la fumée
des joueurs de cartes dans les fenêtres à l'étage
où le journal du soir plie à la future arrivée:
Maison à vendre, lieu préféré, spacieux
prix fixés pour l'acquisition, bien pour ceux
qui connaissent leur métier, téléphone pour détails.

RAISINS DE MER
(SEA GRAPES)

Ils essayent de saisir au bord
du monde
avec doigts noueux, profondes.

Leurs franges tombent au
pointes des pieds,
des buttes
et bords de sable incrusté,
sentant le passage plat
du ressac.

Le ressac serait les tirer
avec sa poignée en mousse souple
qu'il pourrait, nourrir les baies charnues
aux fantômes de requins
qui ont besoin de plus de sang.

Je ne l'ai pas mangé des raisins de mer.

Si tu me dis, ils sont doux
comme des grenades, que la voix
d'Albanese dans *Tosca*.

Si tu me dis, ils sont sure
que les jeunes des citrons, ou
le frisson de jalousie.

Si tu me dis, ils sont amères
comme des mensonges
ou salé comme tragédie.

Et si tu me dis qu'ils goûtent
le fruit dans le purgatoire,
je pourrais mieux
comprendre.

Je ne sais que la mer les veut,
et d'une certaine manière, ils semblent
vouloir la mer.

Et si tu me dis, je te ferai confiance.

Si tu—

et seulement si tu—
me feras

la même.

RÉEXAMEN
(RECONSIDERATION)

L'oiseau
d'Azur satinée
de la tonnelle
de Nouvelle-
Guinée
mélange
charbon de bois et
jus des baies,
et avec un morceau
de l'écorce pour un pinceau
peint l'intérieur
de son nit
en bleu.

Donc, ne pas dire que nous
ne pouvons pas
supporter cette.

Pas vrai
(madame, monsieur).

GAUCHO, CAVALIER ARGENTIN
(GAUCHO)

Le soleil goutte
la glaçage de coucher de soleil
sur la pampa.

À un nouveau feu,
il mange, commes toujours,
avec ses doigts.

Il explique:

S'il tu as besoin une fourchette
tu as besoin d'un plat

si tu as besoin d'une table
sur laquelle le mettre
puis une chaise
pour asseoir à la table
avant longtemps
tu habites avec une femme
et un groupe des gosses
et un chien
qui tue tes poulets.

DALÍ: VIEIL HOMME À LA GAUCHE DE LA MER
(DALÍ'S OLD MAN TO THE LEFT OF THE SEA)

Je suis l'homme encéphalique
étayant ma tête, obtus gonflé
sur le y d'une branche, bâton d'augure
mis à califourchon sur une chaise ordinaire
sur le sable finement broyé
à partir de vieux crânes,
et il est l'écho morphique,
cloche du campanile de la ville,
ballerine transparente.
cerceau d'une vieille femme,
de Bélial incarné, tournant la roue
qui sape une chaîne d'albumine
des sutures
de mon embarras.

Je suis impossible d'habiller
et difficile d'aimer.

BALLES EN SAPHIR DE L'AMOUR PUR
(SAPPHIRE BULLETS OF PURE LOVE)

titre suggéré par J. McLaughlin

Ils disent qu'il est mort en souriant
abattu par les balles en saphir
de l'amour pur, sonnaient à partir
un magasin de secrets,
que son coeur a explosé
et est devenu
une arrière-pensée rayonnante,
que la flaque sous lui
était la couleur de tourmalines
et que l'opale, mouchetée de turquoise
étaient ses larmes.

CONFRATERNITY OF THE GHOST
OF JOHN DONNE (I)

But as it is said
of old cosmographers, that when
they had said all that they knew of a country,
    and yet much more was to be said,
    they said
that the rest of those countries were possessed with giants,
    or witches
or spirits or wild beasts, so that
they could pierce no farther
into that country, so when
we have traveled as far as we can, with safety,
    that is, as far as ancient, or modern expositors lead us
in the discovery
of these new heavens, and new earth,
yet we must say at last,
that it is a country inhabited with angels,
    or archangels,
with cherubim, and seraphim,
and that we can look no farther into it
with these eyes.

Where it is locally, we enquire not;
    we rest in this
that it is the habitation
prepared by the blessed saints of God,
heavens,
where the moon is more glorious than our sun,
and the Sun as glorious
    as He that made it;
for it is he himself, the son of God,

the sun of glory.
A new earth, where all
the waters are milk, and all
        their milk, honey,
where all their grass is corn
and all their corn, manna;
where all their glebe,
all their clods of earth are gold, and all
their gold of innumerable carats;
where all their minutes are ages, and all their ages, eternity;
        where every thing, is every minute
        in the highest exaltation, as good as it can be
and yet super-exalted
and infinitely multiplied by every
minute's addition, every minute
infinitely better than ever it
was before.

Of these new heavens and this new earth
we must say at last, that we
can say nothing.

For the eye of man has not seen,
nor ear heard, nor heart conceived
        the state of this place.

We limit and determine
our consideration with that horizon
with which the Holy Ghost has limited us,
that it is that new heavens
        and new earth
        wherein
dwells
righteousness.

CONFRATERNITY OF THE GHOST
OF JOHN DONNE (II)

But as it is said of old cosmographers,
that when they'd said all that they knew
of a country (and yet much could be said),
they said the rest were possessed with giants,
or witches or spirits or wild beasts
so all would blink and dare a-pierce no farther
into that country; so when we've gone
as far as we are able, and with safety,
far as ancient, or our own expositors
can lead us to discovery of these
new heavens, and new earth, yet we
must say at last, that it is a country
inhabited with angels, or archangels,
of cherubim or seraphim, and that
we look not farther into with these eyes.
Where, we enquire not; we rest in this,
resolve it to the habitation made
by blessed saints of God, and heavens, where
the moon is more glorious than our sun,
and Sun, glorious as He that made it;
for it is He himself, the son of God,
the sun of glory.

A new earth, where all
waters are of milk, and all milk,
as honey, where their grass is corn
and all their corn, of Moses' manna come;
where all their glebe, and all their clods of earth
are gold, and all their gold of innumerable carats;

where all their minutes age-eternal be;
where every several thing, is every minute
cast exalted high, to be as good
as it can be, and super-yet-exalted,
infinitely multiplied by every
minute's next addition, every minute
infinitely better than before.
Of these new heavens, this new earth,
we say at last, we can say nothing.
For eye of man has not seen, nor ear heard,
nor heart conceived the symbols of this place.
We founder to determine and consider
toward the Holy Ghost's horizon veiled,
and that it is entire of that new heaven
and new earth wherein dwells righteousness.

*The two Donne pieces are made by transposition
of prose from "A Sermon of Commemoration of the
Lady Danvers, late Wife of Sir John Danvers.
Preached at Chilsey, where she was lately buried.
By John Donne Dean of St. Paul's, London. 1 July
1627." The first poem is rendered verbatim, only
broken into poetic strophes of free verse, while the
second poem is placed into blank verse, and
amended solely to accommodate the meter.*

POSTCARDS FROM LINCOLN PARK

For decades:

the Cotton Candy Woman
in her enclosure with the dollhouse roof
would never age so long as she stayed,
year by year, plump
and permanently waved of brown, tight curls,
fat arms of twirled cones and
the bites of sweet-nothing, pink
and blue, who dipped, also,
the bricks of harlequin ice-cream
into pans of warm chocolate,
it kissing hard, then weeping
the frozen three flavors a good cry
of confection,
stuck to perfect moments.

The boats in a circle
with their pastel
enamel sides and wood-slat
inlays at the stems,
and the rocking as you stepped into
the one you picked
above the exotic swell of the twelve
deep inches,
and for two tickets,
commandeered it.

The red Tilt-a-Whirl of baskets
bowling up and down the hills

that teetered as we spun,
all the marvels of gravity,
fabulous force, and currents—
Bubble Bounce, Scrambler, Whip,
Round-Up, Trabant that made us sick,
Paratrooper, Himalaya, Rocket-Jets
and Flying Cages, Dodgems driving
each a different color, banging tire-bumpers,
sliding sparks down each electric stick.

Port wine in paper cups
among the Portuguese, clam-cakes cased
in salty grease that blessed
the summer smell of the pavilion,
regiments of picnic tables and benches where
we sat among dukes and duchesses
of the circuit, the court of Lawrence Welk—
Joe Feeney, Irish tenor
who melted my mother, Bobby and Cissy
who were born to twirl among wedding cakes
of the imagination, Jo-Ann Castle and her
barrelhouse ivories,
or the line-up of country and western stars—
Hank Snow and his suit that lit up,
Kitty Wells's gospel truth of the God
that didn't make honky-tonk angels, and
Rex Trailer, our own Boston Cowboy
of Saturday morning TV (with his sidekick Pablo),
signing the pictures.

In the midway, among the small stalls
of curios and games of chance
was the big wheel, where housewives
proud of their vocation played the numbers

to win not bears or trinkets but groceries,
boxes of Tide and Brillo Pads, cans of Spam
and pie-cherries, valuables of a depression
long past, and yet anticipated.

The finest wooden roller coast
north of Coney Island, The Comet—
a passage rite when you were tall
and brave enough to ride it. It heaved
and railed against the normal world
(with the occasional accident)
aside the sedate, man-straddled engine
of the humming train
that surrounded the miniatures
of Kiddie Land; the monolith signed
its pale iconograph
toward the sky, and held forth in
its own shudders
of dominance over the coal-smelling
jalopy go-karts that rumbled and coughed
perpetually below it, those cars that Ma,
who could not drive on the street,
so loved to navigate.

In the Grand Arcade we rolled
discarded duckpin balls, side by side
at the five rings of fortune, tallying
our token strips
for baubles of Chinese plastic
as they plopped;
we slid nickels that turned on
the film-noir of a city street

on an old screen that showed
the walkers in our way,
us frantic at the real steering wheel.
More nickels for the baseball game,
the buttons for fastballs, curves,
and sliders, the bat-snap of the silver ball
that headed for a hole, the pass of the stiff
base runners, the occasional
catapult to the rafters
of the home run as if
it were Yaz or Tony C. at Fenway,
and it was,
it was that, it was.

And the house of another universe.

"Follow the floor" my brother said
to avoid forever inside the mirrors
of yourself, for when you looked up, your life
prismed into past and future, into
calculations that didn't line up.

Escaping, you landed
in the furnished, slanted
Room that Jack Built, pulled
to one wall, where reality, *like* reality,
questioned itself, and you struggled
to pull through into the
Hall of Darkness, stumbling
among obstacles
that appeared not to be there— you tripped
on nothing you expected with your feet
or felt with your hands, reaching to the
glow of the purple ramp, upward.

Atop, the light again, fresh air—
you could wave
to figures but not reach, you could walk
forward, back, forward
on the shifting boards
trying to achieve
the simple goal of another side.

And at end you sat
in the unassuming chaise, only
to have it collapse you to the
carpet, magic, the bump, bump
and bump down to the outside arms
from one Fun House to another, the happy
and the not of this wide life.

When it closed we weren't there.
We were in Florida, where we lived
and had Disney, and children.
They fenced-in Lincoln Park,
let flipped calendars of weeds and trees
and vandals and fires swallow
and burn it. The relics were gone, only
the big spine of The Comet yet rising there
about the dis-and-disassembling.

Finally, they brought
it all down, every bit shaved into grass,
concrete, glass and of becoming
Lincoln Park Commons, condos of
pretend wealth and real retirement,
taking all the breathtaking indoors,

locked away from us
unless we, of love, would open it

like this, in our minds.

COMMUNION SONATA

after Transcendental Etude No. 11,
"Harmonies du Soir," by Franz Liszt

I. Mausoleum

(adagio, lamentoso)

Dull gong.　　　　A dull
gong against the distance of a Sunday,
June morning.

"Hurry up."　　　　"Come along."
The parish's young marrieds run their children up churchsteps
to a throng upon the landing.

As blur in camera's sight, yet clicked
by Christ-time's metal shutter, bluegreen eyes
propel their light along the ground,
up trellised brick, ascending silver gutter
to the rose-rimmed bells whose sway entice
their petals to a semi-circle flutter onto ivory hearts,
and ivory gowns, where she dwells a sweet,
refracted moment, then
walks on.

She walks, out among high mounds, monuments,
a granite Christ-on-Calvary, past dead geraniums,
down an asphalt strip to double-doors
and a pantheon of cold, brown, stone.

Flames suspended on their wicks, the gallery sits
without pictures or forms.

At rows of oaken seats she stands
her cat-feet on green carpets,
a countenance's subtle-sired features
scanning hand-carved signatures 'cross the wall, dropping
magnetized, to a plate that lights—
behind green eyes—
a vivid screen to re-and-redefine
the patterns of her life,
(or lives),
before the first desertion out there among the rocks,
before this too-new wintery interment
off wing of that first palsied prophecy,
leading to incalculable questions
which bounce in echoes off uncracked marble
and rest like sun-dew on the floor,
where they linger
dissipate and
are gone.

*   *   *   *   *   *   *

We are baptized
in uncertain pools of black
cathedral light and fight, we fight
a breakneck pillory of circumstance and sin
seeking only simple breathing,
a suck of milk, a soft caress...
'til cold madonnas leave us clutching
through a lens of holy water for

an *alabaster* breast—
and pinions pressed upon our hours
only bleed the tincture of a memory
for redress.

    She'd squirm
    in the folds of a cradle to be fed; he'd watch her—
    crown of wisps over wide, and widening, aquamarine
    eyes—
    the conscious burning, burning
    beryls of new life.

    She'd take Eu'christs
    careful not to bite or swallow; he'd watch her
    trail of pink skirts as she left the railing,
    her seraphine pink-plastic tiara
    crooked and soon pulled off
    to play the Ballet-Mudslide
    on a morrow.

    She screamed
    as he held her with one arm, climbing
    climbing the Ferris ride that first time,
    to sweep down once again to Mother's waiting
    aprons, waiting aprons and

    she held him, she did, upright when he staggered
    and cried with him in soft duet
    the night they lost his pretty-faced wife,
    velvet curtains
    to a silent love affair

so *where*
and on what avenue to seek them, having long and tongueless
gone?
Through the heavy plaque, through that? Through the tarot,
through some Eastern beads, or toss of Chinese slats?
Or idiot winds that blew
through letters curtly written incognizant of portents,
the ink fast separating to greens and golds
with salted rain upon them? Or do we
at last, gasping
count the pictures left along the mantel
juxtaposed with incense candles? Framed in brass:
"The Wedding," the two together then *ou, " 'Ti Chou on the
Bouncing Laps,"*
or *"Second Wedding"'*s salve, perhaps
lending slender struts of meaning to the search,
a search for what
with whom
and where to find it?

She leaves this place
a vacuum of answers
easing the door
behind her.

The ants
move quicker among their blades as she passes,
their feelers to the skyblue air
unthinking.

II. The Scapulars

(andante cantabile; allegro vivace assai)

Wild celebrant
in white and flashing red performs his mystic transference
of grain to flesh, grapes to blood
enchanting thirteen little penitents
whose crimes have had the time to stray
from chocolate theft
to giggling accords in a backyard of whispers.

About each golden-flecked
and collar-buttoned neck
and on each pair of shoulders, sets
a cotton strap of Christ's life sewn in multicolored thread—
from stable-birth
to the Walk of Palm and Olive, dead,
hung like meat upon a nail but changed,
in fortnights, to an elevated grail which would
"shake and almost crack the axis of this earth,"
so the rector said to his little lambs in the front pew and
anointed with their sweet, exhilarated breath announced:
"so much for death, so much, so much, for death."

The highest purpose flies
to the creation of effect.

A late arrival
genuflects.

He gives them bread.
They bow their heads and turn
a little army, flushing red
toward winking Sister Jacqueline, who'd said

"Your souls will be as purely white as this"—
and taps
once more
a crooked finger on her chest.

      *   *   *   *   *   *   *

As fishers, we
who float on shimmering seas, each
servile to his Simon-self, to his own reach,
hauling the twine of retrospective motion,
the appalling grip-on-grip to find beneath
the sequined, black-drawn drapes of God's mind,
a line that draws and ties
a small, paternally-created son
to one enormous,
inevitable One;

through pain of progeny, the strain of labor,
it follows our ascendant wealth
(like kittens pawing walls of brittle paper),
and as fishers fall
amid the images of sackcloth, and some neighbors—
it can stain the warp and weft
of our collected,
frightened laughter yet remain,
more tauntingly along
the border-stitch of Janie's
fifty-nine
cent

scapular, as lit
by a nine-
cent taper.

      *   *   *   *   *   *   *

To clack of kneelers
the closing keys chorded with a light hand
sift in breeze with consonants of Portuguese,
crossing the street to where three
foreign boys of a foreign Mass
turn tumbles with a dog on dandelion grass, now all
for their Lady of the Untalkative Bench
(who speaks only English
and a little French).

Sun invades
dark inches of an acorn shade
to frame, for blue jade, white these knights
of the Teeshirt Pact—
who bounce and spin their soccer balls
about the spaniel, spun and sprawled
exhausted but, intact, to pull
the dew-kiss of her smile
through the falling, falling track
of one, dropped rivulet.

As noontime blows
grey birds off black wires and arrests
the sepals of yellow-bells shivering on stems
for its light she rises and the boys retire,
Life's Brass Boys, duty done
dissolving their covenants on the run
for a meal of sweetbread,
chicken, and plums.

She wipes the last, wet welling
from those deep, descending browns
of brows, her father's brows
passed through her to everlasting mirrors on
(she knew that, oh, she knew it!)—
she kicks a clumsy,
fawning hedge and like a fool
apologizes to it.

Her shoes step forward
shuddering with a vent
placards of splitting sidewalk cement.
Her eyes
an opal. almondine synopsis, spy
reviving to a warm
and ever warming light
a thousand dewdrop postulates picked
from nineteen summer skies,
all gathered in a cistern of quintessence
swelling the senses with a supple,
symphonic presence far, far removed from pale
rigid, earth-flung fists of mail as she,
child who turns, again, a woman free
to smile light defiance
'stead of double in travail
and port
her living, bright religion like
a sheer, sheer, veil.

III. Coda

(dolce, meno mosso)

Evening, and the children turn
on broad cushions, mouthing soft repeats
of Buxtehude's organ music
pealing in their sleep.

Ab origin, ad finem, ad infinitum.

Before the sun comes again, and on a fluted wind
the subtle nocturne of a baby's cry
dances near the pillow where she lies
star-open-eyed in dreams, and breathing.

One purpose
past the humming streetlights,
greybird shadows strung along the wire,
past their unfeathered young in cornices of a Catholic spire
and beyond the moon—
a purpose evident and ever high
and swaddled in the night's black flannel
reaches, reaches, ever
to survive.

A fortiori, *a posteriori,*
in gloria Dei, gloria Dei, Patris.

SKETCHES FROM THE LIBRETTO
OF THE OPERA, *HELEN KELLER*

CAST

HELEN KELLER (AS YOUNG GIRL)
MRS. KELLER
ANNIE SULLIVAN (AS YOUNG WOMAN)
MICHAEL ANAGNOS, DIRECTOR OF
    PERKINS SCHOOL
MISS PANIER, A PERKINS TEACHER
SMALL CHORUS
ALEXANDER GRAHAM BELL
MARK TWAIN
HELEN KELLER (AS YOUNG WOMAN)
LARGE CHORUS
POLLY THOMSON, ANNIE'S & HELEN'S ASSISTANT
JOHN MACY, ANNIE'S HUSBAND
PETER FAGAN, HELEN'S TEMPORARY SECRETARY
JUGGLER
FIRE-EATER
VAUDEVILLE EMCEE
ANNIE SULLIVAN (AS OLDER WOMAN)
HELEN KELLER (AS OLDER WOMAN)
ELEANOR ROOSEVELT
MARTHA GRAHAM
DANCERS
PATTY DUKE
WINNIE CORBALLY, AN ASSISTANT
EVELYN SEIDE, AN ASSISTANT
CHAPERONE AT NATIONAL CATHEDRAL
SCHOOL CHILDREN
LAST CHILD

STAGING

Three pedestal stages arrayed as a triangle across the stage floor, each spotlighted; screen on each side, one for scrolling the libretto, one for manual spelling, video, and still photos.

TIMELINE

The opera spans eighty years, from Helen at age seven, when she discovers the significance of words (the "well scene"), to beyond her death at 87. Helen survived her teacher, Annie Sullivan, by more than thirty years. Helen died in 1968, and was buried next to Annie in Washington D.C.'s National Cathedral. The opera ends as school children visit the graves.

PLOT SUMMARY

The opera illuminates how Annie Sullivan came to Helen, Helen's initial discovery of words, and her time at Perkins School where she first became a national celebrity. It illustrates how Perkins's director, Michael Anagnos, fanned that celebrity, and how the presence of Helen and Annie at the school created jealousy and animosity among the other teachers. The conflict culminated in "The Frost King" episode where Helen was accused of copying a story that may have been read to her years earlier. Anagnos had touted the story Helen gave him, which was picked up by the press. As a result, he found himself in the middle of the controversy over the work's authenticity. Helen maintained the support of men like Alexander Graham Bell and Mark Twain, both of whom thought the incident ludicrous and vindictive, and campaigned for her publicly.

Annie and Helen left Perkins; Helen wrote *The Story of My Life,* and prepared for her ultimate goal: to attend Radcliffe College. The effort involved two years of study at Cambridge School for Girls. Working without Braille books, the manual-signed, self-induced rigor of Annie reading to Helen affected the health of both women. Helen eventually did attend Radcliffe and passed the standard exams, the answers for which she typed out herself in front of a witness, graduating with honors.

As Helen and Annie began lecture tours that highlighted the problems of the blind and deaf, John Macy came into their lives. Macy was a brilliant scholar and writer, as well as being an ardent Socialist. Macy would manage Helen's burgeoning career in writing and publishing, and became Helen's and Annie's de facto manager. Annie fell in love with Macy, who was very fond of Helen, and the three became inseparable for a time. Later, Macy felt himself the weak link of the triangle. He proved an unreliable manager, lost his affection for Annie, who had aged rapidly and gained weight, and he began drinking heavily. Once, when Helen and Annie were on tour, he accidently burned their Boston apartment, and thereafter lived permanently separated from them. Macy died in 1932.

Annie contracted tuberculosis, and was forced to take a hiatus away from Helen, who was cared for by Annie's and Helen's able assistant, Polly Thomson. While Annie was gone however, an additional secretary was necessary for Helen. Macy arranged for an associate, Peter Fagan, to fill the temporary role. Fagan became close to Helen, and the two had an affair. A clandestine engagement was thwarted by Helen's mother, who took Helen back to Alabama to live with Helen's sister, Mildred. Fagan followed, somehow got messages to Helen, and planned to elope with her. The plans were found out, and

Fagan was forced to leave Mildred's house at gunpoint by Mildred's husband. Fagan tried one more time, but was either scared off or paid off, never to return, as Helen was witnessed waiting all night on the porch for him, bag at her side.

On Annie's return, the pair toured the country on the lucrative vaudeville circuit, providing a serious "act" between comedians, acrobats, and various curiosities. When Annie became too ill to take the stage with Helen, Polly assumed Annie's role. The trio of Helen, Polly, and Annie toured various parts of the world, and Helen made millions of dollars for charities including the American Foundation for the Blind. Among other persons of note who became her close friends: Eleanor Roosevelt, dancer / choreographer Martha Graham, and young Patty Duke, who had played Helen (opposite Anne Bancroft as Annie) on Broadway and in film, the latter winning for Patty an Academy Award.

During her lifetime, Helen wrote twelve books, many magazine articles, and lectured on a variety of subjects: socialism, pacifism, religion and philosophy, as well as the creative life and thought processes of the deaf-blind. Annie Sullivan died in 1936; the loss was a brutal blow. Helen endured however and in fact, thrived over the decades, her celebrity only increasing. Helen died in 1968, at the age of 87. She was buried inside the National Cathedral in Washington, D.C., resting beside her beloved Annie Sullivan, whom she called "Teacher."

THE PHANTOM'S SONG

duet from the libretto of the opera, **Helen Keller**

*[There are three pedestal stages arrayed across the greater
stage. Clutching a doll in one hand, HELEN KELLER (AS
YOUNG GIRL) crosses from stage left, stopping downstage
before the center pedestal on which MRS. KELLER watches
her progress. HELEN feels around, sniffs, and grabs a rose
with her free hand from the rose bush; she pulls it off and
proceeds slowly to stage right, still sniffing the rose, making
"raspberries" and humming sounds, past the last pedestal
stage, stage right, where she stops, circles, and plops herself
down, letting go of the doll. HELEN holds the rose to her
nose with both hands and her sounds continue with random
tones, until one tone is sustained. On the pedestal stage right
is HELEN (AS YOUNG WOMAN), who will act as her own
character, in this case adding a chorus of the mind, and sings
for herself as a child. HELEN (AS YOUNG GIRL) rises, circles
again in place, and making tighter circles, spins several times,
plops down again, probing with her hands, finds her doll and
hugs it, rocking back and forth.]*

MRS. KELLER

God gave me joy for emptiness, a perfect child,
nineteen months of cling and exploration,
words I heard, we heard the words you learned,
to sing your ma and waa your water, run
to light, know yes and no and oh, you *still* so
love the roses!... though I cannot tell you
how they grow. Music made you tap and hum,
and colors lit your bluey eyes with wonder,
while your heart, as through your arms you held

yourself elective to the warm embrace of Mother.
You still come for food and warmth, and hold
your doll as if were you and me, another.

HELEN (AS YOUNG GIRL)

Mmmm....

HELEN (AS YOUNG WOMAN)

(matching tone)

Mmmmama is what your Helen knows....
Mama find your Helen in the rose...

MRS. KELLER

In the past, they'd leave you on a hillside,
pray every day's reminder to forget
the curse, is it, that makes you less than they are
that they trouble to invent, and I regret.
Your father finds it hard to love but loves you,
and cares to act as well as he can care,
who pays the passage for someone to come here,
to our little town a mile past nowhere,
to reach you toward the things beyond the signals
we and you can understand, to make
a softer kind of hard, a kind of somehow
past the awful granteds that we take,
so certain-seeming as an evening star——
and bring you, Helen, to a light less far.

HELEN (AS YOUNG WOMAN)

Mama, you and Papa did your best.
Mama, Papa answered your request.

CHALLENGE TO MISS SPITFIRE

duet from the libretto of the opera, **Helen Keller**

ANNIE SULLIVAN (AS YOUNG WOMAN)

Are you going to dismiss me? I was right and we know
what these teachers at Perkins are like.

MICHAEL ANAGNOS

As it happens, no. You're on probation, yes, it's true,
but this so-special school, the very best of schools for
the blind has been kind to you. Annie... my little Miss
Spitfire!...
You know I'd never cast you out if I could help it,
and I *can,* so you, my most difficult, brilliant student,
will not, if you like, be just cast out, but cast *to.*

ANNIE

And you mean...

ANAGNOS

A job, Miss Sullivan, a seven year-old, a girl,
deaf-blind, in Alabama. The family wants you.

ANNIE

Deaf-blind? What qualifies me so? Deaf-blind!

ANAGNOS

Because you've learned much here, from the work
of Dr. Howe, from poor Laura Bridgman, and me,
and because it's a change for you, a challenge, chance
to do what may be impossible, yet maybe there's good
to be done, and growth, in the child and in you.

ANNIE

But I've not been anywhere, a nobody, and you forget,
I'm three steps from being blind, too.
How can I...

ANAGNOS

Would you leave the child as she is?
A mother calls for you, *this* one, Annie, calls for *you*.
There is no one with your pluck, your drive,
your ingenuity, no one I think of with more to prove.

ANNIE

Could I? I could do it?

ANAGNOS

I think you could. I'll arrange it.
The Perkins School sends Annie Sullivan,
ticket for one, to Tuscumbia, Alabama.
Make us proud, Miss Spitfire.
Make *yourself,* too.

FROM THE WELL-HOUSE

trio from the libretto of the opera, **Helen Keller**

HELEN (AS YOUNG WOMAN)

Every day she spelled to me
the objects of the world,
many things I knew so well
and never called, food and doll
and baby girl, but then
these fingers turned and turned
and I would copy, copy fingers,
make a game, but would not learn

until the water, w-a-t-e-r

at the well, as I pumped it,
wonderful cool something that
was flowing o'er my hand.

ANNIE SULLIVAN (AS YOUNG WOMAN)

Mug, water, mug, water, wet, water.
Cool, water. Mug, water. Cool, water.
Wet, water. Mug, water, wet, cool,
wet, yes, water, cool yes, water wet,
water cool, water, water, water, water,
water, water, water, water on your hand,
wet, cool, on your hand, pump, water,
water, yes water, water, water.
W-a-t-e-r, mug, wa-*what*, yes point! yes,
w-a-t-e-r, water, yes my darling, water!

HELEN (AS GIRL)

Wwwwaaa...

ANNIE

-ter w-a-t-e-r, water my God, water!

HELEN (AS YOUNG WOMAN)

Water, one word bubbling from
the buried years...

Mother said it had been my first word
without pantomime or plea,
before *ma,* and *some,* and *yes,* and *no.*
Waa, Waa-waa for water, water, water...

ANNIE (guiding Helen's hands)

Helen, H-e-l-e-n, Helen, H-e-l-e-n,
Teacher, T-e-a-c-h-e-r, Teacher, T-e-a-c-h-e-r,
Helen, H-e-l-e-n, Helen, H-e-l-e-n,
Teacher, T-e-a-c-h-e-r, Teacher, T-e-a-c-h-e-r,
ground, g-r-o-u-n-d, ground, g-r-o-u-n-d,
grass, g-r-a-s-s, grass, g-r-a-s-s,
stone, s-t-o-n-e, stone, s-t-o-n-e,
fence, f-e-n-c-e, fence, f-e-n-c-e,
stick, s-t-i-c-k, stick, s-t-i-c-k,
rose, r-o-s-e, rose, r-o-s-e,
leaf, l-e-a-f, leaf, l-e-a-f...

HELEN (AS YOUNG WOMAN)

In the moments Teacher walked me
to the big house, stop and go, stop, stop,
stop and go, no longer playing finger games,
but serious the fingers, the feel, my pointing
on my knees and the vast demand for names,
in minutes grew my library up
to thirty things, thirty more than ever came
from the Phantom of my past,
from the nothingness, flinging
open doors to mind and mindscape vast.

ANNIE

Step, s-t-e-p, step, s-t-e-p,
door, d-o-o-r, door, d-o-o-r
Mrs. Keller! Mrs. Keller!

MRS. KELLER (opens door)

Miss Sullivan, what are you...

ANNIE

She knows!

MRS. KELLER

But how, what?

ANNIE

She spells, she knows!

MRS. KELLER

My GOD! She knows?!

ANNIE

She knows! She knows! She knows!

IN THESE BOOKS (TEACHER AND HELEN)

*duet from the libretto of the opera, **Helen Keller***

HELEN (AS YOUNG GIRL) (manually spelled and sung in the mind)

Helen loves stories.

ANNIE (AS YOUNG WOMAN) (spelled and sung)

Helen is I.

HELEN

I love stories.

ANNIE

We love stories. All love stories.
Stories are in books. Life is stories.

HELEN

I know stories. Teacher tells me.

ANNIE

Helen, everyone has stories.
The people in stories are like you and me.
Each life has many stories. They are
real, real stories.

HELEN

Homer makes stories for me.
You give me Homer's stories that I like.
Does Teacher have stories?
Will you tell me your stories?

ANNIE

I will, but here is another story from Homer.
Homer makes his people real.
We can make people that have their stories,
like Homer made Achilles for you.

HELEN

Make Achilles real now.

ANNIE

Achilles has strong arms. Very strong.
Achilles has strong arms.

HELEN

Papa's arms are strong. Papa makes smoke
in his pipe for me. Does Achilles make smoke?

ANNIE

Can he Helen?

HELEN

Yes, he is like Papa! Achilles makes smoke.

ANNIE

Achilles is alone.

HELEN

Papa likes to be alone...
until I find Papa!

ANNIE

Sometimes, people like to be alone.
Sometimes, people don't want to be alone.

HELEN

Before Teacher came, did Teacher like to be alone?

ANNIE

Teacher was alone many times and did not like it.

HELEN

I was alone before Teacher.

ANNIE

Now Helen and Teacher are together.

HELEN

And Achilles and the people in the books.

ANNIE

Helen, you learn so fast. *(aside)*

That is what the world can give to Helen. *(to Helen)*
The world in these books.
The world in these books.

ANAGNOS CELEBRATES

trio from the libretto of the opera, **Helen Keller**

MICHAEL ANAGNOS

She is a sun-child. A divinity. A gift
of Gods who know more than we do.
(But *we* have done our part to guide her, too.)
To think, at eleven, learns to read and write
in French, inside three full phases of moon.
Three months! Vocabulary of a college man!
She thinks things through, thinks 'em through!

ANNIE SULLIVAN

Gifted yes, but still a girl, a girl, not a god,
even a small one. What you're doing is dangerous
for Helen and for me and for you. And the more
you praise beyond the real, the more the others
would tip your high rocking horse on top of us!
She's a girl, a girl, just a wonderful girl!

ANAGNOS

Eleven, to think! And then, this little story,
the birthday present for her *second Papa,*
charming, she wrote it for me, and here it is—
I sent it to our *Journal,* eleven!
Miss Panier? Now *The Gazette* has picked it up!

MISS PANIER (enters stage left)

Mr. Anagnos I must speak to you, alone.

ANAGNOS

It's never done, these wonders.
And *The Sun* reporters want to come!

MISS PANIER (crosses from stage left)

Mr. Anagnos?

ANAGNOS

They're on their way to see what I, what we,
what you and me have done. And just eleven!

MISS PANIER

I must... Can you leave, Miss Sullivan?

ANNIE

Leave? More sneaking around, Miss Panier?
Helen told me you...

MISS PANIER

Mr. Anagnos...

ANAGNOS

Annie...

(Annie leaves, via stage left.)

MISS PANIER

Mr. Anagnos, you must know...
While you were away there was a call.
The Gazette, about a Mrs. Canby.

ANAGNOS

Canby?

(Miss Panier presents the Gazette edition to Anagnos.)

MISS PANIER

That story of Helen's. She did not write it.
This Miss Canby did! Compare...

ANAGNOS

But...

MISS PANIER

Look, look at this.... she *copied* her.

ANAGNOS

I can't believe...

MISS PANIER

Miss Sullivan knew. I could tell by
how Helen answered my questions.
She said as much to me!

ANAGNOS

What? Perhaps you're incorrect. Perhaps...

MISS PANIER

I knew it, knew it all along. They don't
belong at Perkins. You don't deserve...

ANAGNOS

This can't be, but whatever it is... it isn't good.
It isn't good... I see.

THE TRIAL

quartet with chorus from the libretto of the opera, **Helen Keller**

MICHAEL ANAGNOS (both aloud and manually signing)

Helen, when you wrote your little story
that I sent to *The Journal* with my praise,
had you known of The Frost King already?
Did you not make it up yourself? Was
it read to you?... you told me it was yours...

HELEN (AS YOUNG GIRL) (both aloud and manually signing)

No I... it *was* mine, I thought... but now I...

ANAGNOS

What?

HELEN

Are my thoughts mine? Or are all things
and words, what we see and hear.... what
we are told...

ANAGNOS

Were you told? Tell me. Miss Panier says...

HELEN

I wonder if I have a mind...

ANNIE SULLIVAN

Look what you're doing to the girl
you think you made!

ANAGNOS

Miss Sullivan!

ANNIE

She was read no such story
by me or in my presence
and you know Helen!
Her imagination is bigger
than all of us! You of all
people know what she is,
she, herself, not us, not a book,
no one *made* her or could make her,
least of all you!

ANAGNOS

Leave Miss Sullivan!

ANNIE

I'm going nowhere, you can hang me also.

ANAGNOS

Our Miss Panier states that Helen said she...

ANNIE

Miss Panier is a witch that eats children.
Would you like *that* story? She is jealous of
me, jealous of Helen for what she's done
within this school and more important, without!

ANAGNOS

Miss Sullivan, I...

ANNIE

Once you were her champion, you sent me
to Helen, you saw the results. Then you built
her bigger than she needed to be built, than
the miracle she clearly was. And now, look at this,
look at yourself! The Frost King is you!

ANAGNOS

Enough! We will deliberate.

CHORUS

Deliberate! Deliberate! Deliberate! Deliberate!

ANNIE

Deliberately, I think, too.

LETTERS OF BELL AND TWAIN

trio of letters from the libretto of the opera, **Helen Keller**

HELEN (AS YOUNG WOMAN)

The criminal falls far and fast and with her
comes a title earned or fitted not,
I only know the pit of me within
re-lives a trial of sadness as my lot.

I fear my face is torn and tarnished now
and when I write, words say as someone else,
perhaps into a shell the hermit has to plow
and even that is borrowed for a self.

ALEXANDER GRAHAM BELL

Be you my child, for there's no fault and they will listen:
our most original compositions are composed
from separate strains of one and thousand bows.
We all compose from what we read or what we're told
and greatest of inventions comes from things we know.

The heroes of our books and lives discovered
right beneath our noses are as evidently true
as innocents come offering their right and trust.
The miracle of you is that you let us find you—
that we found you is the miracle of us...

MARK TWAIN

I told them, Helen, just the other day
oh, dear me, how unspeakably funny,

idiotic and grotesque the lies
these little pompous people do employ—
as if there's anything in human utterance
except the second-hand, a million hands!
I'll try my best to temper what annoys:

To think these solemn donkeys sought to break
a little child's heart with mealy rubbish—
dull and hoary pirates, setting them
tribunals for to purify a kitten who
might filch a chop from out their royal kitchen!
Don't read my girl!... These bastards born of bled-out
intellect, oh genii of arses, a commission...

HELEN

Now I have told you not to cuss and swear...

TWAIN

And I have told the undressed what to wear...

BELL

And we know what we know about the girl that's setting there.
She'll grow into the finest woman ever anywhere.

TWAIN AND BELL

She'll grow into the finest woman ever anywhere.

WHAT I SEE AND HEAR

aria from the libretto of the opera, **Helen Keller**

HELEN (AS YOUNG WOMAN)

What I see and hear is what you give me,
what I give to you is what I find,
in between the feeling and the scents of a believing
is there anything revealing left behind?

You call it dark, this place that I am living,
but black is just a need within a heart—
what I call white is brilliant light unsealing every seal
of the noisy band that feathers each day's start.

You are the object of me,
and I am the object of you—
I measure things, I tell time
by their motion, anchor some
to make a space that spins
me to the greater world,
an object of devotion.

A flash of smallest me that saved itself
in distant sight and sound reshapes the dishes
filled of fruits that taste of life, and bloom to me a learning
in the fragrance of their bodies, full of wishes.

There is in all of us a way to be
and do and have, to grow and celebrate
our common sense, our simple selves, our Seas of Galilee,
and what I see and hear, my friend, is great—
I see and hear the you inside of me.
I see and hear the you inside of me.

THE PASSION OF THE SLAVES

aria from the libretto of the opera, **Helen Keller**

ANNIE SULLIVAN (AS YOUNG WOMAN)

If they knew, could know, how much I love her,
knew how much as limb to her, I'm loved—
and yet my girl consumes this race,
the race of fingers to the goal of a phrase,
welding to a hundred mates and ways
the dual mania of slaves, of us
one to the other, the melding of our minds
and souls onward to someday's grave—
but for today, the next tome and lesson,
the proof that we can meet the grade
of greater schools prepared for the sighted,
for the easy lave of what they dream so hard,
the unheard that would leave them screaming
for release, for a savior reticent to save,
to be her, be me, chained to the flight
of fingers, eating fingers forming flesh
to blisters; eyes, my dimming eyes
that bleed to read unfeeling texts
of thought that she must understand as real—
how she works, I work, work to thresh
with our incessant fingers (without Braille)
the requisite grain of their hypocrite demands,
to be ready for Radcliffe, the Harvard of women,
as if it were nothing but marvel or parade
and not the world, shouldering the smolder
of these months and weeks and days, to tests
of anything ever enough, to praise.

WHAT I BELIEVE (RADCLIFFE GRADUATION)

chorus and aria from the libretto of the opera, **Helen Keller**

LARGE CHORUS

Radcliffe, now we rise to greet thee,
Alma Mater, hail to thee!
All our hearts are one in singing
Of our love and loyalty.
We have learn'd to know each other
In thy light, which clearly beams,
Thou hast been a kindly Mother,
Great fulfiller of our dreams.
Radcliffe, now we rise to greet thee,
Alma Mater, hail to thee!
Alma Mater, give thy daughters
Each a spark from Truth's pure flame;
Let them when they leave thy altars
Kindle others in thy name.
For our strength and joy in living,
Love and praise to thee belong;
Thou whose very life is giving,
From thy daughters take a song.
Radcliffe, now we rise to greet thee,
Alma Mater, hail to thee!

HELEN (AS YOUNG WOMAN)

Optimism, sure as seems to me,
comes feeling of an ever-present God
in every line and limb of you and me,
and not as some remote, rebuffing king
tilting all His universe at whim,
rolling balls to holes of falling in,

but on the sky careening, bouncing off
the sea to a pure and noble impulse
of the heart, source and center of all minds
and there, the only point of rest.

The shadows that we see, your way, or me
know only part of things and that they change;
but th' unconquerable mind that finds
the North of compasses on turning points
of chosen paths as perfect as our God
directs us still, and makes all evil halt
on way to good, the world within and world
without, of which we correspond from shall
to should, to hope ourselves a golden sense
and salve us a salvation— and it will.

CHORUS REPRISE

Love and praise to thee belong;
Thou whose very life is giving,
From thy daughters take a song.
Radcliffe, now we rise to greet thee,
Alma Mater, hail to thee!

THE COMPANY

trio from the libretto of the opera, **Helen Keller**

JOHN MACY

Yes, I call you Billy, don't know why.

You amaze me with your tender heart
and oh, that will, my little Marxist,
what a bomb thrower you would be...

ANNIE SULLIVAN (AS YOUNG WOMAN)

And that's what you would make her my darling,
brilliant, passionate, but dangerous to know...

MACY

so well....

ANNIE

so well....

HELEN (AS YOUNG WOMAN)

and what about me.... I am three!

MACY

More like two-as-one, plus one—
the one to bang the drum, but it's not
as if I didn't know the merry mathematics
of the firm of Keller and Sullivan, L.T.D.

ANNIE

But we love you, couldn't do without you,
not the writer you are, nor as read,
and if I stop my fingers I can tell you
you are utterly magnificent in bed.

MACY

You might as well spell it, since you
are just as free in love as me, and as I
said, our Billy-girl's a Socialist already.

ANNIE

Helen, your John is quite a fellow.

HELEN

Teacher tell me more, tell me if he
just now swells with pride to be
a part of us, protector and promoter
and the tiller of the waters as our guide.

ANNIE

He is everything left over just for us,
apart a world that wears as property
the you-and-me, as *things* however special,
that are things among *their* legacy and lives.

ENTER PETER FAGAN

duet from the libretto of the opera, **Helen Keller**

MRS. KELLER

I know he's only temporary— watch him.

POLLY THOMSON

He worked with Mr. Macy at *the Herald,*
and he learned her language quickly; now
with Annie convalescing in the tropics,
and Mr. Macy such the way he is,
we needed extra hands to organize
and Helen seems to like him well enough.

MRS. KELLER

Well enough may be too much, watch him.

POLLY

I understand your—

MRS. KELLER

Helen is a bursting woman now,
pretty idol, full of why and how
and where one way must never go for her,
never to endear to men endowed
and to be helpless hind into her ruin,
hopeless to a world I too well know...
watch him.

LOVE SCENE WITH FAGAN

duet from the libretto of the opera, **Helen Keller**

HELEN (AS YOUNG WOMAN)

I cannot sign with silver in your heart
realities that grieve me in this pleasure,
what comes of subtle dreams that others feel
as if invested by a common human right
are barred as of the stones removed from walls
I cannot touch, and so they stop me, can you see,
that if we wed you cannot know a mind
that settles now but settles much for less,
pence for gold and shuttered rooms for worlds.

PETER FAGAN

I see only with the all of me and never eyes,
or ears enclosed with love divested of
whatever claim to free except your life,
arrest in service of your signature,
the goodness of the air you bring and breathe
and though they try, and they will try, to keep us
on the farthest poles of globes away
from each, they cannot reach the woman, you,
who loves the man who asks her, wife, to be.

HELEN

Deep within me I could take you where
I heave and cry of self, a woman more
that feels perhaps than others could, defines

a holy empathy by flower and its tack;
the stamen's dust imbues a rich tomorrow
of its blooms and yet, recoils me,
wintering in springs that sever soul
from body, reach from hold, thanks to all
and nothing, and to where I must grow old.

FAGAN

No more of it, no more of it!
Your fingers tell what I must know!

HELEN

My fingers fly and I disorient!
As often I must fall, just so!

FAGAN

Do you love me, Helen?

HELEN

Yes, as water flows.

FAGAN

Then we'll pledge to us
that heretofore, and ever
as the time may find
that we will marry,
not like the other men-and-wives
but all the better in our seeking
of the purer in our finding,

and we'll live along the binding
of the book and this amending
of your life.

WAITING ON THE PORCH, IN VAIN

aria from the libretto of the opera, **Helen Keller**

HELEN KELLER (AS YOUNG WOMAN)

I have the time of the world,
all of it, and yet it's getting early, late.

I can tell the hours by the oncoming dew,
by the opening mouths of magnolias,
by still no shiver on the grate.
When you came last, and whispered to my hand
the plan, and fled to the rifle on Sister's stoop
I felt her husband's voice against my cheek,
as you did touch me last, and left this roof.

I thread the lines and lineaments
of people, and places, and things—
the ones that rail and the ones that love
and every in between.

Peter, have your life. Teacher has mine.

What you gave me thrilled, thrilled me
till I thought my legs electric, and your kiss
a ripe persimmon off a tree;
the pledge was out of Petrarch or
from Marlowe's fine Leander,
and there's nothing
to be severed— I, you, we.

Alone is my name. Alone as Homer's Helen
in the end. So my love, for moments high
and ever broad as heaven,
I am the Helen of the greater earth,
who finds her bag and shuffles she to bed
before somebody else's clock turns seven.

VAUDEVILLE DAYS

trio and chorus from the libretto of the opera, **Helen Keller**

(there is a juggler and a fire-eater on either audience aisle)

ANNIE SULLIVAN (AS OLDER WOMAN)

All the world loves Helen Keller, the girl of unconquerable spirit. She has fought her way uncomplaining against the greatest obstacles that ever confronted a human being... today she is the Star of Happiness to all struggling humanity.

LARGE CHORUS   (at back stage left)

Wonderful star of light!
Out from the darkness of night,
Sending down a silver ray
Turning nighttime into day.
Wonderful star of light,
Forever shining bright,
Always send your ray to me
Even to eternity.

VAUDEVILLE EMCEE

Thank you Miss Sullivan for bringing Miss Helen Keller to us this evening. Amazing how I moved those roses to the piano, and when Helen came on stage she immediately found them by their scent. She is a wonder! And can she really "hear" the piano by feeling the strings inside?

ANNIE

Yes. In her way, she can hear from the vibrations. She has heard Heifetz by touching the violin, Melchior by touching his lips and throat, and can feel the light tread of dancers.

EMCEE

Dancers! Can she dance?

ANNIE

Yes, she can.

EMCEE

Marvelous.
I have questions from the audience. May I?

ANNIE

I will spell the questions into her hand, and answer.

EMCEE

What is Miss Keller's age?

HELEN KELLER (AS OLDER WOMAN, VIA ANNIE)

There is no age upon the Broadway stage.

EMCEE

Does Miss Keller think of marriage?

HELEN (VIA ANNIE)

Yes, are you proposing to me?

EMCEE

Does talking tire you?

HELEN (VIA ANNIE)

Did you ever hear of a woman who tired of talking?

EMCEE

Do you close your eyes when you sleep?

HELEN (VIA ANNIE)

I guess I do, but I never stayed awake to see.

EMCEE

What do you think of President Harding?

HELEN (VIA ANNIE)

I have a fellow feeling for him. He seems as blind as I am.

EMCEE

Can you enjoy trees?

HELEN (VIA ANNIE)

Yes, they speak to me the silent works of God.

EMCEE

Who are the three greatest men of our time?

HELEN (VIA ANNIE)

Lenin, Edison, and Charlie Chaplin.

EMCEE

Who are your best pals?

HELEN (VIA ANNIE)

Books.

EMCEE

What is your idea of happiness?

HELEN (VIA ANNIE)

Having nothing to do.

EMCEE

Can you really perceive colors?

HELEN (VIA ANNIE)

Sometimes I feel blue
and sometimes I see red.

EMCEE

What could be worse than to be born blind?

HELEN (VIA ANNIE)

To have sight without vision.

EMCEE

Miss Helen Keller ladies and gentlemen!
Helen Keller!

THE PRISON OF US

duet from the libretto of the opera, **Helen Keller**

ANNIE SULLIVAN (AS OLDER WOMAN)

So it has come to this:

Does the drink make me a girl again?
It did once in a while, in your eyes.
Does the silence still the turning world again
a peaceful calm of smiles, in your eyes?
Do the nights I long to tingle still
that penetrate my dreams, demand your lies?
Has future-frame deducted three to two
as footnote of your legacy and mine—
So now there's only you, the whys, the wine.

JOHN MACY

It is too hard, too hard.

What we had through Helen was a treasure,
wonderful a while, as we sang.
What we had of us was icy fire,
'fore it strayed to ashy embers of harangue.
What we never had was true for each—
the who we were before, and longed to be,
what we as two, a vanish-point of reaching
never found together in the prison of
our sacrificing selves–so Teacher, teach.

ANNIE

The prison of us locks my life, you know.

JOHN

I'll stay awhile, if I can, then go.

ANNIE AND JOHN

The prison of us... prison of us... oh.

THREE DAYS

aria from the libretto of the opera, **Helen Keller**

HELEN KELLER (AS OLDER WOMAN)

And so I was asked
if I had three days
to see as you see
the things that I feel
and taste of and smell,
but to *see* as *you* see
well *what would that be?*
Now, *just the three,*
and then darkness
you call it, returns
to me— so set
your mind to work
on the problem of
how it would work,
on the problem of how
you would use *your* own eyes
if you had only
three days to see.

It seems the seeing
miss so much,
the vistas, details
of seconds
turned years
that pass them by.
Me, and those
of senses like me
sponge and savor
everything an
every day provides.

But yes... three days...
the wonder of that
bright idea
that stories prize...

Day One, would let
me go beyond
the visages
I feel and know
to fill the outlines
dear to me,
and dearest, my
dear Teacher,
part of me.

Day Two, the figures
of the greens
that I surmise,
the leaves and trees,
the curve of paths
'fore mountains breezed,
God's painting of
His canvas sky.

Museum trips,
the Met, the history
in the objects of
the things I've learned,
a pageant of time,
of tools and inventions,
fashions that came,
left, and returned.

And then to the art,
the colors of life
copied to carry
and hang on the walls
of our malls and our minds.
DaVinci alive!
Rodin, Monet,
creation of semblance
in tincture and clay.

And of, Day Three—
you wouldn't perhaps,
but I'd walk through the city,
street after street
mixing the people
with birds as they wing
wishing you each
the wonder before you,
before you forget
how to see it, and sing.

MACY FALLING

duet in letters from the libretto of the opera, **Helen Keller**

JOHN MACY

I too was brilliant, awfully, once
before it all consumed me,
faulty cog of wheel too greased
to stop as it assumed me.
My wife, my Irish courtesan
of fire and feel's heat,
grew into phenomenon
of Helen Keller, neat.

I love you, little girl so grown
and Teacher mother made,
but cross the years, a wife became
dull tribute of the trade.
Why do writers drink so much—
it isn't only me;
it's just I see so clearer that
it wasn't meant to be.

So I will curl into a ball
so kittenish and cry—
I don't wish the darkness, dear.
I do wish you goodbye.

HELEN (AS OLDER WOMAN)

Oh, I do wish you goodbye!

HELEN AND JOHN

I do wish you goodbye.

THE WORLD I LIVE IN

aria from the libretto of the opera, **Helen Keller**

HELEN KELLER (AS OLDER WOMAN)

We piece each sensing object to the symbols
and the letters of their names, but they
are objects still to us, you see, objects
ranged and tied to other playful things
beheld or free, and as the baby learns,
analogy and metaphor from things
we've sensed and things we've asked,
so learns the girl and boy, the woman, man,
the form of everything, from things that tie
to things, that tie to things, the different or
the same, the larger then or small, to move
or then be still, and so we learn, and learn
and chew like caterpillars at the leaf,
like ants on steps of Parthenons, instilled
until the edifice is earned, is mapped,
and ants are masters, aren't they, at the end
of every monument and hill, raising
continents of intellect and will.

Patiently the child seeks your dark
until he builds that knowledge of the world
he lives in, and the soul can meet your mettle
in the beauteous world where sun shines heat,
and birds from supple touches sing the throat.
To children deaf and blind the dark is kindly;
in it, they find nothing queer or terrible—
it's their familiar world, even the groping
place to place, the halting, the dependence
on a hand, does not seem strange to them.

Not until they weigh their lives in scale
of your dramas do they realize this mind
of dark, that's different and disabled.
Wafting pity's flight toward those who see
but cannot see, that hear, but cannot hear
their minds and hearts and souls, we, the minors
of minority regret the plight
of those who bind their own infirmity.

ANNIE'S FAREWELL

duet from the libretto of the opera, **Helen Keller**

ANNIE (AS OLDER WOMAN)

Blind like our Tiresias you find me,
waiting for that cloud that you came from,
to rest myself from all you couldn't see
among the carnages my own life had become.

When John died the mass of me had fallen
into depths no woman can re-climb—
all my life I've felt the sapping, sullen
loss of living things, and leaving you, in time.

But you have stepped into your wisdom, darling,
and for your body's needs they can provide—
if you can keep your spirit smooth from snarling
you can take this other world and round it, ride.

HELEN (AS OLDER WOMAN)

When you leave, the outline of me goes
to that great glorious where all must see,
where all the trappings of us fall as clothes
we found ill-fitting as we'd found all our disease.

The outline's what you made me, drew me
from myth of yours to something of a soul
that loves and learns and offers sympathy,
the product of your greatness set upon a pedestal.

So I will try to fill within those lines,
along these walls, and through your door
the path you would have sought for self in kind,
and still discover all you gave to me, and more.

MRS. ROOSEVELT

duet of letters from the libretto of the opera, **Helen Keller**

MRS. ROOSEVELT

Dear Helen,
I meet many people, as I must,
but I so loved the tenor of our hour,
even as we talked between the hands
of Mrs. Henney. Of my isolation young,
I told you things in confidence and here,
a couple more. Don't ask me why I must.

You have inspired me over years, but I
feel that I have shamed me in my thoughts
of you, as I have always feared the dark,
and always most the nightmare cry to someone,
somehow that might bury me alive.
Why did I connect that with your plight?

You have shown me that the dark is light
and that enclosures only close the mind
to everything; that even in our fame
we seek to hide until we once again
can find each other, find we are the same—
I go on working, thank you, in your name.

HELEN (AS OLDER WOMAN)

Many used to say that deaf-blinds cursed them,
that yes, we are the real buried-alives.
Perhaps that *was* in some ways until God
picked Teacher from the all to come and free me,

818

free *us,* too. For other freeing things,
He picked our President, and *he* picked you.
Worlds turn this way, my lovely friend, it's true.

ANOTHER JOAN OF ARC

trio and dance from the libretto of the opera, **Helen Keller**

(entire group center stage, Martha Graham with Polly; Helen [As Older Woman] stands by)

MARTHA (to Polly Thomson, watching Helen)

I see in her a grace that gives what's in the open heart.

POLLY

Mrs. Macy always claimed she had that from the start.

(center stage, dancers prepare)

MARTHA (through Polly Thomson, to Helen)

You are Joan. You get your freedom from God.

(Martha and Helen enter the circle of dancers)

HELEN (holding Martha's hand)

Shall I?... Shall I?

MARTHA (gestures with Helen's hand)

Move with me, move with me now...

HELEN

Yes... Yes...

MARTHA (places Helen's hands on the dancers, releasing)

Now fly...

HELEN (as she begins to follow the dancers, and they dance)

Yes!

(Helen continues alone in the circle as the dancers pass, arms flying gracefully, spinning as she did as a child)

MARTHA (to all)

She releases to a muse, and to herself, and to God...
And we if we could understand this, we could travel
to the vale of this chosen nymph, this child in a yard,
ah!, suffering should be so good, and so to us, unravel.

LARGE CHORUS

Suffering should be so good, and so to us, unravel.

AFTERNOON WITH ANNA

duet from the libretto of the opera, **Helen Keller**

HELEN (AS OLDER WOMAN)

*(walking from stage left, holding Patty Duke's
hand, leading her to two chairs, where they sit)*

This will do us till dinner.
Tell me more, Patty.

PATTY DUKE (using manual language while she sings)

My real name is Anna.
I wouldn't tell you if *they* were here.

HELEN

We all have *theys,* but they can't reach us, really.
Even when they hurt us, they can't reach us.
Thank you for telling me... Anna.

PATTY

I loved being you on the stage. Know why?

HELEN

Why my dear?

PATTY

Because every day, for those three hours,
I was free.

HELEN

Hmmm. Many think being me is being in prison,
but they are wrong. And you, you free yourself
when you play at being me. It's a remarkable
world, my Anna. If we can only let it be.

PATTY

Sometimes it's hard.

HELEN

And so for me. But I tell much from holding someone's
hand. You *will* survive, as I, and find the life you want,
eventually. Now let's laugh, and be so silly!
You know, just before you came I went a quick-step
to the clothesline and took down my big old bras!
I didn't want to scare you!

PATTY

No! (laughs) What's your favorite thing?

HELEN

Martinis! I'm old and can have what I want!
Yes, and one more lovely pleasure— hot dogs!

PATTY

I love hot dogs!

HELEN

You do? Come! Let's boil some up!
It will spoil our dinner!

*(Helen and Patty rise and walk stage left,
holding hands; Helen leading, turns to Patty)*

When things get tough, eat hot dogs, Anna.

And think of me.

TO THE NATIONAL CATHEDRAL

duets and choruses from the libretto of the opera,
Helen Keller

(Helen [As Older Woman] in bed, left pedestal;
Winnie Corbally and Evelyn Seide standing)

WINNIE

Nothing to be done now, just the waiting.
Sometimes she still works her fingers.
Look now, see...

(Helen [As Older woman], works her own fingers)

EVELYN

Imagine, almost eighty-eight. Her mouth...
Does she need water? *(Evelyn grasps Helen's fingers)*
W-A-T-E-R? Helen? Water?

HELEN (responding with her fingers)

Www.....aaaaaaa.

WINNIE

Helen!

LARGE CHORUS

Water!

HELEN (AS YOUNG WOMAN) (appears at right)

Water is the absolution. Sleep, and rise!

LARGE CHORUS

Sleep and rise! Rise!

(Helen [As Young Woman] walks toward the center; there are two chairs beside each other front and center. Annie Sullivan [As a Young Woman] walks to Helen from stage left)

ANNIE

Helen!

HELEN

Teacher! I see you.

ANNIE

Just as you knew!

HELEN

Teacher! I hear you!

ANNIE AND HELEN

Together! *(Annie and Helen embrace)*

There is in all of us a way to be,
and do and have, to grow and celebrate
our common sense, our simple selves, our Seas of Galilee,
and what I see and hear, my friend, is great—

I see and hear the you inside of me.
I see and hear the you inside of me.

(Annie and Helen sit)

*(National Cathedral Chaperone leads children past
Helen Keller and Annie Sullivan in their chairs)*

CHAPERONE

Here in the great National Cathedral rests Helen Keller
and her beloved teacher, Annie Sullivan.

*(the children file from stage right to stage left; the last
child stays behind; she puts a rose on the tomb, and
rising, she turns a pirouette)*

CHAPERONE *(offstage)*

Annie!

(the girl skips off stage left)

LARGE CHORUS

There is in all of us a way to be,
and do and have, to grow and celebrate
our common sense, our simple selves, our Seas of Galilee,
and what I see and hear, my friend, is great—
I see and hear the you inside of me.
I see and hear the you inside of me.

(curtain)

FOR GETTE

The years of words that I have sought to write
I would have bartered for that smile's light,
and kept, I know, for even seconds' sight
the pen at ever rest, the paper white.

Many Thanks

The author extends his gratitude and affection, beyond that already reserved for his beloved wife Gette and family, and in more or less chronological order, to: Joan Burt, Jesse and Keith Pereira, Margaret Mullaly, Eunice Dion, the Martins, Pearsons, and Warrens; Bob Tremblay, Valerie Foley, HSD, Ken Raymond, Hy Sobiloff, Winnie Dimock, Eileen Murphy, James Panos, John Pietruszka, Ken Arruda, Bob Dube, Jerry Mack, Phyllis Pytel, T. S. Eliot, Maurice Methot, Bob Dylan, Jack Kerouac, Larry Dunn, Kerry McKeever, Gerry Ryack, the Moreiras, Karen Proulx, Anne Sexton, LRH, Bruce Kobrin, Barry and Tina Younkers, Dave Vick, Trudy and Don Harris; Maurice Jeffrey, the Gunn family, Henry Gould, Orca's Place, Lucy Harding, Ellen Sander, Amazing Instant Novelist, Maggie Secara, Marianne Wade, Diana Weiss, Barbara Quinn, Noel Haynes, Bethany Bower, Debra Wilk, Terry Godbey, Lucie Winborne, Stephen Caldwell Wright, Gwendolyn Brooks Writers Association, Victoria Richter, Don Bienvenue, Barto Smith, Ori Barto, Gesa Barto; Webb Harris, Dan Schneider, Joe Cavanuagh, Carol Thomas, Janet Watson, Joan Clark, John Foster, Terry Hagans, Lola Haskins, Peter Meinke, Mary-Ann Westbrook, Dan Pels, Gary Broughman, Stephanie Andrews, the Florida State Poets Association, Tina Ayres, Keith Lay, Benoit Glazer, Brian Capley and the Osceola School for the Arts, the Garvises, Holly, Ruth, Jane, and the students of the Twelve Chairs Advanced Poetry Course, the Twelve Chairs Salons, and the Shakespeare Project. To communicate with Al Rocheleau, or to learn more about Shantih Press, the manual *On Writing Poetry: For Poets Made as well as Born,* or The Twelve Chairs Advanced Poetry Course, write or call:

Shantih Press
PO BOX 770640
Orlando, FL 32877-0640
407-592-4527
ARRO40@aol.com

The Poet as a Young Man

CPSIA information can be obtained
at www.ICGtesting.com
Printed in the USA
BVHW040133160219
540171BV00038B/345/P